a stream of dreams

ALSO BY LEON NACSON

Aromatherapy for Lovers and Dreamers
(co-authored with Karen Downes and Judith White)

Aromatherapy for Meditation and Contemplation
(co-authored with Karen Downes and Judith White)

Cards, Stars and Dreams
(co-authored with Matthew Favaloro)

Dream Cards (a 65-Card Deck)

Dream Journal

Dreamer's Guide to the Galaxy

Dyer Straight

I Must Be Dreaming

Interpreting Dreams A–Z

World of Infinite Possibilities

Please visit Hay House USA: www.hayhouse.com
Hay House Australia: www.hayhouse.com.au
Hay House UK: www.hayhouse.co.uk
Hay House South Africa: orders@psdprom.co.za

a stream of dreams

THE ULTIMATE DREAM DECODER
FOR THE 21ST CENTURY

Leon Nacson

HAY
HOUSE

HAY HOUSE, INC.
Carlsbad, California
London • Sydney • Johannesburg
Vancouver • Hong Kong

Published and distributed in the United States by: Hay House, Inc., P.O. Box 5100, Carlsbad, CA 92018-5100 • *Phone:* (760) 431-7695 or (800) 654-5126 • *Fax:* (760) 431-6948 or (800) 650-5115 • www.hayhouse.com • *Published and distributed in Australia by:* Hay House Australia Ltd., 18/36 Ralph St., Alexandria NSW 2015 • *Phone:* 612-9669-4299 • *Fax:* 612-9669-4144 • www.hayhouse.com.au • *Published and distributed in the United Kingdom by:* Hay House UK, Ltd. • Unit 62, Canalot Studios • 222 Kensal Rd., London W10 5BN • *Phone:* 44-20-8962-1230 • *Fax:* 44-20-8962-1239 • www.hayhouse.co.uk • *Published and distributed in the Republic of South Africa by:* Hay House SA (Pty), Ltd., P.O. Box 990, Witkoppen 2068 • *Phone/Fax:* 2711-7012233 • orders@psdprom.co.za • *Distributed in Canada by:* Raincoast • 9050 Shaughnessy St., Vancouver, B.C. V6P 6E5 • *Phone:* (604) 323-7100 • *Fax:* (604) 323-2600

Editorial supervision: Jill Kramer   *Research/editing:* Rachel Eldred
Design: Amy Rose Szalkiewicz

Library of Congress Cataloging-in-Publication Data

Nacson, Leon.
  A stream of dreams : the ultimate dream decoder for the 21st century / Leon Nacson.
    p. cm.
  ISBN 1-40190-150-6 (pbk.)
  1. Dream interpretation—Dictionaries. 2. Symbolism (Psychology)—Dictionaries. I. Title.
  BF1091 .N165 2003
  154.6'3'03—dc21

                              2002152082

                    ISBN 1-4019-0150-6

                 07 06 05 04   5 4 3 2
                 1st printing, January 2004
                 2nd printing, February 2004

                    Printed in Canada

To Isabelle and Liam

CONTENTS

ACKNOWLEDGMENTS

There's no way this book would have ever been completed without Rachel Eldred—two years of cracking the whip and putting up with my excuses. Thank you so much, Rachel.

It has also been a privilege to work with Jill Kramer, the empress of words. And, of course, thank you to everyone in my world—what a buzz, dudes!

— Leon Nacson

INTRODUCTION

I've always loved the expression "Let's cut to the chase." So when I decided to write this book, I was determined to get to the point immediately—and to keep this Introduction short, because everyone tells me that no one reads Introductions! The point, of course, is to tell you what the dream is all about, what you can learn from it, and how it can add more meaning to your life.

Interpreting your dreams is now straightforward. First, turn to the Dreamer's Checklist in the next section to find a list of questions that will assist you. I recommend that you review the list regularly to get into the habit of prompting yourself for meanings.

To interpret individual symbols in your dream, look up each symbol in the A–Z Dream Decoder, take note of the "Quick Interpretation," think about the "Popular Expressions," and ponder the insights that I associate with the symbol. Popular Expressions aren't necessarily listed for every entry, but when they are, please note that sometimes they're descriptive of a certain situation as well as being based on a play on words. For example, in the "Cab" entry, the Popular Expressions are "To talk behind someone's back" and "In someone else's hands," for that's what occurs (both literally and figuratively) when you're in a cab. The idea is to use the information provided as a stepping-stone to develop your own thoughts about the symbol. If I've left out a symbol, use my blueprint to create your own interpretations.

Emotions play a pivotal part in determining the true meaning of a dream. You'll find a number of emotions listed in alphabetical order throughout the book, and in case you're not sure which emotion best describes how you're feeling, I've listed some of the most common ones at the end of the book.

I've searched every source that was available to me to find a collective noun that best describes the assemblage of dreams that it's possible to have in one night. And so it was that I decided to call this book A _Stream_ of Dreams. I look forward to the day when everyone wakes up and automatically thinks, _Wow, what a stream of dreams I had last night!_

THE DREAMER'S CHECKLIST

Before we embark on an extended trip, many of us prepare checklists to make sure we don't forget anything—passport, credit cards, airline tickets, and so on. It's helpful to prepare for a dream adventure in the same way, consulting a checklist of questions that you ask yourself when interpreting your dream.

This is my dreamer's checklist, with typical questions that I'd ask during a dream-coaching session. I recommend that you familiarize yourself with these questions and use them on a regular basis. However, this checklist is by no means definitive, so I encourage you to personalize the list and add any questions that you feel are relevant.

- Is my dream about something that just happened to me?

- Was my dream influenced by something I ate before going to bed?

- Am I being alerted to a physical illness or ailment in my dream?

- Am I living out my worst fears in my dream?

- Is my dream a way for me to develop my memory?

- Is my dream a way for me to develop survival techniques?

- Am I learning more about my relationships in my dream?

- Am I making karmic connections to loved ones who have departed in my dream?

- Is my dream bringing something to a resolution or to completion?

- Does my dream indicate that I'm in conflict about what I think I *should* be doing in my life versus what I'm actually doing?

- Is my dream helping me solve a problem that's happening in my life right now?

- Is my dream about my highest aspirations?

- Does my dream relate to a film or TV program I've just watched, or a book I've just read?

- Is my dream about wish fulfillment—that is, living out my most deep-rooted desires?

- Is my dream about transformation or a change that's taking place in my life?

- Am I revisiting the past in my dream?

- Is my dream alerting me to how I sabotage my deepest desires in life?

- Is my dream so wacko that I'm not supposed to decipher it—it will work itself out in time?

- Is my dream encouraging me to adopt a different attitude about my life—or a certain situation in my life?

Your A–Z Dream Decoder

Abacus

Quick Interpretation: Calculation; precision; self-assessment

Popular Expressions: Count me in; Count me out; Count your blessings

It's impressive what you can do with a bunch of beads and a few sticks! If you're using an abacus in a dream and you've never used one before, is it an indication that you like to work things out the old-fashioned way? Perhaps the dream is about a relationship, indicating a desire to understand *how* things are worked out (as opposed to simply being told the answer as a calculator would do).

The dream may also be career based, indicating that the answers lie in getting back to basics, rolling your sleeves up, and working problems out in a practical way without any modern technology or hype.

If you own or use an abacus in your waking life, then to dream of one may signify that you only trust what you can directly manipulate—or that you're not ready to embrace change.

Is someone else using the abacus in your dream? Are you impressed with their manual dexterity, or are you turned off because a calculator with a digital display is far more practical? Your answer will give you insight into how you feel about the individual.

Also ask yourself if the abacus represents a desire to be included—that is, counted in? Or could it be that it's time to stop complaining about life, as your subconscious is asking you to count your blessings?

Abandonment

Quick Interpretation: Feeling ditched; neglected; unappreciated

Popular Expressions: Abandon a sinking ship; With reckless abandon; Love me or leave me

It's hard to imagine a worse feeling than feeling abandoned. Whether it's by people you love, co-workers, or friends, the question to ask is: Why can't I keep up? Or, why don't I *want* to keep up?

In other words, are those you perceive to have abandoned you moving too fast, and you feel uncomfortable trying to keep up? Perhaps it's all right for them to move that quickly, but it may not be appropriate for you.

On the other hand, perhaps the abandonment has something to do with your having moved ahead. For example, you may feel that your friends have abandoned you. Ask yourself if it's because you no longer have anything in common with them. It may be a positive abandonment; you're now liberated to create a whole new circle of friends and acquaintances. Abandonment always works two ways: Consider whether deep down you want to be set free.

Most children at some point dream of being abandoned. It's an obvious fear; after all, as children we are very dependent on our families for survival.

If you dream that you're an abandoned child, it either suggests unresolved issues concerning your childhood and growing up, or that you're becoming so reliant and dependent on those who abandoned you in the dream that you feel helpless without them.

Perhaps you're abandoning someone or something in the dream? If so, ask yourself if it's time to jump ship on a project you're currently involved in. Is it time to get a new job, embark on a new career, or move to a new city because you've outgrown a location or project? It may be time to abandon whatever it was you thought was important in the past.

Abortion

Quick Interpretation: Termination of relationship(s); profound decisions; endings

Popular Expression: Abort a plan or project; Aborted landing; Bail out of a sinking ship

If you dream of abortion, the most obvious meaning is that you're terminating a project midstream. Is there a project in your life that needs to be aborted? Are drastic steps required because a Band-Aid won't fix the problem?

Ask yourself who's having the abortion and why they can't wait to see how things turn out?

If you're the one having the abortion in your dream and you're not pregnant in waking life, consider whether it's a reflection of your inability to complete projects. Or perhaps you have to accept that a project needs to be nipped in the bud because you're no longer fully committed to it.

If you're the one being aborted in the dream, ask yourself why you feel this way. Does someone want to terminate a relationship with you?

To dream of an abortion—if it's not a literal association—can be a positive symbol, a warning to terminate a relationship or project before it has adverse effects on you or your loved ones. It signifies that it's time to jump ship before it's too late.

Abundance

Quick Interpretation: Fulfillment; satisfaction; gratitude

Popular Expressions: There's plenty more where that came from; Opportunity knocks

To dream of abundance indicates that you're looking at life optimistically. Whether you have a dream about abundance during a time of lack or a time of plenty, it's a reminder that opportunity knocks more than once in a lifetime.

Abuse

Quick Interpretation: Letting go of steam; judgment; misunderstanding

Popular Expressions: Off the beaten track; Can't beat them off with a stick

The best way to get to the heart of what's happening in a dream involving abuse is to ask yourself a series of questions. Are you being abused in the dream? If so, who is abusing you? Is it verbal, physical, or mental abuse? Is it an indication of what's happening to you in your waking life—or what you feel is happening to you in your waking life?

If someone else is being abused in your dream, how did the victim of the abuse react? With courage and strength, or with fear and submission? What did you do about it? And, most important, how did you feel when you woke up?

To dream of abuse is a sensitive issue. It may signify deep torment, or it may be about self-abuse. Are you attacking yourself in some way? If you want to delve into this issue, the best place to start is to examine your dream feelings. If necessary, seek professional help.

Academy (Also see *School.*)

Quick Interpretation: Achievement; acknowledgment; schooling

Popular Expressions: School of hard knocks; Make the grade

This symbol is all about advancement. The academy is a place of higher learning, discipline, a place to develop specialized skills.

Are you a student or a member of an academy, indicating a desire to excel? Or are you on the outside looking in, indicating that it's time to roll up your sleeves once again to improve particular skills?

What type of academy is it? Is it a military academy or an arts academy? The type of academy you dream of will indicate what type of person you are (or desire to be).

Do you feel insecure or threatened at the academy, or welcomed and in your element? How you feel may signify the way you like to work: either individually, without having to consider the opinions and thoughts or others, or in a group, where everyone makes a contribution.

Are you wearing a uniform at the academy, indicating a desire for regimentation? Or perhaps you're dressed casually, indicating that there's no need for fancy displays to show rank.

Every year the whole world turns its attention to the Academy Awards. Do you feel that you deserve recognition for your hard work, or that someone close to you justifiably deserves it?

Accent

Quick Interpretation: Foreign places; heritage; ethnic acceptance/rejection

Popular Expression: Accentuate the positive

The most important question to ask is: What kind of accent is it? Does the accent annoy or please you? Can you decipher what is being communicated, or is it undetectable?

If you don't entirely understand what's being said, are you patient and calm, taking the time to figure it out, or does it annoy you so much that you dismiss the information without a second thought? This may signify either a deep desire to work through things that people are trying communicate to you, or that you simply don't have the time or patience to.

Could the accent be a play on words, signifying that you want to "accentuate" a point? For example, if someone is speaking with a French accent, is it an indication that you want to exude passion and express yourself more romantically?

Acceptance

Quick Interpretation: Acknowledgment; recognition

When you feel accepted, it indicates that others recognize you for who you are. Who has included you in their life? Why do you feel you need to be acknowledged?

Accident

Quick Interpretation: Warning; carelessness; hasty decisions

Popular Expressions: Accidents will happen; An accident waiting to happen; An accident of birth

Whoever said "there's no such thing as an accident" hasn't checked out the traffic circle at the end of my street. It's an auto mechanic's fantasy.

To dream of an accident may be a warning to watch where you're going. Could it be that two worlds are about to collide? For example, are your career and home lives going to clash and create havoc? Or is it that people around you aren't moving as quickly as you'd like them to, and therefore you keep bumping into them?

How do you feel about the accident? Are you distressed and in need of help? Or do you feel that you're in the right? In other words, do you feel that people or incidents in your life are conspiring against you, or do you feel self-righteous about a wrongdoing?

If you're the witness to the accident in your dream, are you lending support, such as first aid? Or are you turning your back because you're horrified by the sight? How you respond may indicate how you're handling a current mishap in your life.

Are people laughing at you because of the accident, or are you laughing at someone else? Are you or is someone else in your dream accident-prone and a constant source of amusement? How do you feel about it?

Each of us reacts differently to accidents, but there's one thing you should stop to consider: Is it time to slow down and perhaps move in a different direction?

Accommodations

Quick Interpretation: Hospitality; refuge; flexibility

Popular Expressions: No rest for the weary; Take a load off

Wouldn't it be great if we didn't need accommodations and could simply curl up under a tree, slip into a cave, or take a nap wherever and whenever we needed to? But, of course, this isn't the way it is.

In your dream, are you looking for accommodations, or are you being accommodated? If you're looking, what do you hope to find? If it's a hotel, is it a five-star hotel or a backpacker's hostel? Do you feel comfortable in the hotel, or do you feel like a duck out of water? If it's a five-star establishment, is it an indication that you want to find a better place to house yourself? Or do you want to escape from something or someone by seeking out new accommodations?

If you're being accommodated, who is accommodating you? Do you feel nurtured and supported by that person, or do you feel like a freeloader? Perhaps someone requires you to accommodate *them?* Are you willing and able to, or does it feel like a burden?

Accountant

Quick Interpretation: Balance; being methodical; taking stock

Popular Expressions: A head for figures; It's a numbers game; You can count on me; Count me out; It doesn't add up

We live in a world where it's almost impossible to get by without an accountant. So, it's becoming more and more popular to regard accountants as white knights in a sense.

Accountants help us cut through red tape. The question is, does the accountant in your dream offer solutions that please you and save you money, or is he or she the bearer of bad tidings, where you find that you owe a lot more than you thought you would?

Is the accountant in your dream a symbol indicating that it's time to get your life in order, keep better financial records, and not spend so much money?

Is it time to take financial responsibility for your life? Do you need to do more to keep your accounts in order than simply throw a bunch of check stubs and receipts in the drawer for your accountant to deal with? Is it time to take control of your finances, relying less on others to help you?

Are you the accountant in your dream, or is someone else accounting for you? If you're the accountant, are you juggling your own or someone else's financial affairs?

If someone else is the accountant, do you respect them and are you interested in what they have to say, or do you feel suffocated by them? The answer will indicate whether you accept, or feel concerned about, your financial position.

Most accountants I've met have wanted to do something else, or *be* somewhere else. Perhaps the accountant in your dream is suggesting that it's time to pack up, move to an island in the Pacific, and paint lush scenery. It would certainly beat counting beans!

Ache (Also see *Pain*.)

Quick Interpretation: Hidden pain; past neglect; anguish

Popular Expressions: Ache for someone or something; Heartache

It intrigues me why some people associate desire with pain. Why do we say we ache for something that's pleasurable? Are we referring to the pain of being without it?

What kind of ache did you experience in your dream? Was it heartache associated with romance, or was it aching feet, indicating a desire to travel? Or was your head aching, indicating knowledge?

The first thing to consider is whether or not the ache is physical. Do you need to consult a physician? If you don't have a physical ailment, ask yourself what it is you ache for. What appropriate action do you need to take to realize your desire?

Acid

Quick Interpretation: Penetration; violent emotion; determination

Popular Expressions: To eat away at; The acid test

The first question to ask is: What's eating away at you? What is it that you want to dis*solve* in order to find a solution? That's the interesting thing about acid as a symbol in a dream—you always end up with a solution.

The symbol of acid may also indicate that other people are treating you unfavorably. Are people in your life giving you an acid reception, or do you feel that you're under a microscope and people are trying to extract answers from you—that you're being grilled?

It may be that you're judging someone's character, or someone is judging your character and putting you through the acid test.

Acorn

Quick Interpretation: Great promises; future investments; hidden rewards

Popular Expressions: Gone to seed; Mighty oaks from little acorns grow

Is there any other food more synonymous with inspiration and possibilities than the acorn? You may remember the expression "Mighty oaks from little acorns grow." Are the acorns in your dream symbolic of your own precious ideas—ideas that you hope will grow to become great achievements? If you're planting acorns in your dream, it may signify the planting of seeds in your mind, seeds that will grow into wondrous things.

The acorns may also indicate that your ideas or thoughts are being protected. Do you feel that you're not quite ready to share your ideas and thoughts with the world yet?

The acorn is also a symbol of hidden treasure. Are you hiding wondrous news or a fantastic idea from someone, or is someone hiding something from you? The acorn indicates that all will be revealed in good time.

At times in our lives, we may find ourselves surrounded by people who are full of promise. Ask yourself if the acorns symbolize such a time in your life. If so, are the people around you simply spin doctors full of hype, or are they people who understand that with patience, ideas will grow into giant oak trees one day.

Activist (Also see *Protest.*)

Quick Interpretation: Idealistic; reactionary; resisting the status quo

Popular Expressions: A slice of the action; Actions speak louder than words

If it's time to stand up and be counted, there's no better symbol than the activist to indicate that you want revolution! At some point in our lives, we get the urge to desert the majority and actively rebel against whatever we don't believe in. Dreaming of an activist may symbolize that now is the appropriate time to act.

Ask yourself what and who you're rebelling against. Is it a just cause? Do you feel like a hero in the cause, or do you need to be secretive and careful because you fear that exposure may mean reprisals? Either way, the symbol of the activist indicates that you're responding to a confrontation in your life (either openly or surreptitiously) by rebelling.

Focus on the cause you're championing to get an indication of the direction you're heading in regarding your future and dreams.

In your dream, are people supporting your cause? If so, it may indicate that in real life, people follow you in the hopes that you will offer them a better future or a slice of the action.

Actor

Quick Interpretation: Make-believe; deception

Popular Expressions: A hard act to follow; Caught in the act; Get in on the act; All the world's a stage

You don't want to wake up because you're hanging out with a superstar in your dream . . . . Actors have always intrigued us because they can give life to make-believe characters.

If you dream of an actor, first ask what emotions the actor brings up for you. Is the actor in a drama, adventure, comedy, or horror movie? That will give you an indication of the themes you're playing out in your own life.

Specific actors have unique symbolism. Strength may be associated with Arnold Schwarzenegger, a suave air with Roger Moore, or a cool sophistication with Nicole Kidman. We typecast actors to understand them, and in turn, when they appear in a dream they can help us understand ourselves.

Determine your association with the actor. Is it an aspect of yourself that you aspire to, or is it a trait you'd like to discard? In your dream, what is the dynamic between you and the actor?

A friend of mine had a dream that she showered with Danny DeVito. Although he's short and stocky, he's regarded as a big Hollywood star, a competent director, and, perhaps, even as an object of desire for some. My friend worked out that she felt she was being judged by her physical appearance. She wanted people to look past her beauty and appreciate her intelligence.

Are you playing a role in the dream? What is it? Do you feel comfortable playing this role? Are you attempting to disguise yourself in a situation? Do you hunger for adulation, relying on other people to boost your self-esteem?

If you feel you never get the chance to say what's on your mind, dreaming of being an actor gives you the space to express yourself.

At a cinema or theater, the audience changes every night and the only constant is the actors, who follow scripts and direction. Would you like to be more in control of your life? Do you feel that you need direction?

Illusion is associated with acting, too. Are you acting the fool, or is someone fooling *you?*

Acupuncture

Quick Interpretation: Ancient wisdom; natural healing; focus

Popular Expression: Getting to the point of something; Make a good point; Point something out; Needling someone; Stick it to someone; Get under someone's skin

It's hard to believe that by inserting needles into your body, an acupuncturist can help heal you of every type of ailment under the sun! But many people swear by this practice.

If you dream of acupuncture, is it an indication that you believe that anything is possible? Is it a desire to accept that life isn't always as it seems? Or do you think that people are gullible and will believe anything?

In your dream, are you the patient? If so, the important thing to note is, what area of your body needs healing? Are you afraid of the needles? If so, ask yourself if someone is trying to needle you. If you're angry, is someone trying to get under your skin? Or if you feel dominated, is someone painfully pointing things out to you that you don't want to see?

If you're the acupuncturist administering the needles, what is it that you're trying to point out to others?

Addict

Quick Interpretation: Escapism; habit; obsessive behavior

Popular Expression: Driven to temptation

An addiction is something you think you can't live without. It's something you're willing to sacrifice friends, family, health, and reputation for.

What are you addicted to? Love, food, sex, money, drugs, sugar . . . try to recall what it is and why you think it's so important. Do you feel that it's essential to your survival?

Is someone else the addict in the dream? Do you look down on them because they have an addiction, or are you sympathetic? To dream of an addict may indicate that you want to surrender to your desires, or perhaps you need to detoxify and break a habit.

If the addict in your dream is a junkie, perhaps it's an indication that it's time to adopt a better diet, the term *junkie* being a pun for "junk food." Are there too many hamburgers and french fries on your menu and not enough broccoli and alfalfa sprouts?

It's important to notice where the addict is. Is the addict in your home or office? If so, what does this tell you about your home or work life?

Perhaps it's time for a spring cleaning, with *junk* being a symbol of the useless stuff in your home that clutters up your life.

Adultery

Quick Interpretation: Lust; rearranged partnerships; jealousy

Popular Expressions: An affair of the heart; You made your bed, now lie in it

Guilt walks hand-in-hand with adultery—they fit together like beer and hangovers.

If you're in a committed relationship and you commit adultery in your dream, is it an outlet for desire? If your partner commits adultery in your dream, is it an issue of trust? If you're not in a committed relationship and you commit adultery with someone who is, is it wish fulfillment, or do you find sex with someone who's attached exciting?

Are you in an adulterous relationship? If so, what is the dream telling you? Do you feel safe in the relationship because you don't have to commit? Or is your behavior an expression of pure lust and excitement?

If you're a religious type and would never break one of the Ten Commandments, then perhaps you're taking liberty in your dream state. Do you still feel guilty even though it only happened in a dream? Or did it relieve tension and you woke up feeling buoyant?

Who are you committing adultery with? If it's with a stranger, a celebrity, or a co-worker, then it may signify lust, or represent an aspect of yourself that you wish to express. For example, if it's with George Clooney or Madonna, perhaps you want to be more outgoing and self-assured.

If you commit adultery with a married member of your family, I believe it suggests a desire to be more intimate with that person. You may want to bond with them and create a closer relationship.

Perhaps you're going through a stage of being dissatisfied with a relationship in your life. If so, the dream may be an expression of your present outlook—that is, the grass is always greener on the other side.

Advice

Quick Interpretation: Acceptance; respect; exploring possibilities

Popular Expressions: A hot tip; Do what I say, not what I do; A piece of my mind; In one ear and out the other; Lip service

We all give it, and we all get it. We all want it, and we all hate it! Who's giving you the advice in your dream? Is it appreciated? Or is it going in one ear and out the other? Have you heard it all before?

Explore your feelings with respect to the advice that's given. Is it good advice that you want to act on? Or do you feel that someone is trying to manipulate you by giving you advice that suits them more than it does you?

Aerobics (Also see *Exercise; Gym.*)

Quick Interpretation: Fitness; movement; animated display

Popular Expressions: No sweat; Run circles around someone; Run for your life; A walk in the park; No pain, no gain

Aerobics is an exercise that only the most coordinated and energetic people can do. It's for people who don't really need to exercise, because, let's face it, if they can do aerobics, they're fit enough!

To dream of aerobics may indicate a desire to be fit and healthy, or it may signify that you've achieved your goals and good health is yours.

If you're participating in an aerobics class in your dream, are you keeping up, or do you feel like a duck out of water? Do you love or dread exercise? Is it no sweat at all, or a painful experience?

Perhaps you're the teacher in your dream and you want to whip other people into shape? Who is in the dream with you? Do you have a desire to get them up and into action?

If you're an aerobics teacher in your waking life, then the indications will, of course, be different. What is the dream telling you about your chosen profession?

Aging (Also see *Old Age; Youth.*)

Quick Interpretation: Maturation; being set in your ways; wisdom

Popular Expressions: Act your age; Come of age; In this day and age; An age-old question; Youth is for the young

We all experience it—some of us in a more dignified manner than others.

Do you feel that aging is a symbol of a loss of power and strength, or a loss of possibility? Or is it a symbol of acquiring wisdom and patience? Do you appreciate life and the way it's unfolding?

If you dream of someone else aging, is it an indication that you want them to act more maturely—or that they're acting more maturely, blossoming right before your eyes?

Agitation

Quick Interpretation: Restlessness; lack of concentration

Popular Expression: Ants in your pants

When you're feeling agitated, it indicates that you're restless and unable to concentrate or focus. What makes you feel restless and uneasy in your dream?

Airplane (Also see *Flying*.)

Quick Interpretation: Travel; elevation; climbing to greater heights

Popular Expressions: Fly by night; Fly off the handle; Waiting in the wings; A fly in the ointment; Wing it; To land something; Something landing in your lap

If you're preparing for a plane trip or if someone close to you is about to fly somewhere, you may have an airplane dream in anticipation of the event. If this isn't the case, then dreaming of an airplane may signify a desire to defy the laws of nature with the aid of technology.

How did you feel about the plane in your dream? Is it an easy takeoff or a bumpy ride? Are you in the air or coming down for a crash landing? Are you comfortable on the plane, or is it a scary experience? People often dream of missing a flight. If this is the case, ask yourself how you feel about it. Do you feel relieved or left behind?

Who is with you on the plane? Do you wish that your relationship with that person would take off? If the person is a co-worker, perhaps you want your career to take off.

Is the plane landing in your dream? Is it a hard or soft landing? Are things landing in your lap by surprise?

What kind of plane is it? Is it modern and fast, or dingy and old-fashioned? The answer may signify where you are in your life at this time.

People who have a fear of flying may dream of a plane crashing. They live out their worst fear in the dream state so it doesn't have such a hold over them when they're awake. If the oxygen mask drops when you're on the plane, ask if it's time to pay attention to your needs before meeting everyone else's.

Finally, dreaming of an airplane may simply mean that you need a vacation.

Alarm Clock (Also see *Time; Watch.*)

Quick Interpretation: Reminders; appointments; rude awakenings

Popular Expressions: The time is now; Right on time; Running like clockwork; Time is slipping away; Wake up with a start

It's interesting that we should call wake-up devices alarm clocks and not wake-up clocks. Why is it that we need to be "alarmed" to the fact that it's time to wake up? Perhaps we're being warned that if we sleep late, we may miss out on something important—like an eight-hour workday!

To dream of an alarm clock may suggest that you're being woken up to reality with a heavy jolt. Look around and see why the alarm bells are ringing. Is there someone else in the dream with you? Are you being alerted to what they're really like?

If you're fortunate enough to remember the time on the alarm clock, consider what that time may signify. If it's late in the day, do you feel as if life is passing you by?

Is the alarm clock waking you or someone else up? If it's someone else, do you feel that they need a wake-up call because they're heading in the wrong direction?

I often dream of an alarm clock when the real one on my dresser is ringing; the only way to ignore it is to pretend it's part of the dream and sleep on!

Alcohol

Quick Interpretation: Intoxication; celebration; distilled ideas

Popular Expressions: A slave to drink; Eat, drink, and be merry; Toasting someone; High on life; Lift your spirits; Live it up

It's interesting that throwing back a few spirits can often lift our own spirits . . . or simply help us cope with life's little challenges.

Do you pour yourself an alcoholic drink in your dream, or does someone else pour you the drink? This may indicate that you're trying to cheer yourself up—or someone else is.

Is the alcohol a symbol of having to be intoxicated to enjoy yourself, or is it simply a social pleasure? How you feel about alcohol is important. Do you think it gives people (including yourself) an excuse to act any way they desire? Is the real you busting to come out but you need a reason to behave the way you do? Or do you think it encourages people to act foolishly?

How do you feel about the person consuming the alcohol in the dream? Are they behaving foolishly or enjoying themselves? It may be time for this person to either take responsibility for their life or live it up a little.

Ale (See *Beer.*)

Alertness

Quick Interpretation: Attention; mindfulness

Popular Expressions: A red alert; Alert someone to a situation

When you're alert, you're very attentive to what's happening around you. You're mindful of the moment. What inspired this type of focus in your dream?

Alien

Quick Interpretation: Foreign places; distant voices; strangers

Popular Expressions: Truth is stranger than fiction; Something that's alien to you; Feeling alienated

It's not for me to tell you whether you've had a genuine alien encounter or not, as I'm not a specialist in that area. However, it's interesting that although we've yet to visit alien worlds, people are certain that aliens have visited ours. This suggests that aliens are more advanced than we are.

If you dream of an alien, ask yourself if you're working with advanced concepts or ideas. Is the alien in your dream there to share information with you or to harm you?

Perhaps it's a time of learning in your life. Is it time to enroll in a course? Perhaps you wish to become more conscious about something or someone in your life. Is it time to embark on a journey of self-discovery?

Are you being dissected by an alien in your dream? If so, it may mean that you need to delve into and dissect your inner thoughts. Do you travel anywhere with the alien in your dream? If the alien takes you on an adventure, perhaps you need to open up to new possibilities, or you have a desire for adventure and exploration.

Is your experience with the alien reminiscent of the movie *E.T.*, where you feel happy, unafraid, and supported? Or is it more like a scene from *Alien,* where you're treated as an inferior species? Do you feel inferior? Do others feel inferior around you?

People new to a country may have alien dreams because they feel that they don't quite belong. Also, it's not uncommon to dream of an alien when you start a new job or relationship, because in these circumstances you often feel different and a little alienated.

The dream could also reflect your ideas. Are they new and far out? Are you ready to share them with others? Should you be selective about whom you share your ideas with?

The X-Files created paranoia and conspiracy theories with respect to alien contact. Is the government covering up the existence of aliens in your dream, or is someone being dishonest with you? Are you being misinformed? Are you deluded?

Fox Mulder wouldn't give up in his search for aliens. How determined are *you* to find out the truth of your situation?

Alligator (or Crocodile)

Quick Interpretation: Hidden danger; firm grip; patience; insincerity

Popular Expressions: Be eaten alive; Jaws of hell; Crocodile tears

Alligators and crocodiles get bigger as they get older, but don't age physically the way humans do. If you have a crocodile dream, ask yourself if you have an investment in staying young.

Alligators and crocodiles are amphibious, which may suggest that you'd like to have a foot in two worlds. Are you the type of person who likes to hunt with the hounds and run with the foxes? Maybe you're being two-faced, or someone in your life is.

The alligator or crocodile may also symbolize adaptability. Are you a flexible person, or would you like to be more flexible? Perhaps someone around you is flexible and it threatens your need for stability.

Ask yourself if the alligator or crocodile is a symbol of patience—these reptiles give the impression that they have all the time in the world.

Do you feel like the reptile in your dream, or are you being chased or hunted down by one? If you're under attack, or about to be attacked, ask yourself if someone in your life is trying to cold-bloodedly ambush you. One woman told me that she had a recurring dream that baby crocodiles were crawling from her filing cabinet at work. It turned out that she felt as if her co-workers were conspiring to get rid of her.

If the reptile in your dream is in murky waters, you may feel a sense of foreboding but not be sure why. Perhaps it's time to act like Sherlock Holmes and find out if someone close to you makes you feel uncomfortable. Perhaps this person doesn't have your best interests at heart.

If you're the crocodile in your dream, it may be that you need to break self-destructive patterns in your life. Is it time to take responsibility for your own shortcomings?

Altruism

Quick Interpretation: Consideration; concern for others

Feeling altruistic indicates thoughtful concern for the welfare of others. Is it time for you to show more consideration toward others?

Ally (See *Friend.*)

Ambition

Quick Interpretation: Goal setting; high aspirations

To feel ambitious indicates the will and the desire to achieve aspirations and goals. What goal do you aspire to?

Ambulance (Also see *Siren.*)

Quick Interpretation: Support; salvation; warning

Popular Expression: Alarm bells ring

The wail of an ambulance siren can be unnerving—unless, of course, you're lying facedown in the gutter and it's coming to rescue you. Its wail then becomes a lullaby.

So, in your dream, is the ambulance a symbol of support, rescue, and deliverance from pain? Is it coming for you or someone else? Who needs help, and what needs rescuing?

Is the ambulance a symbol of something in your life that needs sudden and immediate attention? Consider the location of the ambulance to determine what area of your life you need to look at.

Perhaps the ambulance indicates that something is coming your way and you need to watch out or move over. Maybe it's a warning of impending disaster. For example, if you see an ambulance speeding toward your kids in your dream, it may be time to exercise more parental supervision.

If you're driving the ambulance in your dream, do you see yourself as a savior? Are you driving someone you know to the hospital? If so, who is it? Are you overly concerned about their well-being in waking life? If someone else is driving the ambulance and you're in the back, perhaps you feel that they'll rescue you.

The ambulance may also be wish fulfillment. Perhaps you'd love to be able to drive through red lights, disregard the road signs, and speed off to your destination with a clear and unobstructed path.

Amnesia

Quick Interpretation: Desire to forget; absent-mindedness; being in the present moment

Popular Expressions: A load off your mind; A shadow of your former self; Out of your mind

We'd all love to be able to forget certain people and experiences, but to dream of having amnesia—or that someone else has it—means that the desire to forget is pronounced. It may signify that you tend to live in the past too much, brooding over what you can't change, and that it's time to get past it and move on.

What is it that you, or someone else in your dream, wants to forget? How does it make you feel to not be able to retrieve the information? Is it upsetting or liberating?

Anaconda (Also see *Snake*.)

Quick Interpretation: Restriction; suffocation; being wound up

Popular Expressions: Snake in the grass; Snake through something

Sometimes we may feel that we've been pressured into making a decision. At other times we may feel as if our life blood is being squashed out of us, or that the oxygen in our cells is so compressed that we're about to suffocate. To dream of an anaconda implies pressure and suffocation.

Look at what the anaconda is doing in your dream and who it's harassing. Are you caught in its grip, or is someone else? What are the implications? Is the anaconda a symbol of your pressuring or suffocating someone in your life? Or is it a representation of someone who's pressuring and suffocating you?

Angel

Quick Interpretation: Help; support; imagination

Popular Expressions: On the side of the angels; Spread your wings; Waiting in the wings; Angel on your shoulder

Angels are often described as messengers from God. What area of your life do you feel needs divine intervention? Do the angels in your dream offer reassurance? Do you feel that support has arrived and that your prayers have been answered?

Perhaps the angels symbolize the need for outside help, as it's going to take a superhuman effort to accomplish what you want to get done.

Dreaming of an angel may also indicate that it's time to trust your intuition. Science and logic have their place, but magic can also happen . . . if you believe.

Anger

Quick Interpretation: Feeling threatened; frustration

Popular Expressions: Mad as hell; Mad at the world; Blind fury

When you're angry, it's a sign that you're experiencing a strong emotional response to a real or perceived threat. What is so threatening in your dream? Why do you feel so disappointed and frustrated?

Animal

Quick Interpretation: Nature; domestication; instincts

Popular Expressions: Creature comforts; Nature of the beast; Animal magnetism

We share this planet with a countless number of different species. Wouldn't it be fascinating if one day we could get some feedback from animals and find out what they think about us?!

We imbue animals with human traits. For example, people often say that foxes are cunning, owls are wise, and dogs are loyal. When you dream of an animal, it's important to find out what it represents to you. Some people are scared of rats, yet others keep them as pets. As a teenager, Michael Jackson even sang a love song about a rat named Ben.

Native Americans often use animal totems to seek information and assist them in healing. When you see an animal in a dream, ask yourself what qualities it has that you'd like to emulate. Perhaps you wish to empower someone else with these qualities.

It's important to consider how you feel about the animal, too. For example, are you afraid of it, or do you feel nurtured? Is the animal a solitary beast or part of a pack, flock, or school? How do you feel about its solitude or "pack" nature—strong and empowered, or weak and overpowered?

To determine what the animal in your dream means, you may also want to consider your ethnic background. For example, in early Roman times, the owl was a symbol for *healer,* yet in Eastern cultures it was a symbol for *predator.*

Is the animal free and able to roam unhindered in your dream, or is it caged, in a zoo, or wearing a muzzle or lead? Whatever the circumstances in the dream, they may indicate a current situation. Look at the theme of the dream and the people in it to determine the situation. Do *you* feel free and unhindered, or harassed and caged?

Did you dream of an endangered species? Is this indicative of how you feel other people treat you—that is, as though you don't exist?

The animal in your dream may also signify the way you've been behaving lately. Are you acting purely on instinct? Are you behaving in an uncivilized manner? Or do you feel that acting like an animal is really a virtue, as animals are more aligned with nature than we are? They don't pollute the environment, they don't overpopulate, and they're happy to go about their own business, leaving the worries of yesterday and tomorrow to humans.

Animation (See *Cartoon.*)

Anorexia

Quick Interpretation: Self-image; unacceptance of self; seeking perfection

Popular Expressions: Skating on thin ice; All skin and bones; Cut to the bone

Every time we try to squeeze into last year's jeans and break the zipper, we may desire greater willpower!

No matter who has anorexia in the dream, ask yourself what the heavy weight or burden is that has to be lifted. Why is such drastic action needed to remove the weight? Why is complete deprivation the only answer?

To dream of anorexia suggests little regard for one's health; the will has become so powerful that it undermines the physical body. Are you using your willpower to achieve something in life at the expense of your physical well-being?

If the dream represents a physical ailment (or can be attributed to a real-life situation), please seek professional help or advice.

Ant (Also see *Insect.*)

Quick Interpretation: Organization; hard work; structure

Popular Expression: Ants in your pants

Is there any creature on Earth more industrious, more organized, and more single-minded than the ant?

What are the ants doing in your dream? How do you feel about what they're doing? Do you feel that they're invading your privacy, forcing you to get organized and be efficient? Or do you feel that the ants are supporting you, that you're part of an efficient team that's getting things done?

If you have a large task at hand, to dream of ants may signify the need to branch out, network, and build a team around you.

Is the humble little ant in your dream a reminder that you're capable of achieving extraordinary feats once you put your mind to it? An ant can lift far more than its body weight; what can *you* do that exceeds people's expectations?

Ants have a clear hierarchy where every ant has its place. How do you feel about your social status? Do you feel you're being categorized? Do you want to change your present social standing? Do you want to be queen ant, or do you behave like a queen ant, directing other people to take care of your needs?

If you dream that you've got ants in your pants, is it an indication that you're restless and full of energy? Perhaps your unconscious is telling you to get off your butt.

Antenna

Quick Interpretation: Open to communication; transmitting information; process

Popular Expressions: To have your antennae up; Get picked up

When we have our antennae up, it suggests a desire to extend ourselves so we're more receptive to what's happening around us.

If you dream of an antenna, is it a sign that you're growing spiritually—that is, you're able to pick up all that's unseen and apply it to your life? It may also signify a desire to communicate more intuitively, or that you're on guard and looking out for warnings.

Where is the antenna, and who does it belong to? For example, if it's on your neighbors' house, what is the message you want them to pick up, or what message do you want to pick up about them?

Perhaps you want to be "picked up"—that is, the antenna may be a pun for wanting to be asked out—or perhaps wanting to ask someone out.

Antique

Quick Interpretation: Respect for the past; individuality; uniqueness

Popular Expressions: For old time's sake; The good old days; There's life in the old dog yet

At some point in our lives, we've all referred to "the good old days." To dream of antiques may signify a desire to return to a time when things are thought to have been crafted with a lot more care.

Do you wish that things were a lot less technical and mechanical in your daily life, and a lot more personal?

Is the antique in your dream valuable or an old piece of junk? Look at this in relation to any ideas or plans you've been thinking about lately—that is, how you view the antiques may indicate how you view your own thoughts. Are your ideas outdated and unoriginal, or are they rare and unique?

If the antiques feel out of place in your dream, then ask yourself what in your life no longer "fits." Who is in the dream with you? What is your relationship with them?

If you're a collector or antique dealer, the indications will, of course, be different and may have something to do with work. If you admire antiques, then to dream of them may indicate a desire for time to stand still!

Anxiety

Quick Interpretation: Irrational thoughts; apprehension; dread

Popular Expression: High anxiety

Feeling anxious indicates that you may be entertaining irrational and unsettling thoughts about your future. What are you apprehensive about in your dream? Is there something you're dreading about the coming months or years?

Apartment (Also see *House*.)

Quick Interpretation: Communal living; low maintenance; containment

Popular Expressions: That brought it home for me; On home turf; Getting on top of something; Getting in on the ground floor

We run out of space and can no longer live next to one another. So what do we do? We choose to live on top of one another! To dream of an apartment may be a symbol of wanting to get on top of things.

Are you dreaming of an upper- or lower-story apartment? Dreams that feature upper-story apartments can indicate that you have higher ideals; or lofty thoughts, visions, and desires, while lower-story apartments may signify a desire to keep your feet firmly planted on terra firma.

Apartments offer the best of both worlds—communal living and privacy. As such, they're great symbols for wanting to be more social and communal, without having to give up your independence.

If you live in a house and dream of living in an apartment, it may mean that you want to downsize. Is the apartment a symbol for wanting to simplify your life?

Apathy

Quick Interpretation: Indifference; disinterest

Popular Expressions: Give someone the cold shoulder; Turn the other cheek

When you feel apathetic, it indicates an indifference or disinterest in your surroundings. Who or what in your dream do you feel indifferent toward? Why do you feel disengaged from your emotions?

Ape (See *Animal; Baboon; Monkey*.)

Aphrodisiac

Quick Interpretation: Arousal; stimulation; lust

Popular Expressions: To whet someone's appetite; The world is my oyster; Turn someone on

Where would the human race be without aphrodisiacs? Someone or something has to turn us on to stimulate us to act.

In your dream, who is the aphrodisiac for? Is this person "switched off" and you think they need to be turned on? Is someone giving you an aphrodisiac in your dream? What is their reason for giving it to you? Do they want to take advantage of you? Are they asking you to act in a manner that's out of character?

Perhaps the aphrodisiac in your dream is a symbol for an unconscious desire to be sexually active and lustful without guilt. You can always blame your behavior on the aphrodisiac once it wears off.

To dream of an aphrodisiac may also mean that you need something to spark your imagination and creativity. Is it time to get passionate and aroused to action?

Apology

Quick Interpretation: Understanding; repair; accepting error

Popular Expressions: Forgive and forget; Actions speak louder than words; Swallow your pride

How many wars could have been avoided, lives saved, and friendships kept if people had been brave enough to utter two simple words: "I'm sorry."

If you dream of giving or receiving an apology, is it associated with pride that can't be swallowed? Or is the apology well deserved and well received? If you're apologizing in your dream, what did you hope to achieve? What needs to be repaired?

Who is receiving the apology in your dream? Does it give you (or the person receiving the apology) a feeling of superiority? Do you feel that the apology is deserved, or do you feel that there's no need for the apology, as you weren't offended in the first place?

Also consider if the apology is superficial. Is it a mediocre excuse for inefficiency? Or is someone you know trying to justify poor behavior?

Applause

Quick Interpretation: Acknowledgment; appreciation; gratitude

Popular Expressions: Give someone a big hand; A clap of thunder; Thunderous applause

The sound of a room full of people clapping is (in most instances) very pleasing.

Who's getting the recognition in your dream? Do you think it's appropriate, or is it polite applause? In other words, is it a standing ovation or an indifferent obligation? Look at the people in the dream and its location. This will give you an indication of what it is in your life that you feel you want to—or have to—applaud.

Does the applause signify that you deserve a good pat on the back?

To receive applause in a dream may also be about winning hands down! Are you basking in the glow of confidence and success?

Apple

Quick Interpretation: Forbidden fruit; health; acknowledgment

Popular Expressions: Like mixing apples and oranges; The apple of his or her eye; A bad apple; An apple a day . . . ; Getting to the core of the matter

Anytime someone tells me they dream of apples, I know I'm in for a long conversation.

To date, I haven't come across a dream where *apple* means "health," even though this may be a natural first response to this dream symbol. On the other hand, many people tend to relate to the following apple themes.

If the person has strong religious beliefs, then apples may mean forbidden fruit and temptation.

If the dreamer is a computer whiz or spends most of the day surfing the Net, it may mean they want a new computer (Apple Mac).

Managers, teachers, and other people in authority may dream of apples if they desire acknowledgment. But if my local green grocer dreams of apples, it may signify abundance, because his income is made from selling apples.

Sir Isaac Newton discovered the Law of Gravity after an apple bonked him on the head. So if you dream of an apple, it may be that someone is about to be illuminated by an idea, situation, or person. I once interpreted a dream for a young Tasmanian boy who dreamed that an apple hit him on the head as he was walking to school. To this day, he believes apples signify unexpected danger.

Also consider what you're doing with the apple in your dream. Are you eating it? How are you doing so? Eating it with gusto and confidence may suggest youth, because an older person is more likely to eat an apple tentatively. People who are overly cautious will take small bites, and if you or someone else is peeling an apple in your dream, ask yourself if that person is fussy or meticulous.

Appointment

Quick Interpretation: Arrangement; destiny; a scheduled encounter

Popular Expressions: Make a date; A date with destiny

Everyone's response to appointments is different. We're either always on time, always late, or always early.

Appointments are made to ensure that you meet up with others. To dream of an appointment may signify a desire to establish a definite connection.

Whom do you have an appointment with? Is the appointment a pun for wanting this person to elevate you to a particular position—that is, do you desire to be *appointed* to a certain status? For example, if you make an appointment with a famous football coach in your dream, is it an indication that you have a desire to be appointed to a position on a sports team?

Does someone make an appointment with *you* in your dream? If so, it may mean that this person wants to connect with you, that you want them to *want* to connect with you, or you want to connect with what they *represent* to you.

Argument (See *Fight.*)

Arm (Also see *Body Parts.*)

Quick Interpretation: Dexterity; reaching out; embrace

Popular Expressions: At arm's length; With open arms; Up in arms; To arm someone

Aromatherapy

Quick Interpretation: Trusting your senses; memory; intuition

Popular Expressions: The smell of success; Develop a nose for something

Our sense of smell is often taken for granted. We have institutions for the hearing and sight impaired, but there are no institutions for anosmiacs—people who can't detect odors!

Anything that heightens our sense of smell is powerful. To dream of aromatherapy may indicate that you're honoring your sense of smell, appreciating and attuning to the fragrances and odors that are part of your everyday life.

Are you with someone in your dream who's using aromatherapy? Are they looking to you—or are you looking to them—for a heightened sense of awareness?

To dream of aromatherapy may also indicate a need to get back to nature, or a desire to develop a nose for what is therapeutic and healing.

Arousal (Also see *Aphrodisiac*.)

Quick Interpretation: Stimulation; passion

When you feel aroused, you're stimulated into action. What has sparked your passions?

Arrow

Quick Interpretation: Flight; getting straight to the point; battle

Popular Expressions: A straight arrow; Slings and arrows; Pointed in the right direction; Getting to the point

An arrow always moves forward toward its target. This makes it a great symbol for progression, movement, and getting to the point quickly.

Who fired the arrow in your dream? What was its target? What point are you or is someone else trying to make, and why must it be made swiftly?

If the arrow is coming for you, perhaps someone is attacking you in your waking life, physically or verbally. Consider, too, the famous Shakespearean passage: *"To be, or not to be: that is the question: Whether 'tis nobler in the mind to suffer the slings and arrows of outrageous fortune, Or to take arms against a sea of troubles, And by opposing end them?"* Are you in flight or fight?

The arrow may also indicate that there's romance in the air. Has Cupid fired an arrow in your direction? Is love blossoming in your life?

Art

Quick Interpretation: Culture; creativity; expression

Popular Expressions: Art for art's sake; State of the art; As pretty as a picture;

It's amazing the value we attach to a couple of brushstrokes on a piece of canvas. Is what you see before you in your dream a piece of art or a highly overrated decoration?

Did you create a piece of artwork in your dream? If so, how do you feel about it? How is it received? Do you feel good about it but upset that no one else recognizes its value?

If someone else's work is featured in your dream, do you like or dislike it? Is your response to this person's art indicative of your relationship with them?

It's also important to consider what is depicted in the artwork. How does it make you feel? What do you want to view more or less of in your life?

What materials are used to create the art? Does this illustrate how the artist wants to convey his or her message? For example, is it in soft watercolors or striking oils?

Is the artwork in your dream extraordinarily beautiful but impractical? If so, this may be a reminder that at times we have to do things that aren't logical or rational so that we can create more beauty in our lives.

If the art you see in your dream is created by a well-known artist, is the artist dead or alive? Do you believe that you'll have to die before you're recognized for your creative work, or are you certain that you'll be rewarded for what you create in this lifetime?

Astronaut

Quick Interpretation: Desire to lighten up; exploration; feeling ungrounded

Popular Expressions: It's not rocket science; Reach for the stars; Stars in your eyes; Spaced out; Out of this world

If you want to get away from things, get a job as an astronaut. Then you'll really be able to leave the world behind.

The astronaut is a symbol for being able to see things from a distance; for gaining a new perspective on things in order to appreciate the whole situation.

Who is the astronaut in your dream? Does this person need to take a leap of faith and step out into the unknown?

To dream of an astronaut may indicate that you have a desire to live in a place where you defy the law of gravity, a place where you're weightless and without burdens. It may also symbolize your desire to break new frontiers, move beyond your limitations, and push your boundaries to discover a new place to be or a new way of living.

Asylum

Quick Interpretation: Retreat; control; request for protection

Popular Expressions: It's a madhouse; Nutty as a fruitcake; The inmates have taken over the asylum

The asylum has a double meaning. It can signify a prison or a place of confinement, or it could represent a place of safety and rest.

Are you on the outside of the asylum trying to get in, or are you on the inside trying to get out? How do you feel about your predicament? Whether you're in control or being controlled, how you feel will indicate whether you like or dislike your situation.

At first glance, an asylum may seem like a spooky symbol, but this isn't necessarily the case. To dream of an asylum may also reveal a desire to seek asylum—refuge, protection, shelter, and assurance.

Athlete

Quick Interpretation: Achievement; courage; competitive determination

Popular Expressions: Run rings around someone; Go into overdrive; Be a good sport

Our athletes are our role models. We admire their skill and physical prowess. To dream of an athlete, or that *you* are an athlete, may therefore indicate a desire to show off your athletic prowess, or it could be the acting out of wish fulfillment.

Is the athlete a symbol of a desire for fame and fortune, or a desire for health and well-being? Are you sitting back and watching the athlete on TV, perhaps indicating a projection of an unfulfilled desire?

If you're the athlete in your dream, do you feel that you're achieving your personal best, or are you just going through the motions even though your heart really isn't in it? Does this illustrate how you're responding to the physical challenge of life right now?

If someone else is the athlete, are they well known and famous, or are they an undiscovered talent? This may indicate how you feel about your own abilities. Do you feel that you've reached your full potential, or that you've got a lot of work to do yet?

Are you playing a particular sport? If it's a sport that's totally new to you, it may be time for you to pursue new directions and challenges.

ATM Card

Quick Interpretation: Efficiency; storage

The ATM (automatic teller machine) card enables you to do so much. But the beauty of it is that it's very personal. Does this card in your dream indicate that you want to pass on your personal beliefs to others? Or does someone else want to broadcast their thoughts and philosophies to other people in a secure and personal way? Perhaps you want to keep your personal information secure.

Attachment

Quick Interpretation: Fear of loss; control

Popular Expressions: Tied to one's apron strings; Like two peas in a pod

When you feel attached to a person, situation, or object, it may indicate that you want to impose your will on an outcome. What is it you want to control in your dream, or don't want to lose at any cost?

Attack

Quick Interpretation: Adversary; ambush; infringement

Popular Expressions: A battle of wills; In the firing line; Don't shoot until you see the whites of their eyes; An unprovoked attack; Fight to the finish; To jump on someone

Whether you were attacking or being attacked in your dream, I'm sure the feeling wasn't pleasant. If you're the one being attacked, do you feel that it's justified or unwarranted? If the latter is the case, ask why you see yourself as a victim. Is it an expression of how you feel about your life at the moment? Are outside forces and circumstances conspiring to threaten you in some way?

Is it a physical or verbal attack, or is someone attacking your reputation? Who is it? Is it an aspect of yourself, a colleague, a family member, or a stranger?

It's important that you understand who the adversary is in order to meet them head on. For example, let's say you're being attacked by a group of teenagers. Can it be that you fear new and hip ideas, new ways to express yourself in the world? Do you feel that you're being overpowered by change and don't know how to deal with it? If *you're* attacking the teenagers, then it may indicate that you're forcing new ideas, new beliefs, and new concepts onto others before they're ready. Do you wish to effect some sort of change in the person you're attacking?

Are you hitting the person you're attacking over the head, indicating that you want them to change the way they think? Are you beating them around the ears because you want them to listen?

Also, if you're the attacker, consider whether it's a sign that you're finally breaking out of your shell. Is it your turn to speak and you're taking no prisoners? Is it a release of frustration, and you want to seek revenge on someone who embarrassed or angered you in your waking life? There's no place like the dream world to get even.

Attic (Also see *House.*)

Quick Interpretation: Higher consciousness; storage; sanctuary

Popular Expressions: The moral high ground; Up above it all; Room at the top; On top of things; Above the fray

No matter what the circumstances, to dream of an attic indicates higher thinking. Are you in the attic, or is someone else? Is something being stored up there for later use?

Attics are often used as storage areas, places to keep bits and pieces, mementos, and general nostalgic junk. Are you on a trip down memory lane? Is it time to release the past or revisit it?

Is the attic airy, bright, and open; or dusty, rickety, and full of cobwebs? Does the state of the attic illustrate the state of your mind?

Whenever we embark on spiritual endeavors, we assume that we're reaching higher levels of consciousness. Is this where you think you're going, or where you think you are at present?

Attorney (See *Lawyer.*)

Auction

Quick Interpretation: Unknown value; a show of wealth; good or bad luck

Popular Expressions: Going, going, gone; Make a bid for it; Under the wire

Auctions excite some people, but they don't do a thing for others. How do *you* feel about them? Do they get your blood pumping—for example, do you get excited at the thought of acquiring unique, precious, or discounted items? Or do auctions leave you cold—that is, you feel that your impulses are overruled by reason and you end up paying too much?

How you feel about auctions may signify how you feel about life right now. Do you feel that you're outbidding others and getting a good deal out of life, or do you feel that others are outmaneuvering you, trying to get all they can?

Is your attitude to life that everything has a price and will be given to the highest bidder, or are you more cautious and believe that there's a reserve price that you're in control of?

Is the auction a symbol of disposing of unwanted items for profit, or are you being forced to sell your possessions to stay afloat?

Automobile (See *Car.*)

Avocado

Quick Interpretation: Rough appearance; gentle giant; big ideas

Popular Expressions: Get under someone's skin; He/she's got a thick skin; An old softie

I think the most obvious meaning for an avocado is deception. It looks like a pear, but it has skin you can't bite into and a seed so big it could choke a horse.

The fruit underneath the thick avocado skin is soft, but its center is hard. Therefore, the symbol of an avocado in a dream may suggest vulnerability, under which is hidden a heart of stone. Is this the way you see yourself, or if someone else is eating an avocado in your dream, is this the way you see them?

The avocado is a fruit, but we never include it in fruit salad. It's usually mixed with vegetables and topped with a vinaigrette dressing. Again, is it a symbol for things not being the way they seem?

The skin is so thick that you really don't know what you'll get until you cut it open. Therefore, in a dream, it could be a symbol for surprise packages or disappointment. Or perhaps you need to have a thick skin and approach a particular issue in a hard-hearted way.

However, regardless of the deception, the thick skin, and the heart of stone, an avocado can also be a symbol of satisfaction because it tastes so good! Also, because the avocado seed is so large, it may suggest a desire to reproduce.

Award Ceremony

Quick Interpretation: Recognition; achievement; arduous task completed

Popular Expressions: You reap what you sow; On top of something; A medal of honor; To the victor go the spoils; Getting one's just rewards

There are so many award ceremonies on television today that it's little wonder they take place in our dreams, too. An award ceremony provides the perfect opportunity to acknowledge people who support us.

Are you being thanked, or are you thanking someone else in your dream? If you're thanking someone else, who is it? Does this person deserve a big thank you in waking life?

Are you at an award ceremony and not being acknowledged? How does it make you feel—angry and frustrated, or simply left out? Do you feel overlooked, or do you not take it personally?

At what type of award ceremony were you? Was it the Oscars, the Emmys, the Miss Universe pageant, or were you back at school being presented with an award? What is it you wish to achieve?

Every award ceremony I've attended has run too long. When you go, you're usually only interested in a small part of the ceremony, when either you or someone close to you is presented with or is presenting an award. The rest of it can be quite tiresome. Therefore, to dream of an award ceremony may indicate a long and tedious project that only has a few highlights or golden moments but is still worthwhile.

If you received an award, what kind is it? The answer will indicate the area you want to be recognized in, where you feel you're the most creative. Perhaps the award indicates that you've completed a task to your satisfaction and it's time for you to move on to something else.

Baboon (Also see *Animal; Monkey.*)

Quick Interpretation: Territorial; violent; showing blatant sexuality

Popular Expressions: Go ape over someone; To ape something; Monkey around; Ya big ape

How is it that we associate this adaptive, clever, and resourceful primate with stupidity? Could it be that you feel you're being misjudged, or perhaps you're judging someone else?

Is the baboon a symbol of adaptability? The baboon feels just as much at home on the ground as it does in the trees. Do you feel that you readily adapt to your environment? Are you being called upon to do just that?

Consider, too, whether the baboon is a symbol for sex. After all, it's impossible to miss a baboon that's in heat. The pertinent part of the anatomy is like a beacon, bright red and engorged for the world to see. Are you signaling your availability, giving out the "I'm ready" signal, or is someone being too obvious in their sexual advances toward you?

Baby (Also see *Baby Carriage; Crib.*)

Quick Interpretation: New beginnings; commitments; growth

Popular Expressions: A babe in arms; Baby steps; To baby someone; Cry like a baby; Don't throw out the baby with the bathwater; Handle with kid gloves; Something that's in its infancy; Change is in the air; Giving birth to a concept or idea

A baby is a lot more than a bundle of joy. I don't think anyone will disagree that it's also a big bundle of commitment and dedication.

Whose baby is it? Yours or someone else's? If it's yours and you're not pregnant—and don't wish to be—then it may suggest new ideas, new projects, or new beginnings.

Whether it's related to a career or a relationship, a baby in a dream should remind you that to achieve any goal there must be an incubation period that allows the idea or plan to develop, a development stage where you sketch the idea or plan out, and finally, when it's on its feet, lots of attention and TLC.

Is the baby happy or crying? Does it need changing—again, a good indicator that your project needs attention, and perhaps a change in direction.

Do you need to feed the baby, or is it satisfied and just wants to play? If it needs feeding, is that an indicator that you need to give your project or creation more attention and time?

If it's someone else's baby, do you feel overburdened with their obligations? Or are you honored that someone is entrusting you with what could be the single most valuable thing they have?

Perhaps the baby suggests that you want to be nurtured and looked after so that you don't have to take responsibility for yourself.

Of course, if you're pregnant or desire to be pregnant, the baby has many other connotations, including wish fulfillment.

Baby Carriage (Also *see Baby.*)

Quick Interpretation: Nurturing ideas; transportation; driving force

Popular Expressions: Give something a big push; Love, marriage, then the baby carriage

A baby carriage may be a symbol of wish fulfillment, or a reminder of your obligations. Is your child or someone else's in the carriage? If someone else is pushing the carriage, do you feel that this person is in control?

Bachelor/Bachelorette

Quick Interpretation: Unattached; solitary; uncommitted

Popular Expressions: Footloose and fancy free; Free as a bird; A swingin' single; Breaking the ties that bind

Dreaming that you're single—or that someone else is single and it's an issue—is quite telling, especially if it's not by choice. First, decide if it suggests a desire for a relationship or a need to get out of a relationship.

If someone in your dream is a bachelor or a bachelorette and you admire them, or you feel envious and desirous, then it may indicate that the thought or experience of being single makes you happy. If you don't like what you see and you're annoyed or apprehensive, then the idea of being single may not appeal to you.

What does the single person look like? Is it someone who's old and set in their ways, who has no room for anyone else in their life? If so, this may indicate that you're either afraid of intimacy or prefer to be single.

Is the person a playboy/girl, hopping from nest to nest, breaking hearts? This may indicate that you have no problems with intimacy, but perhaps commitment is an issue for you.

If you're an older person and you dream that you're a bachelor/bachelorette, then you may be remembering a time when you were more happy-go-lucky. Perhaps you'd like to be free of the commitments of married life, children, and paying off a mortgage?

A final consideration concerns study—that is, a bachelor's degree. Is the bachelor a symbol of a desire for acknowledgment of your scholastic achievements, or do you seek to learn something new academically?

Back (Also see *Body Parts*.)

Quick Interpretation: Support; strength; leave behind

Popular Expressions: Get your back up; Go behind someone's back; Back someone up

Bacon

Quick Interpretation: Success; being tempted; desire for affluence

Popular Expressions: Bring home the bacon; Save someone's bacon; Pig ignorant; Something that sizzles

How was bacon ever connected with success and supporting a family? Why did we choose to say "Bring home the bacon" and not "Bring home the beef" or "Bring home the lamb"?!

Who is eating the bacon in the dream, or who owns the bacon, indicating either a breadwinner or a successful person?

If you belong to a particular faith that forbids the consumption of bacon (pork) and you desire it in a dream, it may be indicative of partaking in temptation despite the taboos.

Consider, too, whether it's a symbol for salvation—that is, someone has saved your bacon.

Bag

Quick Interpretation: Travel; success; a put-down

Popular Expressions: Left holding the bag; It's in the bag; Let the cat out of the bag; Let's bag it; Someone who's got a lot of baggage

Anything that's used for carrying or storing something is included in this category—that is, handbags, backpacks, suitcases, purses, or valises.

The symbol of a bag can signify old thoughts, old belief patterns, stored emotions, and unresolved issues. If you're carrying the bag, think about the baggage you're holding on to. Why are you hanging on to it?

If you're carrying the item on your head, the significance is more profound. Items carried on the head may signify thoughts, concerns, and aspirations that weigh heavily on the mind and need to be dealt with quickly.

What type of bag is it? Is it extremely heavy and a real chore to handle? Do you have an express desire to load it, dump it, or get it off you? Or are you managing it with only minor discomfort?

In some cases, the dreamer may see names or initials on the bag. This will immediately identify whose "baggage" you're carrying around with you.

Did you look into the bag? Are the items in it yours? If you identify them as someone else's, again it indicates that you're carrying around someone else's baggage. If the bag is full of junk, ask yourself what you're hanging on to that's useless or out-dated. Perhaps an old belief system may be weighing you down. If the bag is neat and tidy, you may have a deep-seated belief that if you arrange things in your life systematically and put your thoughts in order, then you can clarify your direction.

Bagpipes

Quick Interpretation: Winded; ventilated; signifying a gathering

Popular Expressions: Blowin' in the wind; An old windbag; Full of hot air

If you feel that you're full of hot air—or someone else is—then there's no symbol like the bagpipes to highlight the situation.

In your dream, could the bagpipes be a symbol of not knowing what you're talking about (or someone else not knowing)? Are you (or they) simply a big bag of wind?

The symbol may also indicate respect. It takes a lot of dexterity to play the bagpipes. Ask who's playing the bagpipes and why they're playing them.

Bagpipes can also symbolize pomp and ceremony, valor and heroism. Is there anything more striking than pipers marching before a column of troops as they go into battle?

Bakery

Quick Interpretation: Sustenance; making money (dough); bringing an idea to completion

Popular Expressions: Half a loaf is better than none; A half-baked scheme; A bun in the oven; Breaking bread together

A bakery is warm and inviting, a place to satisfy all the senses. Do you associate the bakery in your dream with warmth and security? Or is it a pun for making money (that is, bread)?

What are you doing at the bakery in your dream? Are you looking for bread, is someone giving it to you, or are you working hard to produce it? What is your relationship to the bread? Is it indicative of your relationship to money?

The bakery may also signify a feeling of success regarding future projects—that is, it's a place where creative projects rise!

Ball

Quick Interpretation: Play; competition; focus

Popular Expressions: On the ball; Having a ball; Take the ball and run with it; That's the way the ball bounces; To bounce back

To think that a simple object such as this is such an important part of our recreational life! It's hard to name a team sport that *doesn't* involve a ball.

Ask who's playing with the ball in your dream. Do you feel they're on the ball, getting things perfect and heading in the right direction? Or are they fumbling with the ball and dropping it, indicating incompetence?

Do you associate the ball with feelings of joy and bliss—that is, are you having a ball? Consider, too, that the ball in your dream may be a pun on "bawl." Are you experiencing a particularly intense and emotional time?

What shape is the ball? Round or oval? Hard or soft? Does it bounce evenly, or does it fall flat? Become the ball. The way it behaves and looks may give you insight into how you feel you're playing the big game called Life.

Ballet

Quick Interpretation: Precision; practice; caution

Popular Expressions: On your toes; A balancing act

Grace, poise, and elegance are associations that come to mind when you think of ballet. It's also associated with discipline, endurance, and flexibility.

Are you watching a ballet or performing in one? Is there a performance of a particular ballet—for example, *Romeo and Juliet* or *Swan Lake?* If so, how does it relate to your current circumstances? Perhaps you're being reminded to stay on your toes—or is another person trying to keep you on your toes?

Is someone the prima ballerina in your dream—in other words, a high-maintenance person who takes up a lot of your time and energy?

Ballet dancers aren't only fit, but extremely flexible. Does the dancer in your dream reflect a desire for greater flexibility in your life?

Balloon

Quick Interpretation: Inflated ego; unrealized dream; a carefree air

Popular Expressions: Went down like a lead balloon; A trial balloon; Up, up, and away; Above it all; Floating on air

This symbol is associated with festivity and celebration. How do you feel about this time of your life? Is it a time of celebration for you?

Are the balloons floating in your dream, or are they on the ground? Floating balloons suggest high spirits, a feeling of buoyancy. If they're on the ground, it may indicate a desire to lift your spirits—or someone else's.

When we float on air, we feel empowered and unencumbered. Where is the balloon? Are there other people with you in the dream? This information will help you determine why you feel good about life.

Also, consider the expression "sunk like a lead balloon." Has something or someone disappointed you in your waking life?

Are the balloons in a cluster, displaying a rainbow of color? Who is holding the balloons? This person may be the custodian of a pot of gold at the end of your rainbow.

Ballroom (Also see *Dance.*)

Quick Interpretation: Social occasions; coming of age; formalities

Popular Expressions: Lead you a merry dance; Belle of the ball

There are ballrooms and there are ballrooms. For some of us, the lights are bright and you have a partner in your arms. For others, the lights are flashing and there's no partner.

Is the ballroom in your dream the traditional type where everyone dances in time, or is it a modern dancehall—an old warehouse where everyone is raging. (If it's the latter, please see *Dance.*)

What's happening in the ballroom? Are you up and dancing, or are you sitting against the wall, a lonely wallflower waiting to be asked for a dance? If the latter is the case, ask yourself if you're scared of rejection. It may be an indication that it's time to be more forthright in your life.

Are *you* in the ballroom? Were you dragged there and forced to attend, or did you choose to go? All in all, is the ballroom a symbol of being joyful and uplifted, partaking in a social occasion that invigorates your soul?

Bandage

Quick Interpretation: Display of pain; healing; support

Popular Expressions: A bleeding heart; Lick your wounds

If time heals all wounds, then what do you need a bandage for?! What is being bandaged up in your dream? Is it a stopgap measure? Are you trying to fix something momentarily without putting much thought or energy into it?

On the other hand, the bandage may be a symbol of tender loving care. Has it been applied to protect an open wound from becoming infected? Is this symbolic of a nurturing relationship in your life right now? Are you sharing TLC with someone, or is someone sharing it with you?

What are the bandages like? Are they clean and sterilized, or soiled and diseased? This may indicate whether or not the treatments you're applying to your wounds are working. If you're treating a wound in your waking life, the bandage may be alerting you to an infection.

What type of wounds are you covering up? Are they being healed or camouflaged?

Bank (Also see *Money.*)

Quick Interpretation: Safety; red tape; wealth

Popular Expressions: To bank on something; Laugh all the way to the bank; Break the bank; Checking something out; Take credit for something

What a bank represents to you in a dream is as personal as your checking-account number. To some it's a symbol of security, safety, and strength; to others, a symbol of debt and repayments.

How does the bank make you feel in your dream? Do you feel abundant, safe, and secure; or overwhelmed, vulnerable, and in over your head? Are you in the bank to deposit money or withdraw it? Are you robbing the bank, or is the bank robbing you? Is there anyone in the bank with you? Are you banking on them for something, or are they banking on you?

If you expect people to keep their word, or vice versa—that is, you're really *banking* on it, then the symbol of a bank may appear in a dream. Or it may be that the symbol appears as a river "bank." If you're sitting on a bank, it may signify that you only want to bank on yourself.

The symbol of a bank may also indicate that you want to turn in another direction, just as an aircraft banks (tips to one side) when it turns.

Is the bank solid, upstanding, and old-fashioned, indicating that you want order, stability, and respect when it comes to financial affairs? Or is it an electronic system with no tellers, indicating that you'd prefer to have more control over your financial dealings?

A bank may also signify that you need to spend more time getting your accounts in order and that you should pay attention to your finances.

Credit cards are so easy to acquire these days that many people spend beyond their means without foreseeing the consequences. Does the bank in your dream indicate that you take credit for things you don't deserve?

Banquet (See *Feast.*)

Baptism

Quick Interpretation: Being reborn; rite of passage; rehydration

Popular Expressions: A baptism of fire; Soaked to the skin; Keeping one's head above water; In over your head

To wash away your troubles and sins is a wonderful feeling. It doesn't matter what faith you follow, baptism in a dream is a universal symbol associated with cleansing.

Who is being baptized in your dream? What are the circumstances of the baptism? Is it a christening or an initiation into a new faith (unwittingly)? Or is an older person being baptized, indicating a change in a belief system?

If you're being baptized in the dream, do you feel reenergized, regenerated, and ready to start afresh? Or are you doing it to please someone else? If you've never been baptized in waking life, is it a symbol of an unfulfilled desire?

To dream of being baptized may indicate that you're ready for bigger challenges. You're ready and willing to throw yourself head first into a baptism of fire.

Bar (Also see *Drinking; Drunkenness.*)

Quick Interpretation: Meeting place; rejection; law

Popular Expressions: Lay down the law; The law of the land; Raise the bar; To bar someone from something

It's hard to get a drink in a bar these days without a valid ID—even if you look old enough to drink, you may be asked to prove it!

In your dream, do you feel that you have to *prove* that you're worthy of drinking—that is, that you're mature enough to handle it? Is the dream about your ability to handle intoxicating thoughts and/or temptations?

What are you doing at the bar? Is it a social occasion with friends and family celebrating over a few drinks? Or are you drowning your sorrows—crying into your beer and telling your life story to the bartending staff?

Perhaps the bar is indicative of a desire to improve yourself in some way. Have you gone as far as you can in a certain area of your life? Is it time to put more energy into it and increase the challenge—that is, lift the bar?

Barbecue

Quick Interpretation: Incineration; creative transformation; social interaction

Popular Expressions: Be my guest; Rake someone over hot coals

There's nothing like a barbecue to complement the beauty of the great outdoors. Is the barbecue in your dream a symbol of wanting to get out in nature and be social? Of wanting to get out of a confined cooking space—that is, the kitchen?

Generally speaking, the barbecue is a symbol of festivity and joyfulness. But if you feel ill at ease about the barbecue in your dream, perhaps it symbolizes being raked over hot coals. Do you feel you're being put on the spot in your waking life?

Consider, too, that the word *barbecue* (that is, being barbecued) implies being done over. Are you doing someone over, or do you feel someone is doing *you* over?

Men often seem to be in charge of the barbecue. If you're female, this dream could indicate a desire to be free from domestic chores. If male, it may be that you'd like to be more dominant in a man's world.

Barn

Quick Interpretation: Storage; love of animals; shelter

Popular Expressions: Close the barn door after the horse has bolted; A roll in the hay

Unless you live in the country, garages are our modern-day barns. We swapped the horse for the car, the plough for the power tool, the hay for gasoline.

Does the barn in your dream indicate a desire to go back to a simpler life when people worked closer to the land?

If you dream of your own barn, is it neat and orderly or a jumbled mess? This could indicate either a desire to clean up your act or to loosen up a bit and just hang out.

Films about trips to the country often depict the barn as a place where one can either lose their virginity or have a good ol' roll in the hay. Consider whether the barn in your dream is a desire to get out of the house and play.

Baseball (Also see *Sports.*)

Quick Interpretation: Success; moving forward; team effort

Popular Expressions: Hit and run; Hit a ball out of the park; Strike out; Make a pitch for something; Cover your bases; Run rings around someone

In a game of baseball, the ultimate achievements include either hitting a home run or making sure someone strikes out. Do you want to hit home runs, or do you want to strike out an opponent?

Your approach to baseball in your dream may illustrate your approach to a real-life challenge. Is your focus on how to achieve your best, or is it on how to bring your opponent down?

If you're pitching, the baseball game may be a pun for "making a pitch." Are you putting forward a proposition in your life?

Are you playing infield or outfield? That is, are you right in there with the action, or are you waiting for something to come your way?

It's important to gauge how fanatical you are about baseball. The intensity of your feelings about the game is a good indication of your loyalty to a cause. Are you a one-eyed supporter, sticking to your team even if they're coming in last? Or are you a fair-weather friend, supporting a team only when it's on top?

Baseball is about team effort, but there's room for individual achievement. Does your baseball dream indicate that personal excellence is possible even when you're part of a team?

Baseball Cap (Also see *Hat.*)

Quick Interpretation: Protection; disguise

Popular Expressions: Talk through your hat; On the team

We place ads on everything these days, including the items we wear. It started with T-shirts, and now it's baseball caps. Athletes often wear caps emblazoned with their sponsor's logo. Is the cap in your dream an advertisement for something? What is it that you want to communicate to other people?

To dream of a baseball cap suggests that something is on your mind. What is it that you're analyzing or contemplating? Or are you being alerted to something? For example, if there's an orange embroidered on your cap, does this suggest that you should be taking more vitamin C?

If you never wear a baseball cap and see yourself wearing one in a dream, is it a symbol of wanting to be younger and more hip, or are you wearing it to hide from someone, indicating a desire to be more mysterious?

If the cap is a loose fit, it may suggest that you can handle whatever is on your mind if you'd only loosen up a bit.

Are you wearing the cap back to front, indicating that you like to do things in defiance of the status quo? Or are you an older person who simply wants to feel young at heart?

Basement (Also see *House.*)

Quick Interpretation: The subconscious; hidden thoughts; storage

Popular Expressions: Under your nose; Down in the dumps

B asements are often seen to be the lowliest part of a building, but they're also the fundamental part, the "base." Is the basement in your dream a symbol that indicates it's time to get back to basics (back to the fundamentals) to understand what's going on in your life?

How deep is the basement? Is it just below ground level, or is it deep in the earth, perhaps indicating the depth of the journey you're presently on?

Consider, too, whether the basement symbolizes something within your unconscious that needs to surface and be brought out in the open.

Bat (Also see *Animal.*)

Quick Interpretation: Sensing; heightened intuition; looking at things differently

Popular Expressions: Right off the bat; Go to bat for someone; Up at bat

W hat was the first bat thinking when it decided that hanging upside down was a cool thing to do?! If you dream of a bat, ask yourself if you should look at things from a different perspective or angle.

Also, consider whether it's a warning to take care and not be impulsive—that is, there's a rush of blood to the head when you hang upside down. Similarly, do you feel that your whole world has been turned upside down? Who's in the dream with you? Are they trying to turn your world upside down?

Bats are commonly associated with vampires. Is something in your life draining you of energy, or are you in a relationship that's draining your vitality?

Is it time for you to get back into the game and be proactive— that is, is it your turn at bat?

Bathroom (See *Toilet.*)

Bathtub

Quick Interpretation: Mistake; cleaning up; danger

Popular Expressions: Skin-deep; Come out in the wash; Throw the baby out with the bathwater; Take a bath on something; Soak something up; In hot water; Running hot and cold

To see a bathtub in a dream can be an exciting or ominous symbol. It's important to notice where the bathtub is. If it's in the workplace, then perhaps you're making unprofitable financial decisions. Equally, if it's in a place where you have some sort of partnership or alliance, it may be a sign that you're cruisin' for a bruisin'. If it's in a home environment, in nature, or somewhere pleasurable, it may be a symbol of cleansing, regeneration, and nurturing.

Who is in the bathtub? Is it you? Is there a feeling of luxury and contentment associated with your bath, or do you feel exposed? Are you relaxing and enjoying yourself, or do you feel that you're about to pull the plug on something?

If you see a bathtub emptied in the dream, are you concerned that your good ideas are being wasted or ignored? Is the baby being thrown out with the bathwater? To dream of a bathtub may indicate that something should be cleaned up in your life. Does something need to be washed or purified?

Are you immersed in the water, or are your arms and legs hanging out? Do you feel that you can't completely cover yourself?

Is it too hot for you in the tub? Are you in hot water, or is someone you know in hot water? On the other hand, the water may be too cold. Are you going cold on something, or is someone going cold on you?

If you continually dream about being in a bathtub, check your body odor. It could be that your dream is telling you what your best friends can't!

Battle

Quick Interpretation: Difference of opinion; projection of wills; outcomes

Popular Expressions: Battle of wills; A running battle; Fight a losing battle; Win the battle but lose the war; Fight to the finish

Each and every one of us has had to fight a battle of some sort in our lives. The question is, what is the conflict about? Are the two opposing forces you and your shadow? In other words, are you battling with an aspect of yourself that you'd prefer to ignore?

Is it a battle between you and a loved one? What are you fighting about? Is this person an aspect of yourself, or are you trying to work through a recent conflict you had with this individual?

How do you feel about the battle in your dream? Do you feel triumphant or defeated? Is this indicative of a situation that's challenging you in your waking life?

Are you fighting in the thick of the battle, or are you observing it? Is the battle being fought chivalrously, or is it undignified and cruel?

Consider your responses in relation to an inner conflict that's taking place within you and begging for resolution.

Also, ask what got you into this predicament, where you feel the only way out is through force.

Beach (Also see *Ocean; Sand; Water.*)

Quick Interpretation: Exposure; fun; being marooned

Popular Expressions: Life's a beach; Bury your head in the sand; Not the only pebble on the beach; Everything under the sun; Getting burned by someone

Unless you're a whale, the beach is a great place to have fun, and it's a symbol of getting away and relaxing. How do you feel about being on the beach in your dream? Is it wish fulfillment, symbolizing a desire to get away from it all? Or do you feel like a whale that's stuck and helpless on the beach, an indication perhaps that your freedom is being stifled?

Are you exposing yourself on the beach more than you normally would in waking life? If so, it may represent a desire to show people more of who you are in a social and playful environment.

Who are you on the beach with? Are you getting "burned" by them, or is this relationship a sign that anything under the sun is possible?

Bear (Also see *Animal.*)

Quick Interpretation: Strength; solitude; hibernation

Popular Expressions: A bear of a problem; Grin and bear it; Can't bear something

Wouldn't it be great to find a comfy and cozy place to sleep through the winter, and then reappear a few months later in time for spring!

To dream of a bear may indicate that it's time to slow down, reflect, and bide your time until it's appropriate to act. In our modern world, we aren't encouraged to sit back and not act. There's a fear that we may miss an opportunity.

Is the bear in your dream aggressive or playful? If it's the former, does it represent a perceived threat—for example, do you feel that someone or something is threatening your territory or loved ones?

If the bear is playful and calm, is it indicative of how you feel about your life at the moment? Are you in absolute control and the master of your environment?

The bear may also be a pun on "to bear." Do you want to bear a new idea or project, and can't bear to wait any longer to share it with the world?

Beard

Quick Interpretation: Camouflage; wisdom; manhood

Popular Expressions: Haven't seen hide nor hair of someone; A blessing in disguise

If you ever want to change your appearance or disguise yourself, a beard is the way to go—if, of course, you're male.

Is the beard a symbol of disguise in your dream? Is someone attempting to hide their true self in your dream? Or are you attempting to disguise something or someone?

The priests of many old religions were required to wear beards. Is the beard in your dream a symbol of spirituality? A sign of turning inward and focusing less on physical appearance?

If you don't have a beard and you grow one in a dream, how do you feel about it? If you're a male, do you feel more or less attractive with the beard? How you feel about the beard may indicate how you feel about growing older. If you're a female, does the beard represent a desire to be more masculine?

If you dream of shaving off a beard, does this illustrate a desire for more precision and excitement in your life—that is, do you prefer a clean, close shave?

Beauty Salon

Quick Interpretation: Makeover; gossip; fountain of youth

Popular Expressions: Beauty is skin-deep; Beauty is in the eye of the beholder; That's the beauty of it; Present a different face to the world; To face something; Turn the other cheek

I f beauty is only skin-deep, then why do we spend so much time going to beauty salons?!

Is someone receiving a beauty treatment in your dream? If so, do they want to present a different face to the world? Of course, if you work as a hair stylist, the implications are clearly work/career related. Ask yourself how you feel about your job.

If you regularly visit a beauty salon, ask yourself why you go. This will help you to determine the meaning of the beauty salon in your dream. For example, if you go to be pampered, are you being reminded that it's time for some TLC?

What do you associate the beauty salon with? With a fear of getting older, or is it a means to boost your confidence and feel more powerful?

Traditionally, the beauty salon is a place of hot gossip. It may, therefore, represent a desire to catch up on the latest news—to be in the know!

Bed

Quick Interpretation: Rest; expression of sexuality; consequences

Popular Expressions: You've made your bed, now lie in it; Get out on the wrong side of the bed; Life's a bed of roses; Pillow talk

W hether we make our beds or not, we still have to lie in them. Have you created an uncomfortable situation in your life that you can't escape?

Is the bed warm and welcoming, a place to regenerate and revitalize? Or is it messy, uninhabitable, and inappropriate for its purpose? The neater the bed, the more confident you feel about having control over your destiny—and taking responsibility for it.

Is the dream sexual? After all, the bed is the most popular place to fool around! Who's in bed with you? Do you want to get into bed with this person in your waking life? If the dream isn't sexual, think of it in relation to business, or a career move. The person you're in bed with may be indicative of a close business relationship—or the desire for one.

The symbol of a bed in your dream may also indicate a wish to get back to basics and put things in order.

Bee

Quick Interpretation: Being stung; activity; networking

Popular Expressions: A bee in your bonnet; As busy as a bee; Getting stung by something; The sting of rejection; Create a buzz around something

Is there an insect more ingenious than the bee? Not only do they pollinate, but they fetch honey, conveniently storing it in a hive for us to collect.

Are the bees in your dream threatening, or are you concerned that you could be stung? This may be a literal fear if you're allergic to bees.

Do you admire the way the bees network and are cooperative with one another to achieve a result? Is this indicative of a situation in your life that calls for more cooperation from either yourself or someone else? Or do you feel that you're part of the crowd and that your participation is overlooked?

Is the bee a symbol of wanting to get involved in a hive of activity, or that you want to escape the hive?

Perhaps you'd like to be more with it, more in tune with what's going on—that is, you want to know what the buzz is.

Beer (Also see *Bar; Drinking; Drunkenness.*)

Quick Interpretation: Fermentation; celebration

Popular Expressions: Someone who has a big head; Something's brewing

Beggar

Quick Interpretation: Outside support; handouts; pleading a cause

Popular Expressions: Beggars can't be choosers; Beg the question; Beg to differ; Plead one's case

We often associate begging with poverty and desperation, yet we can also see it as a yearning for compassion, charity, and understanding.

Are you begging in the dream? What are you crying out for and desperately needing from others? If it's someone else who's begging, are you playing the role of giver in your life at the moment? How do you feel about it?

In your dream, do you give to the beggar without a second thought, or do you ignore the beggar? Do you give enough to make a difference, or do you find a coin of the lowest value and toss that? This may be an indication of how you're treating an aspect of yourself that needs your attention at the moment.

How do you feel about being asked? Is it offensive to you, or do you feel okay about it? If you feel offended, it may indicate that you'd prefer to volunteer your generosity rather than feel that you're expected to.

Perhaps the beggar symbolizes that you hold a different opinion from the people around you—that is, as much as you'd like to see their point of view, you beg to differ!

Bell

Quick Interpretation: Warning; keeping watch; celebration

Popular Expressions: As clear as a bell; Saved by the bell; With bells on; Ring someone up; A ring of truth to it

The sound of a bell can mean a number of different things, from "Lunch is served" to "It's time to pray." What sound is the bell emitting in your dream? Explore how you feel about it. A fast, consistent ring may imply a situation that's grave and intense. If the ring is slow and subtle, perhaps it's simply a reminder. Are you being reminded of an important lesson or event?

Where does the ringing come from? From a church, indicating a spiritual message? Or is it a warning, indicating an emergency such as a fire or an attack? How do you react to the emergency? Do you feel overwhelmed and outmaneuvered? Is it a situation that seems hopeless up until the last moment, but just as you think all is lost, you're saved by the bell?

Bet (Also see *Gambling.*)

Quick Interpretation: Risk; dare; contest

Popular Expressions: A run for your money; hedge your bets; A sure thing

Beverage (See *Drinking.*)

Bicycle

Quick Interpretation: Movement; transportation; balance

Popular Expressions: A bicycle built for two; Just like riding a bike; Put your pedal to the metal; An uphill climb; Back-pedal on something

The great thing about learning to ride a bike is that you never forget! Is the bicycle in your dream a symbol of trust—that is, you know that once you learn how to do something properly, you'll never forget it? Perhaps it's a symbol of encouragement and you're being reminded to draw upon skills you've acquired over a lifetime.

Is it your bicycle or someone else's? The answer will indicate how independent you feel you are.

Where are you riding the bike to in your dream? If you don't usually ride one in your waking life, consider the destination and how you feel about bicycle riding. This will tell you something about how you're moving toward your destination. For example, if you're riding a bicycle to work in your dream and you associate bicycle riding with health and increased energy, is this how you're approaching (or would like to approach) your work?

Are you backpedaling in your dream? Is it time to pull back, reassess a situation, and maybe change direction? Is it time to slow down?

Bird (Also see *Dove; Eagle; Owl; Vulture.*)

Quick Interpretation: Messages; freedom; overview

Popular Expressions: The early bird catches the worm; A bird in the hand; Free as a bird; On a wing and a prayer; To wing it; A nest egg; An eagle eye; A wise old owl; Eat like a vulture; Eyes like a hawk

We call birds our feathered friends. I imagine that it's because watching and listening to them gives us so much pleasure. Or is it that birds deliver messages from up above?

In the ancient world, people believed that birds resided "up there" with the gods, flying down to Earth to convey messages. What is the message that the bird in your dream is trying to convey? To help you find out, determine what kind of bird it is and what you associate it with.

Eagles are often associated with independence because they're kicked out of the nest early. They also fly high . . . and we mustn't forget an eagle's eye! Similarly, if you see a hawk in a dream, think of it in relation to super vision. Do you need eyes like a hawk to ascertain what's happening around you? Or do you feel that situations need *supervision*—that you need to watch things like a hawk?

Is the bird in your dream an owl, implying wisdom? Or do you see vultures, suggesting parasitic behavior? Vultures are also great garbage-disposal units, and therefore an indispensable part of nature.

Perhaps a dove, sparrow, crow, seagull, or pigeon appears in your dream . . . the list is long. To understand the bird's significance, simply think of the character associations you give your feathered friend in relation to your own life.

Birth (Also see *Pregnancy.*)

Quick Interpretation: Renewal; extension of self; emergence of new ideas

Popular Expressions: Breathe new life into something; I wasn't born yesterday; Give birth to an idea

We often associate birth with new beginnings, yet before birth can take place, there must be a period of gestation, not to mention conception.

If you witness a birth (or give birth) in a dream, ask if it's the culmination of a lot of hard work. Is a new idea, concept, or project being born?

Obviously, if you're pregnant or you want to be pregnant, the birth either reflects your current experience or is, perhaps, wish fulfillment. If you have no intention of starting (or increasing the size of) a family, consider the birth in relation to a new career, relationship, or abode.

Who's giving birth? And to what? Is the baby bright, bubbly, and healthy, or is it sickly and unwell? Your answers will indicate how you feel about what has been recently created, whether it's a new relationship, career, or whatever.

In the dream, did you get a distinct image of the partner who was involved in conception? How you feel about the birth will indicate how you feel about the partner. Maybe you're considering a partnership with this person.

If it's a caesarean birth, does this indicate a prominent and renowned birth, as was Julius Caesar's?

Birthday

Quick Interpretation: Celebration; passing of time; origins

Popular Expression: Wear your birthday suit

In the early part of our lives, we can't wait for birthdays to come around, then comes the day when we start to wish that our birthdays occurred every leap year.

Are you celebrating your birthday? How do you feel about the celebration? Is it a celebration of achievement, or do you feel regret—that is, that another year has gone by and you haven't accomplished what you wanted to get done? Who is celebrating your birthday with you? Or are you celebrating someone else's birthday? Your answer will indicate the kind of people you want to celebrate life with at the moment.

Are you blowing out candles on a birthday cake in your dream? If so, do you do it effortlessly, or does it take a few puffs before you're able to blow them all out? This may reveal how you're handling the passage of time—is it with ease, or is it leaving you breathless?

Perhaps the dream indicates that you want to expose who you really are—that is, you want to put on your birthday suit.

Blackboard

Quick Interpretation: Ideas; transiency; knowledge

Popular Expressions: In black and white; In the black; Like fingernails on a blackboard; Chalk something up

Increasingly, blackboards are being superseded by whiteboards. The blackboard is a thing of the past. Is the blackboard in your dream a symbol of outdated ideas? What needs updating in your life?

What are you writing on the blackboard? Are you writing out lines of repetitious sentences because you've misbehaved, or are you solving a problem? Is the blackboard a symbol of feeling irritated—that is, when it comes into contact with certain objects (like fingernails), the sound can be excruciating.

If sound is a feature in your dream and it makes you feel ill at ease, what is it associated with? Is it connected to the message being written on the blackboard? Or does it relate to the person who's writing the message? Is he or she causing the hairs on the back of your neck to rise?

Seeing a blackboard as opposed to a whiteboard in a dream may suggest that you're perceiving the world as mostly dark with a little bit of light, rather than mostly light with a little bit of dark.

Blanket

Quick Interpretation: Security; warmth; superficial covering

Popular Expressions: A wet blanket; A security blanket; To blanket oneself with something

How could we ever dismiss the wet blanket as a killjoy when it can do useful things such as put out fires! Is the blanket in your dream warm and cozy, or is it wet and uncomfortable? If the blanket in your dream is dry, warm, and comforting, then it may indicate how warm and secure you feel at the moment. You know you're safe. If not, it may be that the people or situations in your life that you wish were supportive are not.

Is the blanket a symbol of protection against outside forces, or is it a symbol of deception? What is being covered up?

The blanket may also symbolize a desire to forget something or block it out.

Blessing

Quick Interpretation: Good fortune

Popular Expression: A blessed event

When you feel blessed, you believe that good fortune has been bestowed upon you. What do you feel fortunate about?

Blindfold

Quick Interpretation: Mystery; games; termination

Popular Expressions: A blind spot; Turn a blind eye; Blind as a bat; See no evil; Sight unseen

Unless you're in front of a firing squad, a blindfold symbolizes mystery. The first (and most obvious) question to ask is: What don't you want to see? Is what's happening in your life so frightening that you want to turn a blind eye to it? Or are you completely unaware of what's happening and therefore undaunted because you're blindfolded?

Is the blindfold used as part of a game, indicating a desire to make things more interesting, mysterious, and challenging in your life? Are you excited by the thought of exploring the world with your other senses?

Do you put the blindfold on yourself, or does someone put it on you? How do you feel about being blindfolded? Are you resentful or trusting? Do you attempt to remove the blindfold in your dream, or do you make the most of it despite the handicap?

If you're blindfolding someone else in your dream, why don't you want them to see what's happening?

What kind of blindfold is it? Is it made of coarse material and bound so tight that it constricts your circulation? Does this indicate that you're blind to logical thought and your reasoning powers are restricted? Or is the blindfold made of silk and placed lightly over your eyes by a mysterious dream lover promising a sensual adventure?

Bliss

Quick Interpretation: Ease; comfort; resolution

Popular Expression: Ignorance is bliss

A feeling of bliss indicates a supreme state of ease. What have you resolved? If this isn't a feeling that you commonly experience in your waking life, are you satisfying your need to feel "blissed out" in your dream?

Blood

Quick Interpretation: Life force; ancestry; revenge

Popular Expressions: Blood is thicker than water; It makes my blood boil; Flesh and blood; Blood brothers; A bleeding heart; My heart bleeds for you

Blood isn't only our life stream, it's our pedigree. Where is the blood in your dream? Is it oozing rapidly from an open wound, indicating an outpouring of emotion such as lust, anger, and passion?

Is the blood more indicative of pedigree and kinship—blood being the link to our ancestors—therefore signifying a wish to connect with your past?

Who is with you in the dream? Do you feel they're trying to suck you of your life blood and drain you of power? Or are you giving the blood voluntarily in an attempt to save a life? Is this life an aspect of yourself that you're trying to save?

If you desire inspiration in your life, the blood may indicate that you're on the lookout for new blood.

Of course, for women, it could be associated with menstruation, which may in turn imply a desire to align with nature. It may also be a symbol of release or inner reflection, a time to withdraw from the world and be alone.

Boat (Also see *Sailing; Ship; Yacht.*)

Quick Interpretation: Buoyancy; rising above emotion

Popular Expressions: Don't rock the boat; Miss the boat; In the same boat; The boat sailed without you

If you ever want to be more buoyant in life, getting on a boat is a good place to start. Could the boat in your dream symbolize a desire to be more cheerful and lighthearted?

What kind of boat are you in? Is it a speedboat fully powered and taking to the sea with ease, or is it a leaking tub that takes a lot of hard work to keep afloat? This could indicate how you feel about your ability to stay afloat in life.

Is it a sailboat, indicating self-motivation and the use of natural force to get you to your destination; or is it a yacht (a pleasure boat), indicating a desire to escape and relax? If it's a tugboat, it may indicate burdens and heavy workloads; if it's a container ship, it may signify commercial enterprises; or if it's a naval battleship, it may indicate defense, a show of strength, service, and/or national security.

The idea is to determine what type of boat it is, and then relate the function of the boat to your own life. For example, ascertaining whether the boat is a pleasure craft or a service craft will indicate that it's either time to get away or get to work.

Is there a captain of the boat/ship in your dream? Who is it? Have you given this person responsibility over your life and power to have the final say? Or are you the captain and recognize that you're in charge of your destiny?

Also consider whether anyone is in the boat with you. This may indicate who you feel shares your present predicament—that is, you're in the same boat.

Body Parts

Quick Interpretation: Self; ability; extremities

Popular Expressions: Over my dead body; A body blow; A nobody; A real somebody; Body of evidence; The body temple

Without a body, what would we be? A "no body"! Every part of the body is related to a state of being. For example, the backbone is associated with courage; the head with thinking; the heart with romance and love; the stomach with emotion; the Achilles' heal with vulnerability; and so on.

What part of the body did you dream of? What is its relation to your state of mind? Also consider any phrases associated with the body part, such as "pain in the neck" or "keep at arm's length."

If you have a recurring dream that a particular part of the body is not functioning, then see a physician; it may be your body's way of alerting you to a problem. If there isn't a problem, then consider which part of the body is crippled or restrained in your dream and ask why. Is it a part of your body or someone else's? Does it repulse you? For example, if it's your (or someone else's) feet, is the real issue about mobility and your freedom to get around? Perhaps it's about support. Do you feel you're not getting enough?

If you dream of a skeleton or bones, consider what it is that you want to reveal. Do you need to look at the structure, support, or framework of things? Or could it indicate that you need to rely more on your intuition—as the saying goes, you knew it in your bones!

If you dream of skin, is the message about sensitivity and outward appearances? Are you only looking at what's on the surface? If you see a birthmark, it could indicate individuality or be a symbol of uniqueness.

To dream of a face may reveal the way you see yourself in the world. If the face is heavily made up, does it indicate that you want to make yourself more desirable or hide your imperfections?

If you dream of an internal organ, then consider its function and how it appears in the dream. For example, to dream of a heart may indicate a broken heart, while to dream of lungs may signify a desire for fresh air and ideas.

We're often reminded that the body is a temple for the soul. In relation to the dream, consider how well you're maintaining and caring for your temple!

Bomb

Quick Interpretation: Power; destruction; unharnessed emotion

Popular Expressions: Go off like a bomb; Drop a bombshell on someone; Blow a fuse

When you drop a bombshell, you catch everyone off guard, and it usually indicates that you've changed direction. Is it time you announced new plans or a change in direction to someone close to you?

In your dream, whose bomb is it, and what do they want to destroy? Perhaps it's someone in your waking life who annoys you, pressing your buttons until you're ready to explode. Is the bomb indicative of your life at the moment? Do you feel like you're under pressure?

The bomb may also indicate that it's time to pursue a creative or work project—for example, the bomb is a wake-up call, particularly if it has gone off underneath you! Whatever the case may be, there's no question that you're being inspired to act.

Bones (Also see *Body Parts*.)

Quick Interpretation: Structure; framework; getting to the core

Popular Expressions: Have a bone to pick; Make no bones about it; Work one's fingers to the bone

Book

Quick Interpretation: Knowledge; rules; trouble

Popular Expressions: Throw the book at someone; You can't judge a book by its cover; To book someone (legally); Read between the lines; Read something into it

We all know the expression "You can't judge a book by its cover," but if you dream of a book cover, it can tell you a lot about yourself. Does the cover imply adventure, or do you want to acquire more knowledge?

To dream of a book indicates where you're focusing your attention at the moment. It may be that your subconscious mind is reminding you of a book you need to read to help you understand a question you've been thinking about.

If someone is reading you a book in the dream, what is it you're being asked to listen to? Is it someone you respect who's sharing an important message with you? If you don't respect the individual, does the information being shared relate to the manner in which they interact with you? For example, if your next-door neighbor is reading the telephone book to you, does it mean that they want you to move?

What condition is the book in? Is it tattered but still useful, or is it new with lots of photos and illustrations? Are you being reminded that old age and experience is valuable, or is it time to be childlike and have fun in life?

If you dream of a mystery book, does it indicate that you wish to fully comprehend a situation?

Just as a good movie or play can carry over into the dream state after you've seen it, so too can a book you're reading. It may be that you're trying to understand it further, or that its theme holds a particular meaning for you.

Boomerang

Quick Interpretation: Return to the source; an idea/scheme that backfires; attachment

Popular Expressions: The boomerang effect; What goes around comes around

It constantly amazes me that anyone can get that piece of curved wood to come back! What have you thrown away in your life that you want back?

Who threw the boomerang? Is it someone you feel wants you back in their life?

If you throw the boomerang in the dream and it doesn't come back, how do you feel about it? Consider the boomerang as a metaphor for achievement. Do you feel that what you put out in the world isn't on par with what you get back? Perhaps your hunting skills don't bring you your desired outcomes?

If you're an indigenous Australian, consider the boomerang in relation to your ancestry and tribal customs. Perhaps you wish to reconnect to your heritage. If you're non-Aboriginal, then you may want to learn more about indigenous Australian culture.

Boots (Also see *Shoe.*)

Quick Interpretation: Protection; work; polish

Popular Expressions: Dive in, boots and all; Get the boot; Step into someone's boots

Boredom

Quick Interpretation: Weariness; restlessness; tedium

Popular Expression: Bored out of my mind

When you're bored, it indicates that you're feeling weary or restless about a person or situation due to lack of interest or tedium. What did you lose interest in, in your dream? Why do you feel that it's tedious and uninteresting?

Bottle

Quick Interpretation: Message; refreshment; transparency

Popular Expressions: Hit the bottle; Let the genie out of the bottle; All bottled up; A message in a bottle; Spin the bottle

What is it that you want to bottle up in your dream? Is the bottle a symbol for bottling up emotions that you don't want other people to see?

Is the bottle clear so you can see exactly what's inside? Or is it dark, hiding its contents? If it's opaque, can you tell what's in the bottle? Is it something that you want, or something you shouldn't have? Perhaps it contains a message from or for people far away. Or maybe the message is a cry for help. Is there a genie in the bottle that you want to let out to grant you your every wish? Think about the contents of the bottle and how you feel about what's in there.

Is the bottle a symbol of drinking too much—that is, hitting the bottle?

The bottle may also indicate a desire for intimacy without fear of rejection—if it's being spun in your dream!

Box

Quick Interpretation: Containment; stability; feeling cornered

Popular Expressions: Thinking outside the box; Box someone into a corner

We would be lost without the humble box. What is it in your life that needs storing, moving, or protecting?

Consider the box to be you. What is it made out of? How functional is it? Is it the right box for the job? What does this reveal about you?

The box may also indicate feeling boxed in. Do you feel that you're cornered and lack options? Why?

Bracelet (Also see *Jewelry.*)

Quick Interpretation: Gift; ornament; identification

Branch (Also see *Tree.*)

Quick Interpretation: Offshoot; danger; extension

Popular Expressions: Out on a limb; Branch out

Bread

Quick Interpretation: Wealth; sustenance; livelihood

Popular Expressions: Man does not live by bread alone; The best thing since sliced bread; The bread of life; Make some bread or dough (money); Break bread with someone

Bread is the staple of life. Is the bread in your dream supporting you and satisfying your hunger? Or is it as hard as a brick and not even a chainsaw could get through it, let alone your teeth?

It's important to look at the state of the bread to indicate what you're subsisting on. If it's fresh, then it may suggest that your life is easy to digest at the moment. But if it's moldy and stale, is it time to move on and look for a new life source?

To dream of bread may also indicate that you're about to be inspired and perhaps come up with something truly innovative—that is, it may be the best thing since sliced bread!

If someone is eating the bread and it's not fresh, is it because you perceive the person to be ill-bred? That they're ill-mannered and have no people skills?

If the bread choked you in your dream, or you felt stifled even looking at it, is it that you're dealing with an "in-bred" situation in life that calls for the need to expand your gene pool—that is, your circle of friends or network?

Perhaps you broke bread with someone in your dream, indicating that there's some sort of bonding process going on in your life. Who is the person? Sharing a meal suggests that you're on an equal social footing.

Bread is also another word for "money." Is this what it means in your dream? Do you feel abundant? The type of bread may be an indication. Is the bread multi-grain, full of seeds and opportunity? Does it have a big, thick crust to protect the soft center? Does it smell tasty? Let's hope so!

Breeze (Also see *Wind.*)

Quick Interpretation: Relief; something done with ease; going with the flow

Popular Expressions: It's a breeze; Breeze through it; Shoot the breeze

Bribe

Quick Interpretation: An inducement; influencing favors; secret payment

B ribery and deception are bedfellows. Who is paying you to do what you don't want to do? Or whom do you want to pay to serve your needs/ambitions?

Is the bribe payment for attention, an innocent bribe that's somewhat childish? If so, ask why you feel you can't ask for what you need directly. Perhaps the bribe is work related. Why do you feel you have to be underhanded?

If someone is bribing you in the dream, how do you feel about it? Who is this person? What is your relationship to them in your waking life? How do you react to the bribe? Do you accept or reject it?

Bride/Bridegroom (Also see *Marriage.*)

Quick Interpretation: Commitment; change; new life

Popular Expressions: Bring something to the party; Always the bridesmaid, never the bride; Till death do us part; With these rings, we do wed; Wedded to a concept; A marriage of convenience

T he first thing to consider is wishful thinking. If you're young, fertile, and ready to settle down, then the bride/bridegroom may be a literal symbol of where you want to be. If you're married already and you dream that you're a bride/bridegroom, could it signify a desire to go back to when the relationship began, when things were fresh and exciting? When you dream of a bride/bridegroom, it's important to ask yourself questions such as how you feel about commitment—sharing and joining your life with another.

Is the bride/bridegroom a symbol for a new career, a new place to live, or a new relationship? For example, if the bride/bridegroom is Asian and you have nothing to do with Asian people, ask yourself if Asia is a part of the world you wish to visit and become more familiar with. If the bride/bridegroom is someone you know who works in banking, ask yourself if you'd like to wheel and deal on the stock market and make your money work for you rather than having to work for it.

If it's time for you to spread your wings, move out of the family home, and create your own life, then to dream of a bride/bridegroom is the perfect symbol indicating that it's time to do this, because a bride/bridegroom gives up what is familiar to join a new tribe and begin a new adventure.

Is someone you know getting married? Do you feel excited or left behind? Is there a feeling of enjoyment, of sharing someone's special day, or do you feel afraid, as though the bride or bridegroom is giving away their independence?

If you're the bride/bridegroom in your dream, did you look around as you walked down the aisle to see who needed grooming?!

Bridge

Quick Interpretation: Link; avoidance of conflict; understanding

Popular Expressions: Cross that bridge when you come to it; Build bridges; Water under the bridge; Bridge over troubled waters; To bridge a gap

Is the bridge in your dream a symbol of a shortcut? Do you want to get somewhere faster? Or is the bridge a connection between two points? Ask yourself what's being bridged. Is it a bridging of cultures, or of people who live in the same area? Why is the bridge created? What is its purpose?

Is the bridge powerful, strong, and supportive, indicating that what is being bridged is sound and solid? Or is it rickety and old, indicating a tenuous connection?

Are you looking over the side of a bridge in your dream? What do you see? If you see troubled waters, then it may indicate that you're passing over a crisis in your life, moving on.

No matter what the bridge is made of, the fact remains that it's a practical structure that enables quicker, simpler access between two places. What is it that you want to access more directly in your life with the least amount of effort?

Briefcase (Also see *Bag.*)

Quick Interpretation: Business dealings; legal matters; quick trips

Popular Expressions: Bag of tricks; Let the cat out of the bag

Broom

Quick Interpretation: Cleaning; removal; avoidance; exaggeration

Popular Expressions: Swept off your feet; To sweep it under the rug; A sweeping statement

I think that the first thing we invented when we stopped being nomadic was the broom. Does something in your dream need cleaning up? How do you feel about it? Do you see it as a chore, or are you whistling while you work?

Is the broom new? If so, it may relate to a change in thinking, or if you own your own business, a change in management—that is, bringing in the new broom.

Are you using the broom in your dream to sweep something under the rug? Does this mean that you're not taking responsibility for something that's going on in your life?

Also consider whether the broom is a symbol for mystic powers. After all, no self-respecting witch would go anywhere without her broom!

Brother (See *Family.*)

Buffet (Also see *Feast; Food.*)

Quick Interpretation: Variety; unlimited sustenance; taking more than you need

Popular Expressions: Food for thought; Eyes bigger than your stomach; A full plate

Bug (See *Ant; Insect.*)

Bull (Also see *Animal.*)

Quick Interpretation: Power; being bowled over; lies

Popular Expressions: A cock-and-bull story; Like a red rag to a bull; Take the bull by the horns; A load of bull; Like a bull in a china shop

Bulldozer

Quick Interpretation: To take by force; a clearing out of the old; intimidation

Popular Expression: To bulldoze your way through

If you want to knock something or someone over quickly, a bull-dozer will do the trick. Take note of who's driving the bulldozer in your dream and what's being knocked over.

How do you feel about the bulldozer? Is it a symbol of insensitivity—that is, is it being used to knock over someone's point of view and their right to exist? If so, who's being insensitive? If it's you, who are you being insensitive to?

Bungee Jumping

Quick Interpretation: On a string; bouncing back; exhilaration

Popular Expressions: Look before you leap; A leap of faith

Bungee jumping is the ultimate symbol of a leap of faith. To get up on a platform and trust a piece of rubber to save you from splattering on the ground like a pancake—that's faith!

The practice started as a rite of passage, an initiation into manhood. It involved taking a dive as a boy and limping away as a man. In your dream, does the bungee jump symbolize transformation? Is it a rite of passage into adulthood? Perhaps it's a way of honoring yourself for your achievements.

To dream of bungee jumping may also signify that you're faced with making a very brave decision in your life, and to achieve your goals you must trust others like you've never trusted before.

If someone else is jumping, are you afraid that they're jumping into something unknown, or are you inspired by them? Do you feel that others have more courage than you do?

Bungee jumping may also suggest that no matter how bad things look, you'll always be able to bounce back.

On a lighter note, to dream of bungee jumping may indicate a desire for more exhilaration, spontaneity, and excitement in your life. You can achieve this with a leap of faith and the security of knowing that there's a safety belt firmly attached to your ankle that will save and protect you.

Of course, some of us are simply looking for a thrill, and there can be no bigger thrill than having a scare and coming through it unscathed—even if it's in the dream state!

Burglar

Quick Interpretation: Intrusion; loss; invasion

Popular Expressions: A game of cat-and-mouse; Stealing away in the night; A real steal

Don't you hate it in films when no matter how burglar-proof a building is, there's always someone who makes it look easy to get into it with only a tube of toothpaste, a credit card, and two cotton balls?

What is being burgled in your dream? Is it your home, your place of work, or a friend's house? Your answer will indicate what part of your life you feel is being intruded upon. It may be your career, your private life, or a friendship. Consider who's breaking in and what this person is like in order to determine who or what is intruding in your waking life.

Is the burglar after something specific in your dream? What is your attachment to it? Do you feel helpless in your dream, forced to sit back and watch the burglary take place? Does this indicate that you feel powerless to stop the intruder from claiming your space in your waking life?

Perhaps it's time to reassess your defenses. You may be letting others into your space because you feel they're more clever and determined than you are.

Bus

Quick Interpretation: Fixed route; broken journey; passenger

Popular Expression: To miss the bus

Why is it that every time you're in a hurry, the bus driver decides to take the longest route and stop at every stop? Where is the bus taking you in your dream, or where do you *hope* the bus will take you?

Who's traveling with you? Are you going somewhere together? If you don't normally travel with the person or people on the bus with you, or you don't usually ride a bus, then it could indicate that you want the person/people with you on the bus to travel in the same direction as you in your waking life.

What is the bus journey like? Do you get along well with everyone on the bus and feel confident that the driver will take you to your destination safely? If so, this could indicate that you've embarked on a successful group endeavor in your life. Or is it the opposite and you're uncomfortable sitting with the people on the bus, and/or the bus isn't taking you where you want to go?

Who's driving the bus, and how do you feel about this person? Do you trust them to take you to your destination, or do you feel they'll get you lost?

Do you want to get off the bus in your dream? If so, this may indicate that you want to cut loose and break free from the fixed route that the bus wants to take you on.

Butterfly

Quick Interpretation: Transformation; beauty; something that's short-lived

Popular Expressions: A social butterfly; Float like a butterfly, sting like a bee; Break a butterfly on a wheel

The butterfly is a delightful dream symbol because it represents metamorphosis. One day you're a grub, and the next you're an exquisite creature flitting through the air.

In the dream, do you see the entire metamorphosis from caterpillar to cocoon to butterfly? If you do, this may indicate a desire for a slow and carefully planned transition. Do you see the caterpillar and butterfly but no cocoon? This may suggest that you're happy to get on with change in your life. Do you only see the butterfly? Perhaps you have no interest in the past and find the present a lot more exciting.

Butterflies have a short but brilliant life, which suggests quality of life rather than quantity. The butterfly displays beauty. Do you recognize how beautiful you are even though you may come from humble beginnings?

If the butterfly lands on you or someone else in the dream, then that person may symbolize calmness. Are you calm and relaxed, or does the other person have a peaceful influence on you? This dream scenario may also suggest respect for yourself or the other person—that is, you appreciate their spiritual growth or your own.

The classic symbol of the butterfly is transformation. Ask yourself where you're going and where you've come from. What changes do you want to make in your life? Do you believe that you have to destroy the past to create something new?

Dreaming of a butterfly may indicate that it's time for introspection and silence so you can evaluate a particular situation in your life.

Finally, the butterfly may signify a desire to be admired from a distance.

Cab

Quick Interpretation: Transportation; going places; being escorted

Popular Expressions: To talk behind someone's back; In someone else's hands; Taxi to a stop

Regardless of the country you're in, the cab drivers of the area always seem to come from someplace else! It makes for an interesting history lesson while you're being driven to where you want to go.

In your dream, are you being escorted somewhere, or are you escorting someone somewhere? If you're being escorted, where are you being taken? Do you trust the driver to take you where you want to go and are happy to take a backseat, or are you concerned that they're taking you in the wrong direction or into the unknown? Is the driver lost and confused, or is he or she ripping you off, taking you the long way around? Or do you feel empowered because you're in control of your destination, giving the directions? Relate your response to your waking life.

If you're driving the cab in the dream, does this symbolize taking charge of your life? Of course, if you're a cab driver in your waking life, it's a symbol that relates directly to your work. What is your dream world trying to tell you about your working life?

Also consider whether the cab represents a desire to get where you want to go with no fuss, as the meter is ticking and you can't afford to procrastinate.

Are you trying to hail a cab in your dream to no avail, indicating that you feel that people aren't taking notice of you? Where are you trying to get to, and do you feel that you need to rely on someone else to get you there?

The cab also symbolizes transportation. Perhaps the cab in your dream indicates that you wish to be transported to another place . . . a place you're determined to get to regardless of the cost.

Cabin

Quick Interpretation: Retreat; nature; privacy; vacation; relaxation

Popular Expressions: The perfect hideaway; The pleasure of my own company; Home away from home

A cabin is a secluded place of retreat. Do you long for privacy and the pleasure of your own company? Or does the cabin indicate a desire to hide from the world? Is it time for a respite? Where is the cabin in your dream? Is it in a place you'd like to escape to, in nature, or on a ship? The cabin's location may help you decide where you want to take your next vacation, or where you'd like to spend some time out.

Are *you* in the cabin? What are you doing in there? Is someone in there with you? Would you like to spend some private quality time with this person—that is, escape with them to a cabin in the woods?

Do you recognize the cabin? Perhaps it's the one you traveled to for holidays when you were a child. If so, are you being reminded of days past, when things were carefree and lighthearted?

What is the cabin like? Is it run-down and derelict, perhaps indicating an aversion to a quiet vacation? Would you prefer something more exciting, like a Las Vegas hotel? Or perhaps the cabin is warm and inviting, and it's time to escape to your home away from home.

Cage (Also see *Trap.*)

Quick Interpretation: Protection; control; limitations

Popular Expressions: Rattle someone's cage; A caged animal; To bar someone from something; Boxed into a corner

At first you may think that dreaming you're in a cage means that you're imprisoned, locked up, or confined. If fear is associated with the dream, then this may be true, but the cage may also symbolize protection.

Do you have a desire to lock yourself away from the world, or from the people in your life? We build security "cages" all around us, the most obvious ones being the home and office. The intent isn't to control, but to provide a sense of safety. What do you wish to "bar" yourself from? Whom do you want to bar from your life? Why do you feel you need protection? Seeing yourself caged may also be a symbol of latent creativity: When forced into a corner, newfound strength and creativity is found.

Do you feel that something or someone is imprisoning you in your life? Do you feel restricted? Are you shutting people out, or are you locked in? How do you feel? Is the cage in a dark and dingy place, or do you feel like a beautiful bird in a gilded cage? Are you in the cage or looking at it? Does someone lock you in, or do you lock yourself in?

Is someone else in the cage? Are you helping them to escape, or did you put them in there? Do you feel they deserve to be there because they're a menace to society or to your state of well-being?

Cake

Quick Interpretation: Celebration; passing of time; unrealistic desires

Popular Expressions: Take the cake; A piece of cake; Have your cake and eat it, too; The icing on the cake

Why can't alfalfa sprouts taste as good as cake? If they did, you could eat as much as you'd like without having to worry about fitting into your swimsuit. Who's baking the cake in your dream? What kind of cake is it? A healthy carrot cake, a rich chocolate cake, an angel cake? Your answer will help you determine what you or someone else wants to give as a creative and nourishing gesture.

Does someone bake the cake for you in your dream, or do you bake it for someone else, indicating thoughtfulness and a desire to express love?

Baking a cake may be an expression of harboring unrealistic dreams—that is, you want to have your cake and eat it, too. Or perhaps something magnificent is just around the corner and you're about to put the icing on the cake!

Calendar

Quick Interpretation: Organization; commitments; passage of time

Popular Expressions: Year in, year out; A month of Sundays

Calendars rule our lives in an age where there's more to do than ever before. Are you focused on a calendar event in your dream? Is it in the past or future? Your answer will indicate whether you're living for tomorrow or thinking about yesterday.

Is the calendar in your dream crammed full of dates and appointments, or is it relatively bare? How do you feel about it? Are you glad to be busy, or is it stressing you out? Are you happy to be appointment free?

Is a particular date in the calendar marked out? Why is it significant?

What kind of calendar is it? Is it a sun or a moon calendar, perhaps indicating a predominantly masculine or feminine influence in your life?

Perhaps the calendar represents an unconscious desire to put things in an ordered sequence so they're not overlooked or forgotten.

Calmness

Quick Interpretation: Tranquility; ease

Popular Expressions: The calm before the storm; Peace and quiet

Feeling calm indicates a tranquil state of mind. What has put your mind at ease? Have you resolved something in your waking life that made you feel anxious?

Camel (Also see *Animal.*)

Quick Interpretation: Hydration; judgments; survival

Popular Expression: You should always look at your own hump before you look at others'

It's all a question of geography. If you say "Give me a camel" in some parts of the world, you end up with an animal to take you across the desert; yet in other parts of the world, you end up with a mouthful of smoke. Consider whether the camel in your dream represents something you really shouldn't be doing—something that may be pleasurable on the surface but has deep, adverse ramifications.

What is the camel doing in your dream? Are you using it as a means of transportation? Is it carrying your luggage, perhaps indicating a desire to travel? Is the camel part of a caravan (a group of merchants or others traveling together), revealing a desire to travel with like-minded people for protection? Or are you making a solitary trip with the camel? Your answer will indicate how you see your life—that is, as a team player or a solo adventurer.

The camel also symbolizes survival. Does the camel in your dream represent your strength and willingness to survive no matter how harsh the climate? Are you confident that you have the necessary resources to survive—that is, water—and all that's required is for you to tap in to your reserves?

Also, consider whether you're judging something/someone harshly—the camel being a symbol of looking at someone else's hump before looking at your own.

Camera (Also see *Photograph*.)

Quick Interpretation: Record; memories; the past

Popular Expressions: Put someone in the picture; Get the picture; Camera-shy; A sure shot

Cameras today are easy to use. In fact, many are idiot proof—you just point and click. So if in your dream you see yourself with a modern, automatic camera, it may indicate that you have a desire to enjoy life with a minimum of fuss.

If it's an antique camera, the implication may be that you want to do what you're doing with more precision. Do you have to fiddle with the camera to take a photo: adjust the lens, set the aperture, select the speed, and so on? If so, it may indicate that you want greater control of a situation, and that it's time to take your life off automatic.

The idea of the camera is to freeze a moment in time and record it. So what is it that you don't want to forget? What do you want to capture? What you're photographing may give you insight into what it is you want to hold on to.

Are you shooting for pleasure or for work? If you're a professional photographer, the camera may signify creativity and abundance, or perhaps doubt, depending on the circumstances of the dream.

If someone is pointing a camera at you, does that person want you to stay the same, or are you a poseur? If you have the camera, does it mean you want to direct your own life?

Who do you want to "shoot"? It may be that you want to rid someone from your life.

Candle

Quick Interpretation: Illumination; blessings; rituals

Popular Expressions: Burn the candle at both ends; Can't hold a candle to someone; Light my fire

Isn't it amazing how much light a candle can give off in a movie? Someone lights a candle and you can see into every corner of the castle! What do *you* want to light up?

Who is in the dream with you? Do you think this person is inferior to you? That they can't hold a candle to you? Or do they think you're inferior to them? It's important to note who lit the candle, who's holding it, and what its purpose is. Is the candle being used for celebration, dedication, or to show the way? How does this relate to your waking life?

Do you feel that you're on shaky ground and are easily swayed, like a candle in the wind? Or is the candle being used to bless you? Is there an opportunity to make a wish come true by blowing it out?

Car (Also see *Driving*.)

Quick Interpretation: Mobility; prestige; convenience

Popular Expressions: Backseat driver; Hit and miss; Take your life in your hands; In the driver's seat; Drive someone crazy; Drive someone away; Steer someone in the wrong/right direction; Put your pedal to the metal; Put on the brakes

Cars allow people to move around more freely and quickly. As such, the car is associated with liberation. If you have a car dream, ask yourself if new possibilities are opening up in your life. Do you feel that you're being liberated from someone or something?

Are you driving your own car? How fast are you going? Do you feel that you're in control? Your answer will tell you something about the way you're handling life.

Perhaps someone else is driving your car. Do you feel they're controlling, or trying to control your life?

Are you in the backseat? If you are, do you feel comfortable? You may prefer to be a backseat driver, telling someone else what to do and where to take you. On the other hand, you may hate it and wish you were in the driver's seat. Is someone egging you on to do something you don't feel comfortable with?

Are *you* the car in your dream? Substitute your name for *car* in a sentence—for example: *Leon is moving erratically down the road; he regains control and moves more slowly.*

Observe the color and condition of the exterior and interior of the car. The exterior may signify your external world, while the interior your internal world. What color is the car? What is your association with this color? Is it red, hot, and passionate; or white, clean, and virginal?

How fast are you going? Do you feel comfortable traveling at this speed? A slow speed may suggest that you're traveling in a controlled manner through life and with relative ease, or maybe you're on automatic pilot.

If you're driving a friend's car, ask yourself if you want something that they have, either a possession or a character trait.

Cards (Also see *Poker.*)

Quick Interpretation: Chance; recreation; insecure (house of cards)

Popular Expressions: A real card; Lay your cards on the table

The most important thing about playing a game of cards is ensuring that you have a full deck! Are you playing with a full deck in your dream? If so, do you feel confident that you're in the game?

Is someone dealing the cards in your dream? Who is it? Is it an honest deal, or do you feel something underhanded is going on? What kind of cards are being dealt to you? Do you feel you have a chance of winning, or are the cards unworkable? This may indicate that you feel fate has dealt you either a good or bad hand. How do you handle the cards that have been dealt you? Do you know how to bluff, or do you give it all away with face gestures?

What type of game are you playing? Is it a game of chance where the stakes are high, or is it purely recreational? Is this a reflection of how you choose to play life's game?

Carpet

Quick Interpretation: Warmth; affluence; chores

Popular Expressions: Roll out the red carpet; The red-carpet treatment; On the carpet; Lay it on thick; Pull the rug out from under you; Cut a rug; Sweep it under the rug

How did it come about that the color of the carpet underneath your feet could signify how important you are? In your dream, is the carpet under your feet red?

What is the carpet like in your dream? Is it a magic carpet that's able to take you to distant lands, or is it a dusty, moth-eaten rag that needs spring cleaning? Your answer will indicate how you feel about what is laying at your feet.

The expression "on the carpet" refers to standing before an authority figure for a reprimand. Have you been summoned to stand on the carpet in your dream, or has someone else?

Of course, if you've got something to hide or if you're choosing to ignore the obvious, a carpet may appear in your dream so you can sweep things under it.

Cartoon

Quick Interpretation: Illusions; escapism; exaggeration

Popular Expressions: Paint someone into a corner; Get animated about something; A real character

Dreaming that you're in a cartoon is one of the most exciting dreams you can have. Fear cannot exist in animation land. The characters in a cartoon get shot, stomped on, blown up, and barbecued . . . and they never die! They simply pop back up and shrug off the worst attacks within seconds. If you dream that you're in a cartoon, perhaps it means that you need not worry, as everything will work out and you'll bounce back.

In the cartoon, do you appear as yourself or as a caricature of yourself? If you're a caricature, then the features that are exaggerated can indicate certain circumstances. For example, have the ears been exaggerated, indicating eavesdropping; or has the nose been lengthened, signifying meddling?

What dilemma or adventure are you faced with in the cartoon? And is this a situation you want to deal with in your waking life in a lighter way?

If you're watching the cartoon, who is in it? What are you observing, and does this indicate that the situation can be approached in a lighthearted way? A slapstick or satirical approach to an event may be the way to resolve things.

Whatever the cartoon is in your dream, one thing's for sure: Only you can know "what's up, Doc"!

Cash (See *Money.*)

Cat (Also see *Animal.*)

Quick Interpretation: Independence; companionship; resiliency

Popular Expressions: Cat got your tongue?; Let the cat out of the bag; There's more than one way to skin a cat; More lives than a cat

Throughout the ages, cats have been aligned with the feminine. No self-respecting witch would go anywhere without her black cat.

Cats are symbols of the underworld, the mysterious, and the unknown. Independence is central to their character. Unlike dogs, cats symbolize intimacy without companionship. Perhaps you want to be part of someone's life, but still free enough to be independent?

Cats can also symbolize companionship without subservience. They're the masters of their own domain, and aren't about to fetch your newspaper and slippers for you.

To dream of a cat may suggest a strong sexual undercurrent, due to the crude and slang terminology for female genitalia. Do you have an issue concerning women? Do you only associate them with sex, and lack respect for them?

Cats keep themselves clean. Does the cat in your dream suggest cleaning up your act? Is it time to take responsibility for yourself? Should you spend time grooming yourself for an upcoming project or opportunity?

The cat is also a symbol of reinvention (a cat has nine lives). Would you like your life to be more lively and adventurous? Also consider whether the cat symbolizes a desire for more intimate, feminine company.

Cave

Quick Interpretation: Mystery; hibernation; protection

Popular Expressions: Cave in; In a hole

To some, the cave is a place of mystery and adventure; to others, it's the scariest and most claustrophobic place in the world. What are you doing in the cave in your dream? How do you feel about being in there? Is it a place of hibernation and protection, or do you feel trapped? How you regard the cave may indicate how you feel about exploring dark places.

In your waking life, are you experiencing a time of rebirth, the cave being a symbol of retreat—that is, a place to go to process the old before you step out into the new? Or do you feel trapped in the cave, unable to see a way out, perhaps indicating that you're trapped in a cycle of negative feeling or thought.

Is someone in the cave with you? How do you feel about this person being there? What are you doing together in the cave? Is it an adventure, or do you feel as though you're stuck with them and there's no way out?

The cave is also symbolic of the subconscious. Whatever you're doing in the cave will help you to determine what the message from the subconscious is. What in your life that usually resides underneath the surface is staring you straight in the face?

The cave may also indicate that you're giving up on yourself, a relationship, or a project. Do you feel that you're caving in?

CD Player

Quick Interpretation: Entertainment; crystal clarity; something that's compact

Popular Expressions: Music to your ears; Face the music

CD players are becoming more and more common in dreams. They're replacing the tape recorder, radio, and stereo as a symbol of entertainment.

What are you listening to? Is there a message being conveyed? For example, if it's The Police singing "Don't Stand So Close to Me," does the message have to do with you or someone else being overbearing and possessive? If it's Janet Jackson singing "Together Again," maybe you want to reconnect with a person from your past.

If you grew up in the world of stereos, tape recorders, and transistor radios, then the association you have with the CD player is going to be different from a young person's. Perhaps it's suggesting that it's time to update your technology or ideas, and is a sign not to be afraid of new things.

Ask yourself what the CD player represents to you. Is it a form of entertainment—a distraction—or does it suggest freedom of choice—that is, the opportunity to play what you want to?

Have you misplaced the CD player in your dream, or has it been stolen from you? If you're a young person, this may suggest that you feel that your freedom of choice is being threatened.

Is the CD player in your dream a source of entertainment, or are you annoying people around you with your choice of music? If the latter is the case, this may indicate how you think others perceive you—that is, that they're either for you or against you.

I like to think that the CD player is also a symbol of wanting to make your life more compact. Do you want more precision in your life? Do you wish that it was neater and simpler, with a clearer resonance?

Celebrity (Also see *Star.*)

Quick Interpretation: Fame; desire; public property

Popular Expressions: To show off; Too big for your britches; Fifteen minutes of fame

There aren't too many people in the world who don't secretly (or not so secretly) desire their 15 minutes of fame. The amount of importance we place on celebrity status is extraordinary. Just because someone can remember lines in front of a camera, belt out a tune in time, or expertly handle a ball, they're automatically desirable.

Who's the celebrity in your dream, and what does he or she represent to you—physical prowess, mental skill, or sexuality? Is this what you want more of in your life? Do you wish to be like the celebrity in your dream? Do you believe that you have an equal amount of talent but are yet to be discovered?

Do you turn to jelly when you meet the celebrity? Are you completely dwarfed by the experience, nervous and tongue-tied? Does this indicate a missed opportunity—for example, could you have achieved something important, but you went wobbly at the knees?

What is the celebrity's image, and how do you feel about it? Without the image, is the celebrity just an everyday Joe, all talk and hype and no substance? Or does the celebrity walk their talk? Do you feel you do, too? Is the celebrity a one-hit wonder, a flash-in-the-pan, or someone talented whose popularity has lasted over the years? Do you see yourself as highly talented or a spin doctor?

Do you feel included or excluded by the celebrity in your dream? Does this person make you feel as though you belong and are welcome, or are you treated like a gate crasher? Are you intimate with the celebrity in your dream, or is it a business relationship? This may indicate what you believe your celebrity status will bring to you.

Perhaps it's true that we all get our 15 minutes of fame—some of us in the waking world, others in the dream world!

Cell Phone

Quick Interpretation: Communication; hands-free operations; convenience

Popular Expressions: Talk your head off; Speak your mind

It's amazing to think that the cell phone, in such a short period of time, has gone from being an expensive plaything for secret agents to an everyday accessory.

In your dream, does the phone make you feel safe, because you know that it's at hand in case of an emergency? Or do you feel that it's an invasion of your privacy?

Does the phone ring in your dream? How does it make you feel? Do you think, *Oh, no, they never leave me alone* or *I'm so happy they got through*?

Does the phone suggest that you're a good communicator? That you express your voice and your thoughts confidently, and that your communication is direct, without any wires or cables to interfere?

Are you speaking to someone on the cell phone? What are you trying to communicate? Do you feel empowered or debilitated? If it's the latter, consider the bad press that cell phones have received recently in relation to radiation and its proximity to the ear. Are you expressing concern about this in your dream?

Is the cell phone dropping out or being interrupted in some way, suggesting that you're having trouble communicating? What is it that you find so difficult to express? Do you feel that you're not being listened to?

Does the cell phone indicate a need for commitment? Today, a lot of people sign up for a long-term plan when they buy a cell phone. Are you planning to make yourself more available to other people over a long period of time?

And if you're male, does the cell phone perhaps signify relief . . . as in, smaller is finally better?!

Chain

Quick Interpretation: Containment; protection; burden

Popular Expressions: Pull someone's chain; A weak link in the chain

Chains immediately conjure up images of bondage, being burdened, and bad fortune, and can symbolize such things in a dream. Are the chains holding you against your will? Do you feel weighed down? Do they signify a personal relationship or a career?

Do you feel burdened by the judgments of others? That people are dragging you down? Do you feel that these judgments now represent the truth—that is, other people have built up an image of you that you're starting to believe? For example, someone claims that you're always late and now you only notice when you're late, not when you're on time.

On a more positive note, chains also signify bonds, and bonds link people to create a more powerful force, especially when it comes to fighting a common cause.

Environmentalists often chain themselves to trees to protect forests, and to uphold beliefs and desires for a better future. Do the chains in your dream signify fighting for a noble cause that you believe in?

How do you feel about being chained up? Do the chains enslave you, or are you there by choice—your detention being voluntary?

Perhaps the chains signify looking at the bigger picture—helping you recognize that life is a chain of events. You may be coming to the realization that your actions, or non-actions, are interconnected and create a link between your past experiences and present reality.

Chair

Quick Interpretation: Support; being in charge; sitting back

Popular Expressions: On the edge of my seat; Take a backseat; In the hot seat; To chair a meeting

How could we get by in life without the humble chair? Are you sitting pretty, or do you want to get up and go, indicating a time in your life when you either feel confident and proud with where you are, or restless. Or is someone else sitting in the chair and you're standing over them, suggesting that you need to take control of an inactive situation?

Is the chair offering you support, or is it squeaky and unstable? Ask yourself if you're receiving enough support in your life right now?

Also consider whether the chair signifies a time in your life when you (or the person sitting in the chair) needs to sit back and take things in before making a decision.

Is the person sitting in the chair, or associated with it, in charge of things? Do they hold the chair? If it's you, do you feel you have the final say on what happens in your life? If it's someone else, do you feel *they* have the final say over your affairs? Or is it that you feel you're run by a committee and have to answer to a number of individuals?

The chair may also suggest that some major event is taking place in your life, and you're so excited about it that you're sitting on the edge of your seat!

Chameleon (Also see *Animal.*)

Quick Interpretation: Adaptation; camouflage; ability to assimilate

Popular Expressions: Change your colors; Show your true colors; Hide in plain sight

Mother Nature created the most fantastic eyes for the chameleon. They can look in two directions at once and at any angle. Is the chameleon in your dream a symbol of being able to see things from all viewpoints?

The chameleon also symbolizes adaptability. In your dream, is the chameleon a symbol of your ability to adapt to any situation that presents itself in your life? Is your ability to adapt a positive attribute, enabling you to associate and mingle with a lot of different people from different backgrounds? Or do you feel you lose your sense of who you are and become lost in the crowd?

What is the chameleon doing in your dream? What environment is it in? It's particularly important to take note of where it is, as this may be a telltale sign of where you need to camouflage yourself. For example, the chameleon may be in your workplace, indicating that it's best for you to change your colors to suit the mood of the office rather than demand your own way.

If you don't feel that you adapt to life easily, the chameleon may be a sign that it's time to do so. Also consider whether there's something in your life that's calling you to change your colors. Perhaps it's time to stand up and show your true colors!

Champagne

Quick Interpretation: Celebration; climax; release of built-up stress

Popular Expression: Sour grapes; Pop the cork; Bubbling over

Whenever we want to launch something or celebrate an event, the champagne starts popping. Are you celebrating something in your dream? What are you celebrating? Is it the beginning of something new, or are you acknowledging a moment of success? Is something in your life about to be launched or christened?

Are you drinking the champagne in your dream, or is someone else? What is its effect? Do you (or the person drinking the champagne) feel light and bubbly, or is the champagne making you (or them) sick? Your answer will indicate how you feel about things in your life that are light and uplifting. Do you welcome them, or do they make you sick to your stomach?

Is the bottle of champagne popped open in your dream, indicating a release of built-up stress? Is the hard work over, and now it's time to sit back, kick up your heels, and have fun? Are you able to pop the cork yourself, or is someone else popping the cork for you, perhaps indicating that you need permission to let loose? Also, consider whether the champagne bottle popping open is a symbol for something in your life that has reached a climax.

Charity

Quick Interpretation: Generosity; support; assistance

Popular Expression: 'Tis better to give than receive

When you feel charitable, you tend to engage in acts of benevolence and generosity. Who or what do you feel deserves your support?

Chase

Quick Interpretation: Being followed; a mission; avoiding capture

Popular Expressions: Chase your tail; Cut to the chase; A wild-goose chase; The thrill of the chase; Run for your life

It's wonderful being chased if you're looking forward to being caught! But in a dream, this is usually not the case. More often than not, the dreamer is running from something they don't wish to face. In your dream, are you running from an aspect of yourself, something that you're afraid of becoming, or something that you used to be that you no longer want to be?

If you can't identify who or what is chasing you as an aspect of you, what or who is it that you're afraid of? What do you feel will happen if you're caught? Are you strong enough not to be overtaken? What will happen if you stand and fight?

How you react to being chased is just as important as how you feel about it. Do you stop and confront the assailant, and face the situation? Or do you keep running, confident that you won't be caught?

The primary objective when you're being chased is to escape the person chasing you. Who is it that you want to escape from? Have you planned an escape strategy?

One other thing worth exploring: Being chased in your dream may be a roundabout way of telling yourself to be virtuous and chaste!

Check

Quick Interpretation: Abundance; a promise of payment; acceptance of worth

Popular Expressions: A blank check; Take a rain check; Check your problems at the door

How fantastic! You can sign a piece of paper and swap it for anything your heart desires. Who's giving you the check, or who are you giving the check to in your dream? Does it symbolize wealth, the promise of lots of money coming your way or someone else's? Or does it symbolize mistrust, because you know the check is only a bit of paper with a few numbers written on it that will bounce? Whom don't you trust?

On the other hand, the check may be a symbol of trusting and accepting another's worth—that is, you accept the check as promise for payment, no questions asked.

Whatever the case, the most important thing to do if you dream of a check is to think about it in relation to how you handle your financial affairs. Also, consider the emotion you felt when you saw the check in your dream.

A check can also symbolize that it's time to do a reality check!

Cheerfulness

Quick Interpretation: Lightheartedness; high spirits

Feeling cheery indicates elevated spirits and a lightness of heart. What has brightened your outlook on life?

Cheese

Quick Interpretation: Being churned up; ripening; being number one

Popular Expressions: The big cheese; A cat-and-mouse game; An argument with holes in it

I've always wondered why the big boss, or the person in power, is called "the big cheese." Why not "the big chili"? After all, it's strong, powerful, and knows how to pack a punch!

Does the cheese in your dream represent someone in your life who has authority over you? What type of cheese is it? Hard, soft, aged, tasty, or filled with holes? Relate the description of the cheese to the person you think it represents to determine any correlations. Are you okay with this person giving your life direction, or are they taking liberty with your life and bossing you around? If you're eating cheese in your dream, does it indicate a wish to be the boss? If you're serving cheese to someone else, do you feel subordinate to them?

Cheese is churned, so consider whether it symbolizes the churning of your own emotions. Is someone pushing your buttons or stressing you out? Cheese is also geographical. Every country, from Australia to Bulgaria to Italy, has a different range of cheeses. Is this significant in relation to travel desires or destinations? If the cheese leaves a bad taste in your mouth, is someone from the same region as the cheese annoying you, and your dream is telling you that you're not interested in digesting what they have to offer?

Cheese is used as bait to catch rats. Who's the big rat in your life that you want to trap? Or do you feel that you're being tempted into a situation that could leave you in very bad shape?

Chef (Also see *Kitchen.*)

Quick Interpretation: Creative control; being well prepared

Popular Expressions: To cook up a storm; Too many cooks spoil the broth; If you can't take the heat, get out of the kitchen; Food for thought

Who's the chef in your dream? Is it you or someone else? Think of the chef as a creative director, taking creative control of the kitchen. Is the chef in your dream a symbol of a desire to take creative control? If so, what is it that you (or whoever is the chef in the dream) want to take creative control of? If you're the chef, think about it in relation to how you choose to express your creativity in your world.

Is the chef in your dream cooking up a feast for you, indicating that they care, and want to nurture you? Or are you cooking up a feast for someone else?

Of course, if you're a chef in waking life, think of the symbol in relation to your career. Are you reconsidering your career options, or are you using your dream world as a means to work through creative ideas?

A good chef is always well prepared. Does the chef in your dream symbolize that you're well organized, or that you want to be? Or is the chef a subtle reminder to take some time out; that life has given you lots of food for thought?

Chess (Also see *Game.*)

Quick Interpretation: Planning; ambush; stalemate

Popular Expressions: Like a game of chess; Checkmate; A pawn in someone's hands

You're playing chess in your dream. The first thing to think about is whether you're attacking or defending. Do you feel as though you have a game strategy, with your moves worked out? Or are you simply trying to protect your queen?

Chess is a mind game, unlike, say, Twister, which is more a game for the body. Do you want to develop your intellect? Who are you playing chess with in your dream? Would you prefer to interact with them intellectually rather than physically? Do you want your relationship with them to be more challenging and less superficial?

Or does the symbol of playing chess in your dream signify confidence—that is, you believe you can judge and anticipate the moves and intentions of the people around you?

Again, look at who you're playing chess with. Are you playing against yourself? Does this signify a desire to move beyond self-imposed limitations and barriers, or do you have yourself checkmated—that is, have recent plans and schemes been futile, and you have only succeeded in cornering yourself?

If you can't see whom you're playing against, does this indicate that you feel pitted against the world—as if you're being overwhelmed by unknown opponents and pitfalls and don't really know who's on your side and who isn't?

If you can see whom you're playing against, ask yourself why you want to play mind games with them. Why do you want to outsmart and outmaneuver them? Are you on an ego trip? Or do you feel they're controlling you in some way and it's time to break the chains—or spells—they have over you?

Is the game going to end up in a stalemate, where nothing is resolved? Do you feel that you don't have the resources and ability to bring things to a resolution? Is this the way you feel about life—that at the moment there isn't much point to it, as there never seems to be a positive outcome?

Is the king a prominent feature in your dream? Perhaps it represents someone you know—maybe someone you've spent your whole life trying to protect, perhaps to the point of extreme sacrifice where you gave up your own life. Or are you the king who'd like to see more sacrifice (on your behalf) from the people around you?

Chewing Gum

Quick Interpretation: A breath of fresh air; contemplation

Popular Expressions: To chew something over; Chew the fat; Chew someone out

Chewing gum seems like such a useless activity to engage in—that is, what's the point of chewing if you can't swallow? In a dream, though, it's a wonderful symbol, indicating a desire to give serious thought to something. Is there something in your life that you wish to chew over? Take note of whether you're chewing with your mouth open or closed, indicating whether or not you want others to see what you're mulling over.

If you're chewing gum in your dream, is it sweet and juicy, or is it tough and bland? This may indicate how much you value your words.

The process of chewing is a precursor to digestion. As soon as we start to chew, our digestive system kicks into action. Therefore, is the chewing gum a symbol of wanting to get up and act?

If someone else is chewing the gum in your dream, did they appear uncouth and vulgar; or cool, calm, and collected? This will indicate how you feel about that person.

Chicken (Also see *Animal.*)

Quick Interpretation: Fully hatched idea; fear; riddle

Popular Expressions: Don't count your chickens before they hatch; No spring chicken; The chickens have come home to roost; To be chicken (scared); To lay an egg

One of life's great conundrums is what came first, the chicken or the egg? The answer is, who cares?! The chicken is a great symbol, indicating a desire to let go of trying to answer the impossible. Why do you really need to know?

The chicken is the perfect symbol for fully hatched ideas. What ideas, dreams, or projects have hatched in your life? Of course, if the chicken is sitting on an egg in your dream, does it mean that you're incubating new ideas or projects?

The chicken is also a symbol of fear (think back to childhood taunts), so consider whether the chicken in your dream is a sign that you're fearful of something or someone in your life, or if someone is afraid of you.

The other thing to consider is that age-old question: Why did the chicken cross the road? In other words, are you trying to solve an unsolvable riddle in your life?

Chickens scratch around in the dirt with an uncanny ability to find things to eat when it seems that nothing is there. Do you need to dig around a little more to get what you really want?

Child(ren)

Quick Interpretation: Playfulness; naivete; immature thoughts

Popular Expressions: It's child's play; To kid around; Wide-eyed innocence; Act your age; Youth is wasted on the young

One thing is certain: We've all been there. Consider children in your dream as a beginning, or the blueprint of what shape your life will take.

The most obvious symbolic meanings are playfulness, innocence, and amazement. Is this the way you're approaching life at the moment? Do you feel playful and innocent? Are you amazed by everything you see in your life?

What is the child (or children) doing in your dream? Are you playing with them, indicating a desire to slow down, chill out, and not take life so seriously? Or do you find the child (children) annoying, a distraction from what needs to be done?

The child can also symbolize blissful naïveté. Are you naive about someone/something in your life? Does your naïveté get you into trouble? Does the child in your dream indicate that you desire to be in the know?

Also, consider whether your approach to something/someone in your life is immature. Are you acting like a child when you should be behaving like an adult? Look at the people with you in the dream and your relationship with them to determine whether this is the case.

Is something in your life moving along better than planned? Is what you're doing child's play?

What kind of child do you believe you were? Were you the early bloomer able to handle school and sports, always part of the "in crowd," or were you the nerd, misfit, or ugly duckling who bloomed later in life? In other words, do you believe that all pleasure resides in youth, or that all good things come to those who wait?

It doesn't matter what you think. The important thing is— never act your age!

Chimes

Quick Interpretation: Reminder; passage of time; harmony

Popular Expressions: Clear as a bell; Ring someone's chimes; Chime in

The wind's favorite musical instrument are the chimes. What kind of tune is being played? Do the chimes relax you and soothe your soul, or do they annoy you because they never cease chiming? What do you want to be in harmony with? Do the chimes indicate that you're going with the flow—that is, being blown in the wind, or are the chimes being *struck* in your dream, indicating that someone/something needs to be encouraged to keep in step? Chimes may symbolize that it's time to speak your mind— time to chime in!

Chimney

Quick Interpretation: Escape; gifts; loss

Popular Expressions: Blow your stack; Go up in smoke; Where there's smoke, there's fire; Smokes likes a chimney

Chimneys allow for the release of unwanted smoke, which may indicate that you'd like to clear your head so you can see things better.

If you don't mind a little soot, the chimney can be a great escape route. Are you trying to escape up the chimney in your dream? What do you want to get away from? Or is the chimney a means to get into an abode? Why do you need to go down the chimney? Also consider the chimney's association with Santa Claus. Are you anticipating the bestowal of gifts?

If the chimney in your dream is billowing lots of smoke, it may suggest the release of frustration or stress. On the other hand, it may indicate anger, a desire to blow your stack. The dream world is often the best place to do this, as you don't cause harm to anyone else.

We often use the expression "gone up in smoke" to suggest that something no longer exists. Has something disappeared from your life, or did an idea or goal you were working on fail to yield results?

A very popular expression is "You're smokin'," indicating that projects are moving forward quickly. It can also mean that someone is very appealing physically. Is the chimney in your dream a symbol suggesting that things are really cooking in your life?

Choir

Quick Interpretation: Harmony; cooperation; teamwork

Popular Expression: Preaching to the choir

When angels get together, they form a choir. It would be nice to think that our guardian angels had a good sing-along in between looking out for our souls!

To dream of a choir suggests teamwork. Everyone knows what to do and cooperates beautifully. Are you singing as part of a choir in your dream? Does this indicate that you'd like to sing along with others?

A choir is also a symbol of harmony. Consider what type of choir is in your dream to determine what brings harmony into your life. For example, if it's a church choir, do you find harmony delving into the spiritual or mystical side of life?

Who are you singing with in the choir? Do you feel that you're in tune with this person (or people)? Do you feel they support you? Or is the choir singing out of tune, indicating disharmony?

Look at where the choir is to determine the area of your life it relates to. For example, if the choir is at your workplace, do you feel that life at work is pleasant and in harmony with who you are? That you're cooperating with the people you work with and producing beautiful music together?

When we feel that no one's listening, that our voice is falling on deaf ears, we may feel that we're preaching to the choir. Do you often feel that no one's interested in what you have to say?

Choking

Quick Interpretation: Being speechless; suppression of ideas; high expectations

Popular Expressions: Stuck for words; At a loss for words; Choking (in sports); Get choked up about something

In sports, if a team makes it to the finals every year but never wins, they're referred to as "chokers." Is something in your life stopping you from receiving the ultimate reward?

Who's choking in your dream? What is being choked on? Does this indicate that you or someone else is at a loss for words? What are you (or the person choking in your dream) trying to express that's so difficult? It's important to look around and see what is suffocating you. Is it where you live, the people you're hanging out with, or the way you think?

If you're the one who's choking, is someone helping to dislodge whatever it is you're choking on? Or are they standing back and watching you choke? In other words, are they helping you to express what you need to say?

To choke also suggests that something in your life has stopped progressing. Have you given up on a project because your expectations were too high?

When you're emotional, full of love or empathy, you may get choked up. Has someone or something struck a chord in your heart?

Christmas

Quick Interpretation: Generosity; commercial success; family goodwill

Popular Expressions: Christmas comes but once a year; Christmas cheer; The season of goodwill; Bah humbug; Santa Claus is coming to town

Whether your Santa Claus arrives on a frost-bitten sled or a surfboard, he gets the job done, indicating that Christmas is a time of goodwill for all.

Christmas is also a time when we unite with family and friends. If it's not Christmas time and you dream about it, does this indicate a desire to get together with those who are close to you?

How do you feel about Christmas? Is it a time of joy and celebration, or are you like Scrooge, preferring to ignore it altogether? In other words, do you take pleasure in sharing with others, or do you feel that you want to hang on to what you've got, that you should be the only one to enjoy the fruits of your labor?

In our consumer-oriented society, Christmas is often seen as overcommercialized, and some people think it overrides the true meaning of the holiday. In your dream, does it symbolize something in your life that has lost its true meaning, something you need to put back on track?

If you've been waiting all year to get passionate with some-one and you haven't been able to work up the courage, then Christmas, with its attendant mistletoe, gives you the perfect excuse to go for what you want without fear of rejection.

Church (Also see *Worship*.)

Quick Interpretation: Sanctuary; dogma; ritual

Popular Expression: As poor as a church mouse

Cigar

Quick Interpretation: Odor; ash; big drawbacks

Popular Expressions: Nice, but no cigar; Up in smoke

The first, most obvious symbol association for the cigar is the phallic symbol—Freud would be delighted!

In your dream, decide whether the cigar represents a certain part of the male anatomy, and ask yourself whether you're pre-occupied with it. What type of cigar is it? How do you feel about it? Are you concerned about its length or its thickness?

Are you smoking the cigar, or is someone else? If someone else is smoking it, is it annoying you? Not satisfied with smoking you out, they want to assault your senses, too! Who is this person, and do you feel that they always upstage you in real life?

If you're smoking the cigar, are you celebrating a big change in your life? It's customary to hand out cigars after the birth of a child. Perhaps you're celebrating the birth of a creative project?

Do you enjoy smoking the cigar, or is it leaving a bad taste in your mouth? Who gave it to you, or who lit it? How you feel about the cigar in your dream may indicate how you feel about the individual who gave you the cigar—or lit it for you.

The oldest trick in the book is the exploding cigar. Do you associate the cigar with fear? Do you feel that someone is laying a trap for you or making a joke at your expense?

The home of the cigar is Cuba, a place of rebellion, strength, and determination. Do you want to defy authority? Do you want to be seen as a rebel at any cost?

Cigarette

Quick Interpretation: Danger; habit; time-out (cigarette break)

Popular Expressions: Go up in smoke; Meet your match; A match made in heaven

I can never understand why people think they look cool smoking a dried-out burning leaf covered in paper. The question is, what unhealthy things are you doing for the sake of self-image and outward appearances? Think, too, about the literal correlation. To dream of cigarettes if you're a smoker may be a message from your unconscious to give it up!

In the past, cigarettes were seen as a means to release stress, and doctors would appear on TV with a cigarette in hand, hailing (or inhaling!) its benefits. Today, cigarette advertising is regulated. Is the cigarette in your dream a sign that you must change your tactics to keep up with new information?

What are you doing with the cigarette in your dream? How do you feel about it? Does it symbolize a desire to break bad habits? Or is it a warning that bad habits are easy to create?

Perhaps the cigarette indicates that you need time out—that is, a cigarette break. Or if you feel unduly challenged by someone at the moment, could it be that you have met your match?

If someone is chain smoking in the dream, it may indicate that they require nonstop stimulation to experience life. They can't even take time out to breathe!

Cinema (Also see *Film.*)

Quick Interpretation: Entertainment; voyeurism; escapism

Popular Expression: Get the picture

Circus (Also see *Clown.*)

Quick Interpretation: Out of control; reliving childhood dreams; means of escape from the status quo

Popular Expressions: It's a circus out there; Throw someone to the lions; Walk a tightrope

The circus is often associated with a desire to relive childhood dreams. Is the circus in your dream a symbol of fun, laughter, and entertainment? Is this what you'd like more of in your life, or is this what you're *already* enjoying?

What are you doing at the circus? Are you watching the animals, playing games, sitting in amazement under the Big Top as the trapeze artists perform, or laughing at the clowns? Do you enjoy what you're doing, or do you feel indignant, indicating an intolerance or dislike for childhood pastimes?

Are you working at the circus? A popular childhood fantasy is to run away to join the circus. Do you want to escape the grind and toil of everyday life? Or do you want a break from the status quo?

Also, ask yourself if your life is chaotic at the moment—a circus, perhaps!

Clarity

Quick Interpretation: Confidence; knowledge

Popular Expression: As clear as day

When we experience moments of clarity in our lives, we have a clear and confident sense of knowing, without any doubt. What has lifted the fog?

Cleaning (Also see *Soap; Washing.*)

Quick Interpretation: Rejuvenation; chores; domestication

Popular Expressions: Clean as a whistle; A clean slate; Clean up your act; Clean and sober

Why is it impossible to keep anything clean? Wouldn't it be wonderful if you only had to clean once and it stayed that way? What are you trying to clean in your dream? Is it easy to clean, or do you feel you're wasting your time? What you're trying to clean is important, as it indicates what you wish was unsoiled in your life, free of defects. For example, if you dream of cleaning your kitchen, do you wish to get on top of health matters?

To clean in a dream may also represent a desire to rejuvenate and get on top of things after a particularly difficult time. If you're not the tidy type, then it may indicate a change of heart, a desire to become more domesticated. Also consider the literal meaning, which may simply indicate that your life is full of chores that need to be done.

If you know you've been involved in situations/endeavors that haven't been for your own good, to dream of cleaning may be a straightforward indication that it's time to clean up your act, or that you want to start life with a clean slate.

When someone stops misbehaving, they're said to be "clean." Is it time for you to turn over a new leaf in this regard?

Cliff

Quick Interpretation: On the edge; dizzying heights; nowhere to go

Popular Expressions: To cut corners; On edge; A leap of faith

In dreams, nothing gets the heartbeat racing as fast as when you're standing on a precipice and it crumbles beneath your feet! The first question to ask is: Why do I feel a lack of support? Do you feel brave or insecure? Also, consider whether you feel you're losing ground.

Anything is possible in the dream state, so perhaps the ground doesn't crumble under your feet, but rather, you come to the cliff edge, jump off, and soar like an eagle. Or perhaps you're so scared that you cling to the ground for dear life. Are you afraid of taking an important step in life?

If you're on the cliff's edge and don't fear falling, then this may indicate that although whatever you're embarking on, or currently working through, is dangerous and risky, you feel safe and know that you can handle it.

What lies at the bottom of the cliff? Are there jagged rocks, or perhaps there's a beautiful ocean? Does this indicate that there will be perils ahead, or reassurance—that is, you know you have to step off the cliff but the deep blue ocean will cushion your fall?

If you're at the bottom of a cliff, is it an arduous climb to the top? Or is it a scenic route with a very clear trail that leads directly to your destination? Either way, does it reflect the way you view life at the moment? Are you weighed down with a backpack that's full to the brim? Or are you light on your feet, able to zip up to the top without restraint?

The backpack, as a symbol of extra weight, may not necessarily be holding you back. It may, instead, be full of useful or life-preserving items, indicating a desire to move around quickly—that is, there may be challenging times ahead that require quick action.

Also consider the possibility that the symbol of the cliff may refer to the name of a person. Do you know a Cliff—or a Clifford? If so, think about how the cliff in your dream could relate to your relationship with this person.

Climbing (Also see *Ladder; Mountain.*)

Quick Interpretation: Moving upwards; advancements; desire for achievement

Popular Expressions: Climb on the bandwagon; Climb the walls; Social climber; Reach for the stars; Beyond your reach; The ladder of success

When we feel bothered by others or continually harassed, we sometimes use the expression "being climbed over." In your dream, does climbing indicate that you want people to get off your back and let you be yourself?

What are you climbing in your dream? Is it an easy climb, or do you come across roadblocks? What is standing in your way of getting to the top? What do you do in your dream to overcome the obstacles?

Does the climbing in your dream indicate a desire to move upwards, either socially or economically? Where and what you're climbing will help you to determine this. For example, if you're climbing a ladder in your office, does it represent a desire to get ahead in your career? Also consider this in relation to climbing down.

Are you climbing a tree in your dream, indicating a desire to return to childhood? Or are you or someone else in your dream climbing into a wagon, suggesting a desire to get on the bandwagon?

Also, ask yourself if life is frustrating you at the moment. Are people or circumstances driving you insane, causing you to climb the walls?!

Clinic (See *Hospital.*)

Clock (See *Alarm Clock; Time; Watch.*)

Clown (Also see *Circus.*)

Quick Interpretation: Joy; mask; empathy

Popular Expressions: To clown around; The joker in the pack

It's safer to make a fool of yourself when you're wearing a mask. By simply painting your face, you can get away with doing the most stupid things that make people laugh. Are you looking for an excuse to loosen up and clown around, the clown's makeup providing the necessary camouflage for you to go for it incognito?

A clown brings laughter and joy into people's lives through entertainment. Is that what you're trying to do? Do you desire more laughter and joy in your life? Is it time for you to be zany or foolish so that people find you more endearing?

A clown is also renowned for exaggeration—the exaggerated nose, feet, and smile. Are you exaggerating something in your life? To determine what the exaggeration may be, note where the clown is and what it's doing. Consider this in relation to whom the clown represents in your dream. Also, ask whether someone in your life is putting on a happy face or if you're putting up with a situation that masks a deep sadness.

Do you associate the clown with childhood birthday parties? If so, could it be that you harbor a desire to return to those carefree days when you were the center of attention, surrounded by friends and family, and your most pressing concern was getting through all that wrapping paper?

Clutter

Quick Interpretation: Untidy; overcommitted; hoarding

Popular Expression: One person's trash is another person's treasure

Why do we hang on to things for years and years, believing that one day they may be useful? What needs to be disposed of because it's cluttering up your life? What do you need to let go of?

It's important to ask where the clutter is in your dream. This will help you determine what area of your life you feel is in chaos. For example, if the clutter is in the kitchen, do you feel that you need to pay more attention to your diet? Or if the clutter is in the garage, is it time to clean things up so you can fit the car back in and better direct your life?

How do you respond to the clutter in your dream? Do you get in there and clean it up? Or is it so overwhelming that you try and avoid it? If it's the latter, ask if you have overcommitted yourself to projects or events that you simply can't keep up with.

Don't you love people who can put their hands on exactly what they need even though everything seems to be in a shambles? Clutter is a great reminder that one person's junk pile is another person's filing cabinet.

Cobweb (Also see *Spider.*)

Quick Interpretation: Tangled traps; an ambush; uninhabitable abodes

Popular Expressions: Blow away the cobwebs; Oh, what a tangled web we weave . . .

There aren't many things worse than ending up in cobwebs. The feelings associated with being obsolete and out-of-date are always unpleasant. Do you feel that you're being overlooked, or is there something in your life that finally needs to be put away?

Cobwebs also symbolize that something that was once a marvel to look at is no longer—it's merely a dust collector. Do you feel that something is not as attractive as it used to be?

You can associate cobwebs with slow thinking. Do you feel that it's time to clean out the cobwebs of your mind?

The cobweb is an abandoned home that has outlived its usefulness. The only thing it catches is dust, indicating that you or someone else has moved on. Or perhaps, on a positive note, it's a trap that's no longer dangerous.

Coffee

Quick Interpretation: A break; a lift; feeling wide awake

Popular Expression: Wake up and smell the coffee

Someone related a dream to me recently that left him mystified. In the dream, he gave birth to a cup of coffee! Interestingly, the birth coincided with the arrival of a new baby, his first.

Coffee is a stimulant, yet it's also associated with having a "break"—sitting back, relaxing, and taking it easy. The dream my friend had is directly associated with his child, who's going to provide him with a lot of fun and an excuse for a time-out, but is also going to be a stimulating challenge.

Decide whether the coffee in your dream is stimulating you, and if so, what is it stimulating you to do? Or is it telling you to take a break and chill out? Where did you get the coffee? Home, work, or a partner? Are you being stimulated by, or do you want time off from, home, work, or your partner?

Is the brew too hot to swallow, too cold to enjoy, or just right, the aroma awakening your sense of smell and satisfying your desires? Your answer will indicate how you're experiencing life at the moment. Is the coffee you're drinking instant, indicating that you want a quick fix? Is it espresso, indicating that you're under extreme pressure? Or is it percolated, indicating that you need to slowly mull over and think out whatever it is you're doing?

If you ordered a half-decaffeinated, half full-strength latté with a twist of lemon in your dream, does this indicate that you want it all?

Coin (Also see *Money.*)

Quick Interpretation: Double meaning; concise expression; chance

Popular Expressions: Opposite sides of the same coin; The other side of the coin; To coin a phrase

College (Also see *School.*)

Quick Interpretation: Higher learning; maturation of thoughts/ideas; career advancement

Popular Expressions: School ties; Give it the ol' college try

Compassion

Quick Interpretation: Empathy; understanding

Popular Expression: Walking in someone else's shoes

To feel compassionate is to experience empathy that supports rather than judges. Is it time to walk in someone else's shoes?

Composure

Quick Interpretation: Calmness; peace; acceptance

When you feel composed, you're free from agitation and tension. Nothing can provoke you. What has removed your irritation?

Computer (Also see *Hacker; Internet.*)

Quick Interpretation: Convenience; passwords; stored knowledge

Popular Expressions: A chip off the old block; To pick someone's brain

Computers have changed the face of the world: They think, control, organize, serve, and entertain. What does a computer signify to you?

Are you allowing others to think for you? Are you dependent on the knowledge and advice of other people? Or are you in the driver's seat, imputting and extracting information at your discretion, with the computer at your beck and call?

Are you scared of the computer? Do you not know how to use it, so instead of easing your workload, it has doubled it? Or with the press of a button and the flick of a switch, does the computer simplify your life?

Do you feel that your life is run by computers? Is everything you do recorded and stored for either statistical purposes or to build a personal profile? Do you get the feeling that you're being watched by Big Brother in your dream? Are you surfing the Net, playing computer games, downloading music, or working at the computer? In other words, is the computer taking up too much of your time, or is it helping you do your job?

Is a partner or friend working at the computer in your dream? Do you feel that they're paying more attention to it than to you? Do you feel left out?

Computers also signify having the world at your fingertips. You no longer have to go out to get what you want and do what you have to do—the whole world can be accessed in the privacy of your own home.

Confidence

Quick Interpretation: Self-assuredness; power

When you're confident, you experience a self-assuredness, a conviction that everything is okay. What has empowered you?

Confusion

Quick Interpretation: Mixed-up thinking; lack of clarity

When you feel confused, it's because your thinking is mixed up and unclear. What has perplexed you in your dream? Why are you having trouble clearly defining it?

Contentment

Quick Interpretation: Satisfaction; joy

When you're content, you're satisfied with what you've created in life. What has given you satisfaction?

Convent

Quick Interpretation: Serenity; dedication; union with spirit

A convent is a community of like-minded people on a spiritual path. Would you like to unite with others on a spiritual journey rather than walk alone?

What are you doing at the convent? Are you studying or visiting? How do you feel about being there? Is it a place of serenity and peace where you know that you'll be safe?

If you're studying at the convent, does it symbolize dedication? Do you wish to devote your life to the study of the spirit, an indication that you want to connect the physical and metaphysical aspects of your life?

If you're a nun in your waking life, the significance of the dream will directly relate to your chosen path. Are you experiencing a crisis of faith? Also ask if the convent symbolizes a desire to adopt good habits.

Cooking (Also see *Barbecue; Chef; Kitchen.*)

Quick Interpretation: Nourishment; creative expression; chores

Popular Expressions: You're cookin'; What's cookin'?; Too many cooks spoil the broth; If it's too hot, get out of the kitchen

Cop (See *Police.*)

Cosmetics

Quick Interpretation: Camouflage; cover up; beautify

Popular Expressions: Make up your mind; Make up ground; A makeup test; Make up with someone

In the past, men used cosmetics to strike fear in the hearts of adversaries, while women have used cosmetics throughout the ages to attract a suitable partner.

In your dream, are you using the cosmetics as camouflage? What are you attempting to cover up, distort, or accentuate? Are you using cosmetics to give others a false impression of what you're really like? Are you covering up what you perceive to be your imperfections, or are you highlighting your strengths?

Have you used the cosmetics on a particular part of your body? For example, are you applying luscious red lipstick to bring attention to your mouth and what you're saying? Or perhaps mascara to exaggerate your eyelashes, signifying that you're "wide open" to new experiences?

Who's applying the cosmetics—you or someone else? Perhaps you're imposing change on yourself, or someone else is trying to impose change on you. Or are you applying cosmetics to some-one else? Look at the individual and ask yourself if you're trying to improve their life in some way. Why is it that who they are isn't enough?

Does the cosmetic makeover in your dream have a direct effect—that is, you feel you're more desirable and attractive—or does it serve to give the wrong impression?

Also, consider whether there's someone in your life you'd like to "make up" with, either an aspect of yourself or someone in your dream whom you're close to.

Cosmetic Surgery (Also see *Body Parts.*)

Quick Interpretation: Being two-faced; new outlooks; being stretched

Popular Expressions: Mutton dressed as a lamb; Put on a dif-ferent face; Saving face; Face first; About face; To face some-thing; Put on a brave face; Go under the knife

Most of us admire and have a deep respect for Mother Nature, but sometimes we question her attention to detail when we look in the mirror. Why couldn't the nose be a little shorter, the chin a bit more square . . . and why did the eyebrows have to meet like that?

If you dream of cosmetic surgery, are you the one under the knife? How do you feel about it? Do you believe that you're sim-ply improving your natural beauty, and cosmetic surgery is no dif-ferent from going to college—you're improving your appearance as you would your mind? Or do you want the cosmetic surgery to erase an image of yourself that you've always hated? If so, ask if you're having cosmetic surgery for yourself, or to improve your image in the eyes of others?

Examine why you feel that you need to undergo such a dra-matic change and how you feel about undergoing the procedure. Are you changing a particular part of your anatomy? Is it your face, implying that you want to face things differently? Perhaps it's time to put on a brave face? Or is it a symbol for being two-faced?

Is it breast surgery, indicating a desire to be more nurturing (breast enlargement), or a desire to withdraw from nurturing (breast reduction)? Perhaps you want to feel more sensual and provocative, or you want to be less desirable so that you're not the focus of lustful thoughts.

If it's genital surgery, does it indicate a desire for role reversal? Do you want to be more feminine or more masculine? If the surgery is performed on the feet, do you want to put your best foot forward to give a good first impression? We all know how hard it is to erase a bad first impression.

The most common reason people get cosmetic surgery is the desire to turn back the hands of time, to stop the clock. Don't you appreciate time's natural imprints? If you dream of cosmetic surgery but have no desire to go under the scalpel, ask if it indicates a refusal to accept change.

Cosmetic surgery isn't simply a symbol of vanity or egotism; in a dream, it can also suggest proactive choice—that is, you can get rid of anything you don't want in your life.

Costume

Quick Interpretation: Camouflage; new identity; changing roles

Popular Expressions: Dressed to kill, Dress someone down; Wear someone out

Why is it that the biggest, toughest, burliest men always dress up as women at costume parties? What are they trying to do—balance the masculine with the feminine?

To dream of a costume suggests camouflage or a new identity. Are you wearing the costume in the dream? What type of costume is it? The type of costume it is will indicate how you wish others to perceive you in your waking life. Do you want to create a new identity? Is it time to change roles? How do you feel about the change of identity?

If someone else is wearing the costume in your dream, how do you feel about it? Is it simply a bit of fun, a change in identity for the day? Or is the costume confusing you, a reminder that people are never as they seem?

Perhaps you're wearing a costume in your dream because you want to present a different side of your personality, one that's only allowed out on special occasions!

Couch

Quick Interpretation: Relaxation; laziness; self-analysis

Popular Expressions: A couch potato; To couch something in certain terms

Why is it such a big sin to lie around on a couch? It seems that whenever you do it, someone is compelled to create things for you to do! What are you doing on the couch in your dream? Is it a place of relaxation, indicating a desire to take time out, or are you acting lazy—that is, being a couch potato?

Is someone else on the couch in your dream? How do you feel about it? Do you want them to get off the couch and into action, or do you think they should enjoy their time of respite?

Also consider whether the couch symbolizes a time in your life when you're being self-analytical—that is, lying on the psychologist's couch to understand more deeply how you think and feel.

"To couch" can mean to lie in ambush. Whom do you want to trap?

Cow (Also see *Animal.*)

Quick Interpretation: Domestication; chewing things over; versatility

Popular Expressions: 'Til the cows come home; Have a cow; A sacred cow

Crash

Quick Interpretation: Lack of attention; out of control; an ending

Popular Expressions: Crash and burn; Crash course; To crash (fall asleep); A computer that's crashed; Stock market crash; Party crasher

The same word that's used to describe a violent collision is also used to describe going to sleep. Are you tired or inattentive? What is it that has crashed in your dream? Who's involved in the crash? Is anyone hurt? If you're hurt, ask if the dream is a warning, indicating a time to take care.

If the crash involves other people, what is your response? Do you get in and help, or do you sit back and watch? How do you feel about your response? Is it appropriate, or do you feel that you're not doing enough to help? Do you feel helpless?

What causes the crash? Is it lack of attention, indicating a need for focus? Or is it lack of control, suggesting that it's time to slow down? The crash may also signify a wake-up call, a dramatic way of letting you know that something has come to an end and it's time to let go.

When someone turns up at a party they weren't invited to, we say they "crashed" it. Do you want to be part of something even though no one has asked you to?

Credit Card

Quick Interpretation: Simplicity; credit; false economy

Popular Expressions: Give someone credit for something; Extra credit; Give credit where credit is due; A cash cow; Play now, pay later; In debt up to your ears; Paper or plastic?; Charge!; On borrowed time; Buy something on "time"

It's strange to think that a small piece of plastic with numbers on it can open up so many possibilities. Does the credit card in your dream imply wealth, safety, and confidence? Is that how you see yourself—full of possibilities, with unlimited resources? Or does the credit card make you feel overcommitted, in debt, and out of control? If so, does this indicate that you feel as though you're living on borrowed time, spending what you have yet to earn?

Is it your credit card or someone else's? If it's someone else's, ask if you're giving them the credit they deserve, or if you're undervaluing them? Or perhaps you're overvaluing them and feel that you're living in their shadow?

If it's *your* credit card, then do you feel that you're getting the credit you deserve? Are you hoping for greater convenience and simplicity in your life? Convenience is what that piece of plastic is all about.

The credit card in your dream may also symbolize a desire to be accepted at face value without having to prove yourself. When you hand over a credit card, you're showing people that you have money without having to actually prove it.

Crib (Also see *Baby; Baby Carriage.*)

Quick Interpretation: Rest; dishonesty; game

Popular Expressions: Robbing the cradle; Crib sheet

To dream of a crib or a cot can indicate hard work for some and relaxation for others. It all depends on whether you're watching over the crib or are in it. Do you need support and nurturing, or would you like to provide gentle care to someone else?

The crib in your dream may also indicate dishonest behavior. To crib is to plagiarize. Is someone taking credit for work you did, or are you taking credit for work someone else did?

Crime

Quick Interpretation: Danger; injustice; offense

Popular Expressions: If you can't do the time, don't do the crime; Crime doesn't pay; Crime and punishment; The punishment doesn't fit the crime; It's a crime

The interesting thing about crime is, it's a matter of geography. In one part of the world, a particular action may be against the law, but in another, it isn't. For example, try driving in England on the same side of the road that you drive on in America!

What type of crime is committed in your dream? Is it perpetrated against you, or are you the perpetrator? If it's the former, how do you react? Do you try to confront the perpetrator of the crime, or do you want to but you don't know who committed it? Do you feel that you've been wronged in some way? Do you feel that someone or something is trying to get a piece of you? Or do you feel your life is threatened at the moment? Also consider whether the crime in your dream represents a situation in your life that you feel is unjust.

If you're the criminal in your dream, what is your crime? Is the dream a way to resolve guilt about a situation in your life that you feel is your undoing? Whom did you commit the crime against? How do you feel about this person?

A crime is an offense. Has someone or something in your life highly offended you? Or do you have a desire to offend in order to make a statement?

Crocodile (See *Alligator.*)

Quick Interpretation: Hidden danger; firm grip; patience; insincerity

Popular Expression: Crocodile tears

Cross

Quick Interpretation: Sacrifice; martyrdom; heavy responsibilities

Popular Expressions: A cross to bear; Double-cross; Cross my heart and hope to die; To be cross with someone; Cross-eyed; To cross someone's path; To cross-examine

Why is it that when we're cross, we're angry or annoyed? Is it because we feel that we're being crucified? What are you doing with the cross in your dream? Are you using it to protect yourself? What do you feel you need protection from?

Ask yourself if the cross symbolizes sacrifice. Do you feel that you have to make sacrifices in your life right now? What are these sacrifices, and how do you feel about having to make them?

If you're Christian, then consider the cross in relation to your religion. Are you being called upon to have more faith, or is your faith in question?

Do you feel burdened at the moment, weighed down with too much responsibility—as if you're bearing a cross? Is the cross a symbol of martyrdom? Are you prepared to carry the load, as you see it as your lot in life? Or do you want to put the load down but feel conflicted—on the one hand, you want to follow your own dreams, but on the other, you feel that you must do what you think is expected of you?

If someone else is holding the cross, how do you feel about them? Do you feel that this person is untrustworthy—that is, has double-crossed you?

When we vote with our conscience instead of toeing the party line, we're said to cross the floor. Can the cross in your dream symbolize a desire to go with what's right instead of with how others want you to act?

Crying (See *Tears*.)

Crystal

Quick Interpretation: Healing; clear thinking; breakthrough

Popular Expression: Crystal clear

Crystals have many sides and surfaces that light bounces off of. Does the crystal represent you in your dream, illustrating the many facets of your beauty and individuality?

Whenever you dream of crystals, one of the first things you should do is find out the attributes that are associated with that particular type of crystal. For example, amethyst is said to help purify and clarify thought. Crystals are said to be valuable healers, so consider your dream crystal's meaning in relation to your own life. Is the healing advice for you or someone else?

If you're drinking from fine crystal in your dream, then perhaps this indicates that things are becoming crystal clear in your life.

Curse

Quick Interpretation: Misfortune; bad luck

When you feel cursed, it indicates that you're entertaining thoughts of imagined misfortune, that you feel a sense of foreboding? Does someone have power over you in your dream? Is your power taken from you, or do you hand it over?

Dance (Also see *Ballroom.*)

Quick Interpretation: Success; freedom; being in partnership

Popular Expressions: Make a big song-and-dance about it;
Dance your way through life; Step lively now; In step;
Wallflower; Two left feet

There's only one thing worse than leaning up against a wall and waiting to be asked to dance—walking across the dance floor, asking someone to dance, and being refused! Is it fear of rejection that keeps you glued to the wall?

Are you at a dance in your dream? What type of dance is it? Is it an old-fashioned type of dance, with participants taking part in the fox-trot and waltz? Or is it more like a dance party, fast and electric, with the participants only interested in dancing solo? If it's a dance that involves a partner, does it symbolize a desire to be in partnership, either work or love related? Or do you prefer to dance alone, suggesting individual freedom?

If you're dancing with a partner, are you dancing in step, or is it awkward and embarrassing, indicating that perhaps you should not be in partnership with this person?

Are you dancing in your dream or sitting back watching? If it's the latter, do you feel that others are enjoying life but you can't? How do you feel about what you're doing? If you're dancing, is it a time of release and celebration in your life? Perhaps you're enjoying a recent success. Do you feel footloose and fancy free? Also, consider whether there's something in your life that you feel is receiving undeserved attention—that is, that there's no need to make a big song-and-dance about it.

Dancing is a great ice breaker. It lets you get intimate, in a sense, with a stranger. Perhaps your subconscious is telling you to embark on a new adventure, step out, and take a risk.

Darkness

Quick Interpretation: Lack of clarity; caution; inspiration

Popular Expressions: It's darkest before the dawn; Kept in the dark; A shot in the dark

The great thing about being in the dark is that you know you'll soon see the light . . . just before it gets dark again! Who's in the dark in your dream? If it's you, what are you in the dark about? To help you determine what it may be, think about where you are in your dream. For example, if you're at a friend's place, do you feel that they're keeping you in the dark about something?

If someone else is in the dark, is there something you should be telling this person? Or is it that they're confused at the moment and you're concerned? To be in the dark also suggests proceeding with caution. Is there something in your life that requires you to do just that? Do you need to feel around and get accustomed to the dark before you move?

If you feel comfortable in the dark, is your unconscious telling you not to worry, that all will soon be revealed, and that the darkest hour is before the dawn?

Our sense of sight is the only sense that isn't able to fully function in the dark. Is your dream of the dark reminding you to exercise your other senses? You don't necessarily have to see to believe.

Date (See *Appointment.*)

Deafness

Quick Interpretation: Silence; sanctuary; blocking out unsolicited opinions; refusal to hear

Popular Expressions: Fall on deaf ears; Deaf as a post; Don't like the sound of things; Hard of hearing

We have all, at one time or another, desired complete and absolute silence, even from the voices of our minds. Is deafness a symbol suggesting that you want to take time out to enjoy sacred silence?

One of the most obvious symbol meanings for deafness is disliking the sound of things. Who's deaf in your dream? If it's you, what don't you like the sound of? What do you refuse to hear? If it's someone else, do they dislike the sound of what you're saying?

If you're deaf in your dream, how do you feel about it? Do you experience worry and anxiety because you think you may miss an important piece of information? Or are you glad you can't hear what's being said? Does it provide sanctuary, a way to block out unsolicited opinions? Perhaps you feel that no one is listening to you in your life, that everything you say is falling on deaf ears!

When people ask, "Are you deaf?" they're really saying, "Aren't you willing to listen to me and do what I say?" To dream that you're deaf may be a symbol for self-determination, for directing the course of your own life without needing to live up to other people's expectations.

Death (Also see *Funeral.*)

Quick Interpretation: Transformation; completion; new beginnings

Popular Expressions: Bored to death; Done to death; Fight to the death; A dead end

The big *D!* There are documented cases where people have dreamed of someone dying in a dream and it has happened. But this is only a tiny average given the number of people who have dreamed of death. In most cases, death symbolizes completion.

After every act of destruction, there's an act of creation. Death dreams are common throughout adolescence, where we experience the death of the child and the birth of the adult.

If you see someone close to you dying in a dream, it may mean that your relationship with them is undergoing a complete metamorphosis. If someone you're not close to dies in a dream, consider your association with this person. It may be that you're releasing an aspect of yourself that you no longer desire or require.

If you see yourself dying in a dream, ask if it represents change. It may signify a time of renewal and growth in your life. Where you die is also significant. For example, if you die at work, it may suggest a job or career change.

Who or what is killing you? How do you die? How do you deal with it? Are you ready for the transformation or scared of it? Is it a happy or heavy dream? What area of your life do you think it reflects: family, career, or relationships?

How you feel about the dream will indicate whether you're living in the past (regret), enjoying the present (joy), or looking toward to the future (anticipation).

Debt (Also see *Credit Card; Check; Money; Mortgage.*)

Quick Interpretation: Responsibility; poor judgment; recognizing obligations

Popular Expressions: A bad debt; Forever in someone's debt; Up to my ears in debt; IOU

It's not as bad to run into debt as it is to run into your creditors. If you're in debt in your waking life, to dream of it may be your way of coming to terms with what lies before you and determining what course of action to take. It may also be a way for you to deal with feelings that accompany such a situation. If you're in debt, determine whether your dream offers any insights that may help you get out of it.

If you're not in debt in your waking life, yet dream that you are, are you concerned about your financial situation at the moment? Are you taking risks with your money? Debt also suggests taking responsibility for your financial affairs and recognizing obligations. Is it time you took control of your financial affairs?

Also, consider whether the symbol of debt indicates bad judgment. Are you using poor judgment in managing your financial affairs?

Debt is also a great symbol for acknowledging that you owe someone something. Is it time to even the score with someone?

Dentist (Also see *Tooth*.)

Quick Interpretation: Filling in; inability to speak; dread; search for youth

Popular Expressions: Like pulling teeth; An eye for an eye, a tooth for a tooth; Fight someone tooth and nail; Long in the tooth; At a loss for words; That's a real mouthful; Hit a nerve

I believe that having checkups twice a year is more than enough time to spend at the dentist! However, if you dream of a dentist, the obvious question to ask is: Should I make an appointment? Your dream may be telling you that there's a problem.

The next thing to ask yourself is, what is the dentist doing in the dream? If the dentist is extracting perfectly good teeth, does it mean that you find it difficult to articulate and express what's on your mind? If decayed or rotten teeth are being extracted, then it may signify that you want to cut the gossip.

Does the dentist hit a raw nerve? How do you feel? What do you think you're touchy about, and how can you deal with it? Is the dentist working on someone else in the dream? If so, who is this person, and do you want to drill them about something or extract something from them?

Going to the dentist often provokes unfounded fear and unnecessary dread, which is usually associated with anticipated pain. However, the end result is healthy teeth that not only look more attractive, but allow us to chew our food properly. Is there something you're dreading even though you know it's for your greater good?

Finally, we all get "long in the tooth," and with today's focus on age reversal and stopping the clock, to dream of a dentist may indicate that you're searching for ways to remain youthful.

Depression

Quick Interpretation: Despondency; apathy; limitations

Feeling depressed indicates that you're despondent and apathetic, and that your belief in the future is governed by limitations. Why do you believe the situation is hopeless? What is making you feel inadequate?

Desert

Quick Interpretation: Desolation; extreme conditions; isolation

Popular Expressions: Shifting sands; Build something on sand; Sands of time; Stranded on a desert island

No desert has *always* been a desert . . . it was once either a lush rain forest or an ocean. To dream of a desert is a great indicator that nothing is permanent except change.

The desert in your dream may also suggest that you might be dealing with extreme conditions in your waking life. Is your environment particularly hazardous at the moment? How are you coping?

What are you doing in the desert? Are you traveling through it, indicating a quick ride through desolate conditions? How you feel about being in the desert will indicate how you feel about isolation, particularly if you're there alone. If you're in the desert with other people, are they helping you through a lonely time in your life, or are you helping them through one?

The desert may also symbolize hydration. Do you feel that your life is particularly dry at the moment and it's time to get wet? It's also a symbol of survival. Is your unconscious telling you that although things are at a melting point, you'll adapt?

Desk (Also see *Office; Work.*)

Quick Interpretation: Work; commitment; study; authority

Popular Expressions: A desk job; Stuck behind a desk

Nowadays we spend more time at our desks than we do in bed. No wonder it's become a great place to sleep and have sex! Are you sitting behind a desk in your dream? What are you doing there—working or studying? Do you feel comfortable sitting at the desk, indicating a desire to sit down and get serious about working through a particular issue in your waking life?

To sit behind a desk may also indicate authority. Do you feel empowered sitting behind a desk? Is it a symbol of order and taking charge, or is the desk weighed down with papers and you feel snowed under? How is this a reflection of your waking life?

If you have a desk job in your waking life and feel uncomfortable about sitting at the desk in your dream, does this indicate a desire to change jobs?

When you've outlived your usefulness and your superiors think it's almost time for you to retire, you get a desk job. Does the desk in your dream symbolize retirement, or a time to consider a job that's not so physically demanding?

Detachment

Quick Interpretation: Release; surrender

You know you're experiencing detachment when you're able to let go and surrender to the unknown. What have you released?

Devil

Quick Interpretation: Temptation; the shadow self; retribution

Popular Expressions: Better the devil you know than the devil you don't; Play devil's advocate; Between the devil and the deep blue sea; Having a devil of a time

When reversed, *devil* spells *lived*. Do you think you have to act like the devil to live? How does the devil appear in your dream? As a Pan-like character with horns and hooves? Or does it appear in human form? How it appears will indicate whether you're dealing with the devil head-on, or dealing with devil-like behavior.

Who is the devil in your dream? If it's you, are you throwing all caution to the wind and reveling in temptation? Oscar Wilde wrote in *Lady Windermere's Fan:* "I can resist everything except temptation." Are these your sentiments at the moment? If someone else is the devil in your dream, do you feel they're being led into temptation?

The devil may also symbolize your shadow self. Is the devil encouraging you to see things about yourself that you don't like? Also, ask yourself if it's time to disagree with someone or something even though it's not apparent why you should—it might be to your advantage to play the role of devil's advocate.

Perhaps the symbol of the devil indicates that you're doing just fine and there's no need for change at the moment because it's better the devil you know.

Diamond (Also see *Jewelry.*)

Quick Interpretation: Strength; affluence; desirability; completion

Popular Expressions: A diamond in the rough; Diamonds are a girl's best friend

Why are diamonds a girl's best friend? Boys love 'em just as much! Do the diamonds in your dream appear as jewelry or simply gems? If you dream of diamond jewelry, it's a symbol of completion. If you dream of diamond gems, you may feel as though you're a rough diamond and need to do a lot more work on yourself to feel a sense of completion.

Who has the diamonds in your dream? Are they yours, indicating affluence? Or are they a symbol of strength? What are you doing with the diamonds? If you're showing them off, do you wish to show off your wealth or strength? Or if you're hiding them away, do you fear that your wealth or strength will be taken away from you?

Do the diamonds in your dream belong to someone else? Do you feel envious of, or are you impressed with, this person's show of strength or affluence? Diamonds also symbolize desirability and engagement. Do you wish someone would get down on bended knees and propose to you with a big, glittery diamond?

One of the most perfect transformations in nature is when a dirty hunk of coal becomes a perfect crystal-clear diamond. Is your subconscious reminding you that the pressure and stress in your life can make you a stronger and brighter person?

Dictionary

Quick Interpretation: Definitions; clarity; discovery

Popular Expressions: It's only words; From the word *go*; A way with words; Word of mouth; Look it up; A defining moment

It's wonderful how it's impossible to create a definitive dictionary. Every day new words are added to our vocabulary. Is the symbol of the dictionary in your dream a reminder that expression and verbal communication have no limits?

A dictionary is a great way to bring clarity to a situation. What is it that you wish to clarify in your life? Are you trying to find a particular word in the dictionary? What word is it? What is it trying to tell you about what's happening in your waking life? Look at what's happening in your dream and who is in it to help you determine what the message is.

Who does the dictionary belong to? If it's yours, does this indicate your desire to define or explain yourself? Or if it's someone else's, do you wish to define or explain them? The dictionary also symbolizes discovery. Are you on the lookout for something new in your life?

What language is the dictionary in? If it's in a language that's foreign to you, ask yourself if you have an unconscious desire to find out more about that country. It could be that you wish to define the language of that place so you can understand and accept its people.

The dictionary is a perfect symbol of an inner longing to be in step with others. Whenever we're unsure of a word's usage, we refer to a dictionary to reach common agreement. Do you want to be in agreement with others?

Diet

Quick Interpretation: Getting rid of excess; vanity; well-being

Popular Expressions: Throw your weight around; Worth your weight in gold; A pound of flesh; Take the pounds off; To pound something

Half the world is trying to work out how to get more food in order to survive, and the other half is trying to work out how to eat less food in order to fit into a bikini! Who's dieting in your dream? If it's you, are you dieting in your waking life? What kind of diet are you on? Is it a diet to lose weight, or are you dieting for health reasons? What is the dream trying to tell you about your diet?

Dieting is often associated with getting rid of excess. Are you or the person dieting in your dream experiencing a need to pare down—that is, take in and use only what's absolutely necessary?

Vanity is directly related to dieting, so to dream you're on a diet may indicate that you're concerned about your looks. Are you dieting only to look good? Dieting symbolizes a desire to take in less to achieve more (desirability, self-esteem, and so on). Does this apply to you?

Dinosaur

Quick Interpretation: Outdated ideas; inability to adapt; things coming to an end

Popular Expressions: Old hat; An old fossil; Out with the old; The end of an era

Our fascination with dinosaurs never wanes, which is quite extraordinary given that the dinosaur species disappeared millions of years ago. Is the dinosaur in your dream a symbol of intrigue with the past?

The dinosaur also symbolizes unexplained extinction. What has become extinct in your life? Look at where you are and who you're with to determine what it may be. The dinosaur is also associated with outdated ideas or ways of being. Is an idea or way of being in your life outdated? Is it time to give up the old for the new?

To dream of a dinosaur may also suggest that you or someone in your dream is unadaptable. What is it that you (or the other person) cannot adapt to? Are you (or they) unwilling to change? Is the dinosaur a motivator, encouraging a change in direction before it's too late?

Also consider whether something in your life is coming to a natural end, or if you're obsessing over things in the past. Is it time to direct your attention to the present?

When ideas and actions are outdated and inappropriate, we call them "dinosaurs." Is it time to modernize your outlook on life, and adapt to new ideas and new ways of doing things?

Disability

Quick Interpretation: Low self-esteem; self-judgment; moving beyond limitations

Popular Expressions: Lend a helping hand; No can do

The only people who believe something is a disability are the people who don't have the disability. People with disabilities always find ways to overcome them.

Who has the disability in your dream? If it's you, and you don't have a disability in real life, take note of what part of your body is disabled and consider it in relation to what you feel you can't do at the moment. For example, if your hand is disabled, do you feel that you can't handle an important situation that has arisen in your life?

To dream you're disabled may also indicate that you're dealing with self-esteem issues. Why do you feel you're not capable? To determine what it is you feel you're incapable of doing, take note of where you are and who you're with.

If someone else is disabled in your dream, what is your response? Do they make you feel uncomfortable, or do you offer to lend them a hand? How do you feel about your response? Do you feel guilty because you don't know how to help them? Or do you feel that your help is unnecessary and that the person is quite capable despite their disability?

To dream of a disability may also suggest that you're doing your best (or the person with the disability is) to move beyond limitations.

Some people wear their imbalances like a badge, as though it makes them special. They announce, before you even get a word in, that they're afflicted in some way. Check and see if you're unconsciously playing the role of the victim.

Disagreement

Quick Interpretation: Resolving conflict; standing up for yourself

Popular Expressions: Shoot daggers at someone; Agree to disagree; Stand up for yourself; Let off steam

What a boring world it would be if we all agreed with each other. The tension created when opposite views clash actually makes life interesting. Are you trying to spice up your life by openly disagreeing with another person?

Who's disagreeing with whom in your dream? If *you're* disagreeing with someone, is it helping you to resolve a conflict you have with this person in your waking life? Is it a way of letting off steam? How you feel when you wake up will help you determine whether this is the case—a lightness of heart is a good indicator. To dream that you're disagreeing with someone may also suggest that you're standing up for yourself and refusing to let someone else tell you the way things are.

If two strangers are disagreeing in your dream, how do you respond? How you do so may indicate how you deal with conflict in your waking life, or how you're dealing with a particular challenge that's facing you at the moment.

At some point in our lives, we must stand up and be counted. If this is the case in your dream, then disagreeing can mean you're on the best team of all—your own!

Disappointment

Quick Interpretation: High expectations; unrealized dreams

When you feel disappointed, it indicates that expectations you had about a person or situation weren't realized. Who or what has let you down? Were your expectations unrealistic?

Disaster (natural)

Quick Interpretation: Sudden change; beyond control; feeling victimized

Popular Expressions: Everything's turned upside down; A wave (or flood) of emotions; In the eye of the hurricane

Has there ever been a disaster that didn't reap some benefit for someone? This is very true for natural disasters. After a brush fire, drought, or flood, there's always space for new life. Ask yourself what in your dream needs regenerating.

The most common natural disaster dream is the tidal-wave dream. If you accept that water is a classic symbol for emotion, then the tidal wave indicates overwhelming emotion. Are you caught in a tidal wave, are you running from one, or are you watching a tidal wave hit from a safe place? How do you feel that it reflects your waking life? Are you dealing with a highly emotional situation at the moment, or do you *feel* a great deal of emotion?

If you don't dream of a tidal wave, what type of natural disaster is it? An earthquake or volcano? Either will indicate sudden change. Has your life recently been turned upside down? Do you feel that everything is beyond your control? Are you in an explosive situation? Do you feel like a victim?

Think about how you respond to the natural disaster. Does this reflect how you're responding to a difficult time in your life right now?

To dream of a natural disaster is also a great indicator that the things that no longer serve you will be destroyed completely (and naturally) so you can get back on track.

Dissatisfaction

Quick Interpretation: Lack of contentment; unmet expectations; separation

When you feel dissatisfied, it indicates that you're discontent with how things are or how they've developed. What is it that doesn't meet your expectations? Why do you feel disgruntled?

Divorce

Quick Interpretation: Separation; completion; independence

Popular Expressions: Split the scene; A split decision; Divide and conquer; Two heads are better than one; Separate but equal

Why do people say they're divorced? Aren't they either married or single? Is it because they need to announce that they were once in a relationship—or once capable of having a relationship? If you're in a committed relationship, do you wish to separate, or are you playing out your worst fears?

If you're currently going through a divorce, or have just been through one, your dream world is clearly helping you process a difficult time in your life. Take special note of the details in your dream; they may help you determine the most appropriate course of action so you can protect yourself as you pass through it.

Perhaps the divorce involves friends or strangers and has nothing to do with you personally. Think about the divorce in relation to something that may need dissolving in your life. Perhaps it indicates a desire to split something up. Do you want to separate from a situation in your waking life to resolve a dispute?

It's very important to look at the reason behind the divorce, as it may indicate how far people can push you before you separate from them.

Doctor (Also see *Hospital.*)

Quick Interpretation: Health; warning; authority

Popular Expressions: Just what the doctor ordered; Trust me, I'm a doctor; Doctor something up; Physician, heal thyself; With surgical precision

The first thing we think of when we hear the word *doctor* is healer. However, it's also a title for high academic achievement. Ask yourself if the doctor in your dream is a symbol of well-being or the attainment of knowledge.

When you dream of a doctor, the first thing to consider is your own health. Is the doctor a symbol suggesting that you need to take better care of yourself? If you're in the doctor's waiting room in your dream, does it indicate that you're taking your time about checking out a certain health concern? If you're in surgery, what needs healing?

If you're a doctor in your waking life, consider the dream in relation to your profession. It may be helping you process a difficult situation at work.

What is your relationship to the doctor in your dream? Does this person have authority over you or someone else? Do you trust the doctor's authority, or are you concerned that you (or they) are in the wrong hands? Do you feel you're trusting someone else with your (or their) health when you should only be trusting your own advice?

If you're the doctor in the dream, who are you taking care of? Is it someone you must take care of in your waking life? Perhaps you dream that a friend or family member is a doctor, signifying that you have put your health in their hands. How do you feel about it?

When we creatively tinker with things we want to cover up because they could get us into trouble, we doctor them. What have you screwed up that needs unscrewing?

Document

Quick Interpretation: Formality; records; proof

Popular Expressions: On the record; Sign on the dotted line; Signed, sealed, and delivered

Documents imply something official. Does the document in your dream provide a feeling of security, or do you feel uncomfortable about it because its formality is restrictive? Is the document used as proof in your dream? How is it received? Is it accepted as a valid record, or is it overlooked, leaving you upset and frustrated? Does it directly reflect your waking life—that is, you feel that not even formal records can guarantee trust and honesty.

Also ask whether the document indicates an absolute certainty about something in your life, something you don't mind putting on the record.

Dog

Quick Interpretation: Friendship; loyalty; protection

Popular Expressions: It's a dog's life; You can't teach an old dog new tricks; Every dog has its day; Barking up the wrong tree; Bark worse than their bite; On a short leash; In the doghouse

Dogs ooze unconditional love. They will follow you to the end of the earth, lick your smelly feet, and be there when no one else is.

What type of dog appears in your dream? Is its breed defined geographically—that is, is it a German shepherd, Irish setter, or French poodle? This may indicate that you have an affiliation with that particular country. You may have a desire to visit the country, or you may associate an aspect of the country with yourself. For example, if you dream of a French poodle, do you wish to be better groomed? Is manner and etiquette important to you?

Is the dog in your dream protecting you, or do you feel threatened? Is the dog's bark worse than its bite? Is someone in your life making things more difficult than they have to be? Are you making a lot of noise and not following through with action?

Do you hunger for companionship, or does someone you know desire that type of relationship? If you dream of someone else's dog and you know the owner, ask if they're seeking your friendship.

What are you doing with the dog? Are you exercising it, playing with it, or showing it off? What does this say about you? To dream of a dog show may symbolize respect, pride, hard work, and attention to detail.

If you don't like dogs, perhaps you feel that it's a dog's life. Do you feel that you're living in the doghouse? Do you dream of a working dog? How do you feel about your working life? Are you working for people who respect you, or do you feel enslaved?

Finally, have you heard about the dyslexic atheist? He didn't believe in Dog.

Dolphin

Quick Interpretation: Safety; communication; intelligence

Popular Expressions: Neither fish nor fowl; The best of both worlds

No human feels unsafe in the presence of dolphins. They provide a sense of peace, tranquility, and safety. They symbolize communication between two worlds. I like to think that when you see a dolphin in a dream, it means you have a foot in two worlds—that is, you're equally at home in the air and in the water. Do you want to be more versatile? Do you wish to be more at ease in your environment?

Communication is a key symbol when you dream of a dolphin. Without words, they're still able to communicate their feelings to us. Is there something you need to communicate in your life? Or do you wish to promote greater understanding on an issue?

Dolphins are also associated with the intellect and intelligence. Do you thirst for intuitive knowledge? What the dolphin is doing in your dream may give you a clue as to what you have to do to acquire it.

The dolphin also symbolizes salvation. We've all heard tales about dolphins saving shipwrecked mariners. Do you need to be saved from something?

Dolphins are often seen frolicking effortlessly in a harmonious environment. Therefore, dreaming of dolphins may indicate that your life is without struggle and you're looking at it with a greater state of awareness. It could also be that you desire unusual friends. Once you bond with a dolphin, you know the friendship is solid and unique.

To dream about dolphins in captivity (in cement ponds or swimming pools) has special significance. Is someone controlling you? Is someone controlling your creativity?

Is the dolphin in your dream performing tricks? Are you doing this very thing to get someone's attention? If so, maybe it's time to stop performing—after all, you're a free spirit.

Donkey (Also see *Animal*.)

Quick Interpretation: Stubbornness; strength; hard work

Popular Expressions: Donkey's years; Do the donkey work; Talk the hind leg off a donkey; Make an ass of yourself; Ass backwards

Door

Quick Interpretation: Entry; threshold; new opportunity

Popular Expressions: As one door closes, another one opens; Bring something to a close; Behind closed doors; Through the back door

The door (or gate) as a dream symbol can mean isolation or open invitation. Is the door in your dream open or shut? Are you walking through a door in your dream, or has someone else opened one, perhaps indicating that they're entering your life? How do you feel about it?

The door is a great symbol of new opportunity. Is the door in your dream a symbol of something new opening up in your life? If you open the door, what's behind it? Are you eager to explore?

Dreaming of a door can also symbolize that you're delving into different aspects of yourself. If you opened a door and walked through it in your dream, does it indicate that you want to find out something new about yourself? Or are you standing on the threshold, uncertain as to whether you should open the door or not?

Doors have a habit of slamming shut. If this occurs in your dream, it may mean that definite and decisive actions should be taken to bring something to a close.

Dove (Also see *Bird.*)

Quick Interpretation: Peace; love; freedom

Popular Expression: Lovey-dovey

Peace, harmony, love, and devotion are the attributes associated with the dove. Relate the significance of this symbol to aspects of your life that need love and healing.

Dowry

Quick Interpretation: Commitment; unfair treatment/demands; tradition

Popular Expressions: Icing on the cake; Bring something to the party

A dowry is a gift that's received (in some cultures) when you decide to settle down in domestic harmony. How do you feel about the dowry? Are you receiving it or are you giving it? Do you feel it's enough to get you started, or are you concerned that's it not enough and that your prospects are strictly limited because of it?

Do you feel *you're* enough, or does the dowry indicate that you feel you have to enhance your desirability to become a prospective partner?

Drinking (Also see *Bar; Drunkenness; Water.*)

Quick Interpretation: Replenishment; spirituality; intoxication

Popular Expressions: Drink to your health; Lift your spirits; Quench your thirst

Why is it that we drink to people's health? Is it because drinking amber fluid lifts our spirits and makes us feel better? Are you drinking alcohol in your dream in the hopes of lifting your spirits?

It's extremely common for people to dream of drinking water or some other replenishing fluid and not feeling satisfied. It's a clear and strong indication of thirst.

If your dream isn't directly associated with replenishment or hydration, is it about survival? If you poured the drink for someone else, are you helping them through a crisis or difficult time in their life? Or vice versa if they poured the drink for you?

Drinking is also associated with spirituality—that is, quenching your spiritual thirst. Look at where you're drinking or who gave you the drink to determine if it represents a desire to find spiritual replenishment.

Driving (Also see *Airplane; Bus; Car; Train.*)

Quick Interpretation: In control; purpose; escape

Popular Expressions: Drive your point home; What are you driving at?; Driving someone away; In the driver's seat; Being driven (intensely motivated)

Driving is related to control. Whoever is behind the wheel has the power. Does this symbol indicate that you want to take more control of your life and its direction?

Are you driving the vehicle in your dream, or is someone else? If you're driving it, where are you heading? Are you moving assuredly toward your destination, or are you driving around in circles? How does this reflect upon your life?

If someone else is driving the car, are they in charge of your life? How do you feel about it? Are you quite happy to take a backseat while they direct your course, or do you want to take charge of the wheel? Perhaps you're giving directions and the driver is ignoring you.

Are you trying to make a point about something in your waking life but aren't sure what it is? Where you're driving to or what you're driving in may help you to determine what it is. Or are you certain about the point you want to make—that is, determined to drive your point home?

Whenever someone becomes fanatical about a situation, cause or project, they're driven. Does driving symbolize that you're becoming a zealot, or a rebel with a cause?

Drum

Quick Interpretation: Announcements; being in step; attention

Popular Expressions: Beating to the same drum (or a different drummer); Beat someone up; Beat a dead horse; Drum up support

Are you beating a drum in your dream? What is it that you want to announce to the world? Do you feel that no one ever hears what you say and the drum is one way to communicate your thoughts and feelings assuredly?

If someone else is beating the drum in your dream, are you marching to their beat? How do you feel about it? The drum may also be a symbol of being in step with other people, dancing to the same rhythm to create united focus.

Does the drum indicate that you're united with a group or cause in your waking life—that is, marching to the same drum? Or does it symbolize a desire to get people involved in a just cause, a desire to drum up support?

Drunkenness (Also see *Bar; Drinking.*)

Quick Interpretation: Loss of control; celebration; numbing emotion

Popular Expressions: Drunk as a skunk; In high spirits; Live it up

Being inebriated is often a magnification of who you are. There's the happy drunk, the violent drunk, and the noisy drunk. Which type did you dream of? Does this indicate how you wish to behave in the world? Do you feel that you can't behave this way or that it's inappropriate without the alcohol? To be drunk in a dream may also indicate that you want to embark on a spiritual journey. How do you behave when you're drunk in your dream? Are you in total control? Does this indicate your desire to loosen up and live a little?

If someone else is drunk in your dream, how do you feel about it? Are you repulsed, annoyed, afraid, or amused? Is this what you think the consequence of consuming alcohol will be?

Is the drunkenness part of a celebration? What is its effect on the celebration—uplifting or ruinous? This may indicate how you feel things will develop if you let your hair down.

Dusk (See *Sunset.*)

Eagle (Also see *Bird.*)

Quick Interpretation: Power; great achievements;
seeing the big picture

Popular Expressions: Soar like an eagle; An eagle eye;
A bird's-eye view

Could it be that the earlier you get thrown out of the nest, the higher you fly? Baby eagles hardly have time to sprout feathers before they're kicked off the highest perch. Is the eagle in your dream a symbol of early independence?

The symbol of the eagle is synonymous with strength and sovereignty. Do you feel particularly strong in your life at the moment? What is it that you feel strong about? Perhaps the eagle in your dream signifies that you want to see things from a higher perspective, to see the big picture?

Of course, ask yourself the important questions such as "Where is the eagle?" and "What is it doing?" to further help you determine its meaning. For example, if the eagle is looking through your bedroom window, does it mean that it's time to get out into the world? Or is it time to soar like an eagle?

The eagle is also associated with clear vision—that is, being eagle-eyed. What is it that you can see with 20/20 vision?

Earrings (Also see *Diamond; Jewelry.*)

Quick Interpretation: Ornaments; beautification; attraction

Popular Expressions: Have something coming out of your ears; I'm all ears

Ears (Also see *Body Parts.*)

Quick Interpretation: Listening; sounds; antennae

Popular Expressions: Bend someone's ear; In one ear and out the other; Have an ear for something; I'm all ears; Hear me out

Earthquake (Also see *Disaster, natural.*)

Quick Interpretation: Disruption; change; turmoil

Popular Expressions: Move heaven and earth; Shake things up

Easter Egg (Also see *Egg.*)

Quick Interpretation: Fertility; rebirth; "sweet" sensations

Eating (Also see *Anorexia; Feast; Food.*)

Quick Interpretation: Making ideas/thoughts digestible; hunger

Popular Expressions: Eating away at you; Eating me up inside; Chewing things over; That's hard to swallow; A real mouthful; Food for thought

Egg

Quick Interpretation: Wholeness; new potential; hidden treasures

Popular Expressions: A nest egg; Put all your eggs in one basket; Egg on your face; Egg you on; Hatch a scheme; Walk on eggshells; Break out of one's shell

If you see eggs in a dream, the most obvious meaning is fertility. Each of us started out as an egg, fertilized by a sperm. The Easter egg, too, is a symbol of fertility as well as resurrection.

Are you sitting on eggs waiting for them to hatch? This may indicate that you have a lot more work to do to achieve your goals. Or are you treading on eggshells, indicating that you need to be more sensitive?

In your dream, are you or is someone else breaking out of a shell? Does it mean that this person is growing up, developing a character of their own, and becoming more self-assured? Does the egg signify that you're being "egged on" to do something you don't want to do, or go somewhere you don't want to go?

Is the egg in your dream hard-boiled or does it have a soft center? If it's the former, it may indicate a desire to be more assertive and definite in your opinion. Or is it that you've had a tough journey and have gone through a baptism of fire that's left you hard-boiled?

If the egg has a soft center, maybe you want to experience more gentleness in your life. Perhaps you wish to be more gentle, or you expect other people to be.

If you dream that egg is splattered all over your face, or splattered all over someone else's, are you or someone else dealing with an embarrassing situation?

Election (Also see *Politician.*)

Quick Interpretation: Acceptance; favorable judgment; thirst for power

Popular Expressions: Win the popular vote; Cast your ballot; Vote with your feet

More and more, elections are becoming popularity contests and a question of charisma rather than content. Does the election in your dream indicate that you want to be more popular and acknowledged for it?

If you're elected in your dream, what office is involved? Being elected indicates responsibility not only to yourself but to other people. Is this what it suggests in *your* life? How do you feel about it?

Being elected also represents an acceptance of who you are and what you stand for. If it's you who's elected in the dream, do you feel that it's a sign of approval? Or if you dream that someone else is elected, do you accept the result or do you want a re-count, indicating that you're either willing to accept the majority view or that you'll stick to your own opinion?

Also think about the election as a thirst for power. Ask if the person who's being elected has a desire for more control over other people's lives.

Of course, if an election is about to take place in your waking life, you may dream about it, indicating that it's time to make a decision about which way you're going to vote.

An election can also mean that it's time for you to leave a debilitating or toxic relationship. You realize that it's time to vote with your feet!

Electricity

Quick Interpretation: Energy; transformation of power; a sudden shock

Popular Expressions: At the flick of a switch; A bright spark; A power surge

Don't you think it's incredible that a fast-flowing river can allow you to hear your favorite Beatles song? Electricity is energy derived from converting other forms of energy—for example, water, air, or fossil fuel. It converts natural energy into a more convenient form—that is, energy that's available at the flick of a switch. What simple thing can you do in your life to feel revitalized and reenergized? Meditate, go for a walk in nature, or visit a friend?

Electricity also symbolizes high energy. Are you or is someone else in your dream full of vim and vigor? How do you feel about it? Or do you have too much energy, distracting you from your need to relax?

Is the electricity powering up an object in your dream—for example, an appliance or light? How well is it powered? Your answer will indicate how well you feel an aspect of your life is powered. For example, if the electricity is attempting to power up a flickering light in your dream, this may suggest that at the moment you lack the energy to think through ideas.

If you dream of some type of electrical incident such as an electrical storm, it could indicate that you want to channel your energy into something more powerful. Electricity can also signify a sudden shock. Has something shocked you into awareness recently?

To dream of electricity also begs the question: What is electric about your life at the moment?

Elephant

Quick Interpretation: Toughness; good memory; uselessness; exploitation

Popular Expressions: An elephant never forgets; A white elephant sale; Seeing pink elephants

You're sure to remember a dream with an elephant in it because elephants never forget! Ask yourself what it is you don't want to forget. Look around at who else is in the dream to help you determine what it is you want to remember or are being reminded of. For example, if the elephant is with someone you know to be a spendthrift, are you being reminded to be careful with money?

The elephant is also a symbol of being thick-skinned. Do you or does someone else in your dream have a hide as thick as an elephant's—that is, you or they don't get upset easily?

Elephants are valuable to poachers because of their tusks; the whole magnificent beast is done away with to get them! Does the elephant in your dream indicate a desire to be valued for all of your talents and not just one? Are people taking advantage of you in order to exploit a particular attribute?

Elephants are gentle giants. Is that how you see yourself? Tough on the outside but gentle within? Also consider whether the elephant's long trunk is a gentle reminder to keep your nose out of business that doesn't concern you.

Elevator

Quick Interpretation: Movement; ascent/descent; feeling uplifted

Popular Expressions: Not lift a finger; Give someone a lift; Move up in the world; Taking the easy way out; Push someone's buttons; Getting high; Down in the dumps

The elevator is a great symbol for getting to high places with a minimal amount of effort. In your dream, do you want to get as high as you can with no exertion?

The most obvious dream symbol meaning is movement, either upwards or downwards. Are you ascending or descending? If you're ascending, can it be that you want to move up in life? Or if you're descending, do you want to come down from your perch?

Where is the elevator taking you (or someone else) in your dream? This will indicate where you (or they) are moving up or down to. For example, if you dream you're descending to a subway station, it may represent a time in your life when you're being taken to deeper levels of understanding.

If you dream you're stuck in an elevator, think about it in relation to feeling stuck in your life. Is someone stuck in the elevator with you? Is your relationship with them at a standstill?

To dream of an elevator may also indicate that you're experiencing something that's uplifting in your life, or maybe someone is pushing your buttons and bringing you down.

Emergency

Quick Interpretation: Sudden change of direction; quick thinking; a test

Popular Expressions: Fight or flight; All hell breaks loose; A matter of life and death

If we were more selective about what to prioritize in our lives, I'm sure we wouldn't have so many "emergencies." So much day-to-day stuff we think we *have* to do isn't life threatening and can afford to be handled in good time. What is the emergency in your dream? Is it a matter of life and death, or are you making a mountain out of a molehill? What do you feel needs your immediate attention?

How do you respond to the emergency? Efficiently and promptly, or with trepidation? This may indicate how quickly you can think on your feet. It will also indicate how you react when the unexpected happens—that is, fight or flight.

Also consider whether the emergency in your dream is a test to see how well you respond when chaos hits. Is the emergency a symbol of neglect? Perhaps a simple problem that could have been solved long ago is now out of hand?

Emotions

I believe it's just as important to look at the emotions that arise in dreams as it is the symbols. Emotions are simply the way you react (or choose to act) to an experience. Such reactions or actions are expressed as feelings. Even though there are only two basic primordial responses to every situation, fight or flight, there are countless shades in between. In this book, you'll find some of the most commonly expressed feelings. For example, if you feel angry when you wake up from a dream, you can look up "Anger" and/or "Frustration." Beneath these entries, you'll find a definition of each feeling to help you identify it. You'll also find one or two poignant questions included to assist you in focusing on the cause or source of the feeling. I encourage you to explore the full heights and depths of your feelings, as they will assist you in interpreting your dreams. (Also see "Emotions at a Glance," page 421.)

Empowerment

Quick Interpretation: Power; authority

Popular Expression: In the driver's seat

When you feel empowered, you know you've given yourself the power and authority to move forward in your life. Why do you feel that you're back in the driver's seat?

Encyclopedia

Quick Interpretation: Knowledge; cataloging present achievements; priorities

Popular Expressions: Look something up; A photographic memory; Right at your fingertips

Wouldn't it be great if you could swallow an encyclopedia and bring up the information you need at will? It would certainly make you the most popular person at a Trivial Pursuit party.

An encyclopedia is a symbol of accumulated knowledge. What are you doing with the encyclopedia in your dream? Are you reading it, or is someone else? Does it indicate that you'd like to increase your knowledge? Or is the person with the encyclopedia in your dream expressing a desire to increase theirs? What is it that you (or they) are trying to find out? If the encyclopedia isn't being read in your dream, how are you interacting with it? This may indicate how you choose to relate to the acquisition of general knowledge.

In an encyclopedia, each entry is direct and straightforward, detailing the facts only. What in your life do you want to deal with in a direct and straightforward way? Also consider that for each entry in an encyclopedia, the facts are given priority—you don't just chuck everything in. Do you need to give priority to certain things in your life and recognize that it's often impossible to capture everything? Usually it's only possible to capture your own interpretation of things. Is this what you need to do right now?

An encyclopedia is also a catalog of achievements and events. What achievements or events in your life do you wish to record for future reference?

Encyclopedias can also signify that you don't have to worry about remembering facts, figures, times, and places, as this information is always available at your fingertips.

Engagement

Quick Interpretation: Promises; formalizing relationships; important decisions

Popular Expressions: Take someone in hand; Hold someone's hand; Promise the moon; Test the waters; A trial run; Take the plunge; Engage someone in conversation

Isn't it great that you can try out a relationship before you make the final commitment? If you're not engaged or about to be engaged in your life, then to see yourself or someone else engaged in your dream may indicate a desire to test the waters and give the situation a trial run before you commit. Engagement also symbolizes formalizing a relationship in anticipation of a desirable conclusion. Whom do you want a commitment from? Do you feel that it's time to make a commitment?

Is it a long- or short-term engagement? Perhaps it's a message from your unconscious telling you to either take a long, hard look at a situation before you commit, or that it's time to jump in there and try it out.

If you're unattached, the engagement may be wish fulfillment. Being engaged is an outward display that someone is interested in you, especially if a diamond boulder hanging from the third finger of your left hand is blinding people. Is it a symbol of acceptance and love, showing that you're desirable?

To get engaged to someone in a dream may not mean you're going to walk down the aisle with this person. It could simply mean that you want to develop lines of communication with them—perhaps become engaged in a conversation or project.

Envelope (Also see *Letter; Post Office.*)

Quick Interpretation: Surprise packages; feeling surrounded; protection

Popular Expressions: Push the envelope; Stamp of approval; Signed, sealed, and delivered

It's nice to open envelopes—unless, of course, there are bills inside! Do you open an envelope in your dream? How do you feel about opening it? Perhaps this indicates how you deal with "opening up" to people. What are the contents of the envelope? What needs to be unsealed in your life?

Examination

Quick Interpretation: Test; exposure; checkup

Popular Expressions: Stand the test of time; Test the waters; Under the spotlight; Making the grade

You look down at your test papers, beads of sweat on your forehead—you're being examined in a dream again.

Even the most knowledgeable person dislikes the thought of having to remember things under pressure, especially if they haven't prepared. Take a look at the context of the dream. Are you at school, a university, or at some other institution? What subject are you being tested on? Does it give you clues as to what you feel you're being tested on in life? Are you nervous or afraid?

Maybe something in your life is putting you under pressure. Why do you feel the need to be tested? Is it a time of learning for you, or are you trying to prove yourself? People on spiritual quests, who search for a deeper understanding of themselves and their lives, often dream of examinations. It signifies learning and a desire to "test" oneself.

Examination dreams are often disliked. Is it because we fear exposure? Are you about to embark on an adventure that you feel unprepared for? Perhaps it's the lack of preparation rather than the test itself you fear. What are you about to prepare for? Do you feel you haven't dedicated enough time to something?

Regardless of how life may be testing you, there's nothing like preparation and confidence to get you through.

Excursion (Also see *Vacation.*)

Quick Interpretation: Release; seeking brief pleasures; desire to expand awareness

Popular Expression: Hit the road

When we go on an excursion, a special purpose is always involved. What was the purpose of the excursion you went on in your dream? What knowledge did you wish to acquire?

Does where you're going in your dream indicate where you want to go to seek a time of brief pleasure in your life?

To dream of taking an excursion suggests a time of release— a time to break routine and get out and enjoy the world. It also indicates a desire to expand awareness, to extend your comfort zone and explore life.

If you're being supervised on the excursion, look at where you're going and ask whether you should be looking for a mentor to help you get to this place. If the excursion isn't supervised, then it may be an indication that you feel you're on the right track and have the necessary skills to get to that special place by yourself.

Execution

Quick Interpretation: Final judgments; enacting decisions; accomplishment

Popular Expressions: Cut-and-dried; Come under fire; Cut someone dead; Execute a shot

Executions imply definite endings. Who or what do you want to close the door on in your life?

Who's being executed in your dream? If it's you, why is it happening? Do you feel you deserve to be punished for something you did? Or if it's someone else, do you feel they deserve to be punished? Or do you think the punishment is unjust?

To dream of an execution suggests that you're making a final judgment about something in your life and bringing it to a determined finale. It may also symbolize that misadventure in your life has reached an end.

Also consider the verb *execute*. Is it time to execute a plan of action in your life? Execution can also be a symbol of achievement—that is, you can execute the right note or a beautiful shot (say, in basketball). So consider the possibility that it's a symbol of accomplishment in your endeavors.

Exercise (Also see *Aerobics; Gym.*)

Quick Interpretation: Action; desire to get fit; carrying out a decision

Popular Expressions: Working up a sweat; Working out one's problems; Exercising control; Putting your dreams into action

Wouldn't it be great if you could hire someone to do all your exercise for you? You get the muscles; they get paid.

To dream of exercise indicates a desire to get active. Are you exercising in your dream, or is someone else? What do you want to get active about or put into action? Or do you watch the other person exercise and wish you were just as active—that you had the energy to follow your goals and dreams?

Also consider whether it symbolizes a desire to get fit. How do you feel about the exercise in your dream? Do you want to get up and into it, or do you feel intimidated? Given that exercise is an important part of life, think about your dream in relation to the exercise you do (or don't do) in your waking life. Is it time to undertake more exercise, or time to ease off?

We exercise our bodies or minds to improve our lives in some way. To dream of exercise may imply the discipline necessary to achieve goals. Exercise can also symbolize a desire to release emotion—that is, water is popularly know as a symbol of emotion, and when we exercise, we perspire.

Eyeglasses (See *Glasses; Sunglasses.*)

Eyes (Also see *Body Parts*.)

Quick Interpretation: Improving your vision; looking at things differently; personal perceptions

Popular Expressions: I can't believe my eyes; Make eyes at; See eye-to-eye; An eye for an eye; See the light

Face (Also see *Body Parts; Cosmetic Surgery.*)

Quick Interpretation: External appearance; coming to terms with something; deceptions

Popular Expressions: Being two-faced; Face up to something; At face value; Saving face; Facing one's problems; Put on a brave face

Failure

Quick Interpretation: Unmet expectations; lack of success

The feeling of failure is the experience of not having lived up to expectations—your own or others. What situation not did conclude satisfactorily? Why are you disappointed?

Fairy

Quick Interpretation: Magic; joy; nature

Popular Expressions: A fairy-tale ending; Living happily ever after

I don't know many people who have seen fairies, but I know a lot of people who'd love to. It's a fantastic symbol that suggests that anything is possible if you believe it. How does the fairy appear in your dream, and what is it doing? Does it help you fix a situation, or is it just playing? The answers to these questions will help you determine how you feel magical forces work in your life. If you're an adult and you dream of a fairy, it may indicate that you wish to have a more simplistic, childlike, and innocent viewpoint on life.

The fairy may also symbolize a desire for a harmonious or happy outcome in a current situation. After all, we'd all love a fairy-tale ending.

Faith

Quick Interpretation: Belief; trust; confidence

Popular Expressions: Hope, faith, and charity; In God we trust

When you have faith, it indicates that you're able to put your belief and trust in something or someone, confident that all will be well. What has instilled trust in your life?

Fall

Quick Interpretation: Out of control; being ungrounded or unsupported; in a slump

Popular Expressions: Headed for a fall; Take the fall for someone; Fall in love; Fall from grace

You've woken with a thud. You know you've just taken a fall in your dream and made a crash landing back into your body.

Why are we so frightened of falling when the sensation in itself is so exciting? What we're really frightened of is being unsupported and crash-landing. If you dropped from a tall building and 20 strong firefighters stood underneath you with a net, you wouldn't be as afraid because you'd feel supported.

Falling in a dream may suggest that you feel unsupported in life. Why don't you feel supported? What can you do to support yourself? Notice what you're falling from in your dream (a cliff, a ladder, or out of thin air) and if you don't wake up first, take note of what you fall on or into. What's the context—work, relationships, or a social situation? This will give you a clue to the areas of your life in which you feel unsupported.

If you dream you fall off a ladder, first check the ladders around your house to make sure they're safe, then ask yourself if someone was supposed to be holding the ladder for you. If you see someone else falling in a dream, ask yourself if they need support. Or perhaps they're falling from your grace? What do they represent to you? Perhaps an aspect of yourself is falling away?

Look at your life, too. Are you anticipating a downfall at work, in a relationship, or in another area of your life? Fall is another name for autumn, a time when the leaves drop off the trees. Is it time to hibernate and get ready for the regeneration of spring?

Research has found that when astronauts dream in space, they dream that everything floats! Perhaps the fall in your dream is simply a physical sensation.

Fame (Also see *Celebrity; Star.*)

Quick Interpretation: Unfulfilled desire; double-edged sword; exposure

Popular Expressions: Fifteen minutes of fame; Famous last words

Family

Quick Interpretation: Inclusion; identification; familiarity

Popular Expressions: Familiarity breeds contempt; You can choose your friends, but not your family; The black sheep of the family

Our family provides us with a sense of belonging. No matter how healthy or dysfunctional a family is, you're always part of it. To dream of your family, or members of your family, can have deeper meaning or simply suggest a desire to be included in a group. It's important that you note how you feel toward your family member(s) in your dream. What is your relationship to them like? Are you going through a rough patch? Is your dream helping you process heavy or difficult emotions?

When you see a member of your immediate or extended family in a dream, ask what issues you're being confronted with that involve this person. The last time you were with this individual, what transpired, and how does this relate to your dream?

Does the relative in your dream represent a characteristic or trait in you that you don't like? Are you becoming more like your family, or less like them? Are you comparing yourself to, or competing with, someone in your family? Are you constantly measuring yourself against their achievements or failures?

Is the relative a dependent who relies on you for their survival? Or do you rely on the relative, perhaps leaning on them too heavily? Explore how you feel about your dependency, or their dependency. Is it reassuring or a drag?

Family dreams can also indicate that you're working through past issues. Perhaps you're working to change the relationship you have with them, or maybe you're dealing with childhood issues.

Dreams of family are common, and their meaning ultimately depends on how you perceive your relationship(s) with them to be. The dream can reveal important feelings and thoughts, so take careful note.

Are you part of another family in your dream, indicating a desire to develop new relationships? We can choose our friends, but we can't choose our family. Does the symbol of the family in your dream therefore suggest that you should make the best of what you've got?

Fan

Quick Interpretation: Cooling down; new ideas; change of direction

Popular Expressions: A breath of fresh air; Up in the air; Fanning the flames; Cooling it; Be "cool"; A fan of someone; The s— hits the fan; Be blown away by something

This symbol perfectly illustrates the use of puns in dreams, but let's begin with the most obvious meanings. Does the fan symbolize that you want to be cooled down, refreshed, or rejuvenated? Do you need a breath of fresh air? Does someone give you a fan or turn one on in the dream? Does this indicate where your inspiration is coming from at the moment?

If *you* turn the fan on, then it may indicate that you desire to change your way of thinking. Perhaps it's time to start thinking laterally. If you're excited about a current project or romance, the fan may signify the need to cool down and look at the situation more calmly.

Does the fan represent a desire to be blown away—that is, to be excited, surprised, and moved? Or do you want to blow people away with an idea or project? As a pun, the fan may also represent adulation, respect, and desire. Are you a fan of an individual, a thought, or a philosophy?

If the fan is cooling down lots of other people as well as you, it may indicate a desire to be admired. Who's with you? Would you like respect and adulation from them?

The hand-held fan has been used throughout the ages to evoke mystery, sexuality, and allure. Do you want to cover up your thoughts and ideas and have them shrouded in mystery? Do you feel that the fan protects you or makes you a more desirable and mysterious person?

Just as fans create a superficial breeze, perhaps you want people to think that you're much cooler than you really are.

Farm

Quick Interpretation: Production; understanding the seasons; hard work

Popular Expressions: Give away the farm; Buy the farm; The funny farm

At some stage in life, most of us have wanted to get away from the city and enjoy farm life. It's a symbol of the great outdoors, getting close to nature, and difficult but healthy labor. If you're a city slicker, then maybe you'd like to get away from the concrete jungle and embrace Mother Nature. If you work on the land, the dream is clearly related to your everyday life. Is the farm in your dream better or more run-down than your own? This may indicate a desire to improve your lot, or a fear that your farm may degenerate.

If things are going haywire around you, or people are behaving irrationally, you may also dream of a farm, a symbol of the funny farm!

Father (See *Family.*)

Faucet (See *Sink.*)

Fax Machine

Quick Interpretation: Communication; announcements; superseded technology

Popular Expressions: To the letter; Signed, sealed, and delivered; Leave a paper trail

Did you know we've got a transporter room like the one on the Starship Enterprise in every office? The problem is that it only works for bits of paper!

What information do you want to deliver an exact replica of quickly? What's on the piece of paper that you're faxing? Is it clear and legible, or is it a washed-out fax with a line down the middle, which is difficult to read? Your answer will indicate how you feel you're receiving your information, or how good a communicator you think you are. It may also reveal how good your network is.

To dream of a fax machine may imply that you'd like to show people exactly who you are and how you feel.

Fear

Quick Interpretation: Danger; lack of safety

Feeling frightened may indicate that your senses have been alerted to impending danger—real or imagined. What has surprised you and left you feeling unsafe?

Feast (Also see *Food.*)

Quick Interpretation: Abundance; gluttony; rewards

Popular Expressions: Feast your eyes on this; It's feast or famine; A full plate; Eyes too big for your stomach

A feast is a fantastic dream symbol—unless you're on a diet! The most obvious symbolic meaning is bounty. Are you enjoying a time of plenty in your life? What is so abundant?

Are you taking part in the feast, or sitting back and watching others take part in it? If you're taking part, do you see it as a reward, or are your eyes too big for your stomach and you feel like a glutton? If you're watching someone else take part in the feast, do you wish to join in, or are you disgusted with the voracity of their appetite?

Who's holding the feast? Is this person asking you to look at them more closely—that is, to feast your eyes on something? Feasts and celebrations go hand-in-hand. What are you celebrating?

Feather

Quick Interpretation: Desire to lighten up; laughter; cleaning up (feather duster)

Popular Expressions: A feather in your cap; Birds of a feather flock together; Ruffle someone's feathers; Light as a feather

Does the feather in your dream indicate that you need to lighten up? Is your unconscious telling you not to take life so seriously? Or does the feather belong to someone else, indicating that it's time for *them* to lighten up?

What kind of bird did the feather come from? Look at this in relation to your associations with that bird, and ask whether the feather is a symbol of a desire to adopt the attributes you associate with it. For example, if you dream of an eagle's feather and you associate the eagle with freedom, are you seeking to be free from someone or something in your life?

What are you doing with the feather in your dream? Do you find it, indicating good luck? How do you feel about the feather or feathers in your dream? Lighthearted and uplifted, suggesting a fun time?

Perhaps you saw white feathers in your dream, symbolizing cowardice. Has someone committed a cowardly act, or do you feel that *you* have? How do you feel about it?

Also consider whether you feel judged or typecast because of the people you hang around with—as the saying goes, birds of a feather flock together.

Feet (Also see *Body Parts*.)

Quick Interpretation: Movement; support

Popular Expressions: Get your feet wet; Get cold feet; Two left feet; Put your foot in your mouth; Arch rivals

Feline (See *Animal; Cat; Lion; Tiger.*)

Fence

Quick Interpretation: Containment; safety; defense

Popular Expressions: Mend fences; Sit on the fence; Come off the fence; To fence something

I've never met anyone who wants to be fenced in, but we all are in some way. To dream of a fence indicates that you want to feel protected and secure but be able to come and go freely. The question is, who or what do you want protection from, or to give unrestricted access to?

The fence can also be a symbol of containment. What are you trying to contain in your life? Look at what is within the confines of the fence to see what you're trying to keep together.

Perhaps the fence is a symbol of safety, of keeping unwanted intruders out and creating a strong defense. Look at what type of fence it is to determine whether it's a symbol of defense—that is, is it a solid fence that's hard to penetrate or get over? On the other hand, it may be a picket fence, a symbol of a desire for old-fashioned values.

How do you feel about the fence in your dream? Is it a symbol of feeling fenced in? Or is it a symbol of claiming your territory—that is, you wish to mark out what's yours?

Maybe it indicates a desire to remain neutral in an argument, to sit on the fence.

If someone wants to get rid of stolen merchandise, they go and see a "fence," who converts it into cash. Is this what the fence in your dream represents?

Festival

Quick Interpretation: Celebration; good spirits; tradition

Popular Expressions: Let your hair down; In high spirits; Living it up

If you're on a personal-development quest, then dreaming of a festival is great because it indicates that you're in high spirits! Is the festival in your dream a symbol of celebration, of letting loose and living it up? What type of festival is it? Is it a rock festival, a folk festival, a food festival, or a festival that celebrates an important aspect of life such as art or culture? The type of festival you dream of indicates where you feel you can go to loosen up.

What are your feelings and thoughts about the festival in your dream? Do you have fun there, indicating that you need a break from your routine, or that you wish to create a sense of strength or high spirits in your life right now?

If the festival is an annual event that you attend every year, and you feel empowered every time you dream of it, then clearly you're looking for a simple way to recharge your battery.

A festival is also a symbol of tradition. How do you feel about the traditions you uphold in your life? Is the festival a reminder of your ethnic background and ancestry?

Festivals give individuals permission to take time off work and be carefree and jovial. Could it be that the festival in your dream is giving you permission to loosen up? Perhaps you need to give yourself a mental holiday from the work that's on your mind.

Field (See *Meadow*.)

Fight

Quick Interpretation: Defense; attack; conflict of interests

Popular Expressions: Fight fire with fire; Fight like cats and dogs; A fight to the finish; Throw a punch

Today, big title fights are a symbol of getting rich quickly. Most heavyweight boxers throw a few punches and collect millions of dollars without raising a sweat. Does the fight in your dream symbolize a desire for quick fame and fortune? Is it a fight to the top?

What are you trying to defend? Or are you attacking someone or something in your dream? In life, we either fight to defend our beliefs, property, and so on, or we attack because we don't agree with another's beliefs or wish to have power over someone. Look closely at the fight in your dream. Are you defending against an attack from an outside force, or are you attacking because you feel that you must bring someone to justice?

It's common to dream of throwing punches and not being able to connect with the person you're throwing the punches at. Or maybe you're able to connect, but the punches have no power or strength behind them. Do you feel that you're fighting against someone or something in your life but getting nowhere?

If you're not fighting in your dream, who is? What do you do about it? Do you leave them to it, or do you interfere? How do you feel about your response? Do you feel that it's necessary to let them fight to sort things out, or do you feel that it's best to stop the fighting so they can talk through what's happening?

Whenever you dream of a fight, it's important to consider whether it represents a conflict of interests, either between you and someone else, or between two points of view you hold.

If your fight is in a ring, do you want to be judged on your fighting ability without the need to demolish your opposition, indicating that you're able to prove a point without having to give a knockout blow?

Film (Also see *Television*.)

Quick Interpretation: Following directions; escapism; entertainment

Popular Expressions: The picture of health; Get the picture; Larger than life

There's no genie that can transport you to a foreign place or time in the future as quickly as a film. What are you watching, and where is it taking you?

After you've established what type of film it is and have identified your feelings and thoughts about it, think of it as a distinct experience from watching television. To watch a film in a dream suggests seeing things that are larger than life. It also suggests watching things as a community rather than as an individual or a family. Who are you in the cinema with, and what is your purpose for being there? Is it a symbol of romance or escapism?

No profession propels a person to fame as fast as being a movie star. If you see yourself on the screen in your dream, does it represent an unconscious desire for your 15 minutes of fame?

Fire

Quick Interpretation: Purification; passion; warmth

Popular Expressions: Fight fire with fire; Come under fire; Play with fire; Light someone's fire; A fire in your belly; Fuel a fire; Put out fires; Fan the flames; Rekindle a relationship

Fire is a powerful symbol. Many indigenous cultures use fire in initiation ceremonies. It's associated with transformation and initiation—a rite of passage into something new. Fire is the only element we can't pollute. It may, therefore, also signify purification. Ask yourself how you react under fire. Is something out of your control? How are you handling it? Perhaps you feel like you're in the line of fire.

Fire can symbolize motivation—that is, being all fired up by an idea, concept, or relationship. Or it may be that you're angry. People have dreams that their place of employment is burned down. Later it's revealed that they fear being fired.

How do you feel about the fire? Is it warm and nurturing, or is it extremely hot and uncomfortable? If a fire is raging in your dream, are you or someone else trying to put it out—or fuel it? Perhaps you feel that someone in your life is trying to extinguish your life force or energy. Or perhaps they're increasing your energy.

On the surface, brush fires look like uncontrolled destruction, but in fact, a brush fire is a symbol of regeneration. Some plants can't survive without the aid of one. Does the fire in your dream signify a desire to rekindle something in your life?

If you often dream of fire, perhaps it's time to get rid of that overly warm blanket!

Fireworks

Quick Interpretation: Celebration; flamboyant behavior; creative explosions

Popular Expressions: Go down in flames; A flash in the pan; An explosive situation

When situations in your life take off or come to fruition, you may dream of fireworks. It indicates that things have just exploded in your life. Who lit the fuse, or what did it take to light the fuse? Is the fireworks display choreographed and properly organized, or is it chaotic, with fireworks exploding accidentally? This may signify that when a great opportunity comes your way, you'll feel it's a result of your planning and forward thinking, or that opportunity knocks randomly and is beyond your control.

If you're feeling lethargic and unmotivated right now, then the fireworks may indicate that you need to light a rocket underneath you to get you up and going.

Fish

Quick Interpretation: Spirituality; going with the flow; searching

Popular Expressions: Big fish in a small pond; Have bigger fish to fry; There are plenty of fish in the sea; Fish around for something

The fish is a wonderful symbol of going with the flow. Is that what the fish in your dream symbolizes? Is it swimming contentedly downstream, indicating that you feel that your life is traveling along at a steady pace? Or, if the fish is out of the water, is it an indication that *you* feel like a fish out of water? What in your life don't you feel comfortable about?

Perhaps the fish signifies that you feel like a big fish in a small pond. Do you like holding sway over the other fish, or is it time to get out of the small pond and undertake new challenges?

Are you eating a fish in your dream? If so, do you need to incorporate more protein into your diet? Or are you trying to catch a fish, indicating a desire to commune with nature and simply relax?

The fish is also a symbol of Christianity, so consider the fish in your dream in relation to your thoughts on religion.

Flag

Quick Interpretation: Respect; dedication; patriotism

Popular Expressions: Flag at half mast; Flagging someone down

A flag represents national identity, comradeship, patriotism, and tribal unity, and is a great way to stir up people's emotions.

In your dream, what is the flag's place of origin? If it's your own country's flag, does it stir up a sense of pride, or is it a cause for embarrassment? If it's another country's flag, do you feel like burning it, or are you full of admiration? If it's the latter, then it may indicate a desire to travel to that country, or to be more like its people. If your feel anger or aggression in your dream, then what is it about the flag's place of origin, or its people, that offends you?

Does the flag symbolize fighting for a just cause, or enforced patriotism? Does it signify impending danger or safety, like the flags you see on a beach when a lifesaver is on the job? Perhaps the flag is a symbol of knowing where you belong. For example, when you go to a sporting event, the flag indicates what side you're on, ensuring that you don't end up in the opposition's territory.

Are you or is someone else in your dream raising or lowering a flag, indicating either rising opportunities or diminishing returns? If the flag is at half-mast, it may indicate melancholy and sad feelings—a period of loss and mourning. Who or what saddens you at this time?

When a country declares independence, it creates a new flag to show the world that it's a republic with its own head of state. If you dream of making a flag, then it may signify a desire to create change in your life on a grand scale, a complete reinvention of yourself and your situation.

Flexibility

Quick Interpretation: New concepts; innovation

When you're flexible, you're able to readily adapt to new ideas, concepts, or situations. What has instigated a change of heart?

Flood (Also see *Disaster, natural.*)

Quick Interpretation: Feeling overwhelmed; baptism; impending danger

Popular Expressions: A flood of memories; To open the flood-gates; A wave (or flood) of emotion; It's water over the dam

Flower

Quick Interpretation: Attraction; forgiveness; coming of age (blossoming)

Popular Expressions: A rose by any other name would smell as sweet; On the scent; The flower of one's youth

To see flowers in a dream can represent a heightening or lifting of spirits. Are you looking for a natural high?

What are you doing with the flowers in your dream? To receive or give flowers in a dream indicates that someone is showing you that they love and care for you, or you're showing someone else you love and care for them. Flowers can also be a symbol of forgiveness. Are you giving the flowers, or is someone giving them to you as a sign of forgiveness?

What kind of flowers are featured in your dream? Red roses suggest romance, yellow roses friendship, chrysanthemums Mother's Day, jasmine the coming of spring, and so on. What do you associate with the type of flowers in your dream? If you dream of a lily, think of it in relation to the saying "to gild the lily."

Are the flowers in full bloom, indicating a blossoming, a coming of age? Is something or someone blossoming in your life? Or are they only buds, indicating the delicate beauty of youth? What do you feel is about to unfold?

Also consider that flowers are associated with our sense of smell. What do you want to sniff out in your life? Flowers can also symbolize resolution. Do you want to make peace with someone or something in your life?

Flute (Also see *Musical Instrument.*)

Quick Interpretation: In tune; release; lip service

Popular Expression: Blow in the wind

Flying (Also see *Airplane.*)

Quick Interpretation: Freedom; inspiration; overview

Popular Expressions: Get off to a flying start; With flying colors; Fly me to the moon; Rise above it all

Most people love flying dreams, since the dreamers feel a sense of liberation as they soar through the sky or float around the bedroom. I've never met anyone who hasn't enjoyed the experience of flying in a dream. However, the experience of a flying-in-an-airplane dream is different.

If you have a flying dream, ask yourself what you're flying over. This may be what you want to rise above. If you're flying over your home, maybe you feel as though you're being bogged down by household chores. If you're flying over a large city, maybe you want more activity in your life, or perhaps you want to escape the concrete jungle. Do you see a group of acquaintances chatting and wish to rise above idle gossip?

The most common feeling associated with flying is exhilaration, a sense of freedom. You can do whatever you want and aren't scared of falling. It speaks of a desire to liberate yourself from mundane, day-to-day activities.

A lot of people who dream of flying say it signifies a time in their lives when everything is flowing smoothly and they feel in control of their destiny. Other people say it gives them the strength and motivation to take responsibility for something in their lives that they feel is spiraling out of control.

Other types of flying dreams, such as flying in an airplane or helicopter, aren't usually as exhilarating. Sometimes they occur before you or someone else is about to take a flight somewhere. But if that's not the case, it's important to notice where you're flying to in the dream, how you feel about it, and why you feel you need technology to help you rise above it all.

Fog (Also see *Pollution.*)

Quick Interpretation: Mystery; hidden danger; melancholy

Popular Expressions: Full of smoke and mirrors; Haven't the foggiest notion; In a fog

Fog is, in fact, low-flying clouds, so to dream of it may suggest a wish to be more grounded. It's important to note how you feel while you're in the fog. Are you lost and unsure of your footing? Or are you comfortable, knowing which direction you're heading in and that you're on solid ground? Your answer will indicate whether you need to see things to believe them, or whether you're willing to proceed in life even though you're not clear where your life is heading.

If you dream of smog rather than fog, then it indicates that you feel the air around you is polluted. Perhaps you're blinded by emotion (the particles of water in the air), as well as the negative projections (thoughts and feelings) of others. If you're creating the smog, what is it you feel is negative about yourself that you don't want others to see?

If you dream of a mist rather than a fog, it may symbolize emotions that are becoming more prominent and apparent to you. What are you emotionally attached to at the moment? What is the best way to deal with it before it becomes torrential rain?

When we're confused and at a loss, we are said to be "in a fog." The warmth from the sun is the best way to lift the fog. Perhaps you need a little ray of sunshine in your life.

Food (Also see *Diet; Feast.*)

Quick Interpretation: Gratification; hunger; celebration

Popular Expressions: Food for thought; Feast or famine; Eat your heart out; A taste of the good life

Does the food in your dream reveal an imbalance in your life? It may indicate that you think it's time to go on a diet, or that you need to put on weight. What type of food do you dream of? Is it healthy and natural, or greasy junk food? This is a good indicator of what kind of diet your body would like you to adopt.

Do you prepare food in your dream for a celebration, or is the preparation a chore? In other words, is the food preparation an extension of your creativity, or do you just want to fill your empty stomach?

Is the food from a particular region of the world? Ask yourself if you have a desire to travel to the place from which the food originated.

Our planet is one giant restaurant. Everything on Earth is food for something else. Where do you see yourself in the food chain? Are you predator or prey? Consider this in relation to your relationships or career.

Food is what sustains and nourishes us. What sustains and nourishes you? After all, we are what we eat.

Foreign Country

Quick Interpretation: Adventure; greater understanding; new horizons

Popular Expressions: Come up/down in the world; It's a small world; Carry the weight of the world on your shoulders; A world of possibilities

It's amazing how diverse human beings are . . . with all their different languages, cultures, beliefs, and ways of living. Foreign shores are exotic locations where we get to experience diversity. Look at the foreign country you're dreaming of to determine how you want to diversify.

What are you doing there? Are you visiting, indicating a desire for travel and new experiences? Or are you in your country of birth, indicating a longing to return?

How do you feel about being in a foreign country? Do you feel scared or unsure of the language, the people, or the place? Or are you about to embark on a travel adventure, and the dream is a way for you to process any feelings of uncertainty you may have about stepping out into the unknown?

If, in your waking life, you've never really given much thought to the foreign country that appears in your dream, then is it time to do so?

The most important thing to do is to think about the foreign country and how it impacts or influences your waking life. Do you have friends or family living there? Do you wish to visit the place? Do you love the people? Keep asking yourself these questions in relation to how the foreign country appears in your dream to determine its meaning.

If the foreign country you visited in your dream is extremely familiar yet you haven't been there in your waking life, consider that it may be a past-life dream. Are you stepping back in time to resolve a past-life issue with present-day knowledge?

Forest (Also see *Jungle; Tree.*)

Quick Interpretation: Narrow-mindedness; natural surroundings; biodiversity

Popular Expressions: Can't see the forest for the trees; Not out of the woods yet; Don't have a limb to stand on; Out on a limb

Why is the forest so enchanting? Is it because so much of what's really going on is camouflaged? Is the forest in your dream a place of wonder and mystery, or an overgrown jungle full of dead ends? This could symbolize how cluttered or uncluttered you feel your mind is at the moment. If you dream of a clearing within a forest, it may suggest that you feel centered amid confusion, calm amid chaos.

Do you feel that the forest is being invaded and pulled down to make way for new developments, perhaps indicating that your sanctuary is being invaded and your privacy is being encroached upon?

Often answers to the most perplexing problems are so simple, but how often do we not see the forest for the trees?

Forgiveness

Quick Interpretation: Resolution; acceptance

Popular Expression: Forgive and forget

When you express forgiveness, you release a person or situation from ill feeling without seeking retribution. What have you resolved?

Fortune-teller (See *Psychic.*)

Fountain

Quick Interpretation: Refreshment; beautification; display

Popular Expressions: Fountain of youth; Take a bath on that; Gushing with emotion; My cup runneth over; Make a big splash

Ever since we saw water gush from the center of the earth, we've had to artificially re-create the effect in our front yards. Fountains are associated with creativity, abundance, and youth.

As a dream symbol, the fountain often has a very positive impact on the dreamer. It's a great metaphor for the release of emotions that have been bottled up inside.

Does someone witness (or receive) the release of your pent-up emotions in your dream? Can you now be more calm around this person in your waking life? Or is it the other way around, and the fountain symbolizes the release of someone else's pent-up emotions? Whom the fountain belongs to will help you ascertain who's releasing the emotions and making such an exuberant show of it.

A fountain also symbolizes recycling—that is, its water is often recycled. Are you making the most out of the little you have? Do you recognize that you don't need much to do well, and that your best attributes, when used appropriately, can make you a big achiever?

A fountain can also signify an affluent culture or domicile. Is the fountain in your dream a symbol of wealth? If it's your fountain, perhaps you've become more comfortable with your ability to create wealth.

Let's not forget that the fountain is also a symbol of youth—that is, the mythical fountain of youth. Is your dream telling you that it's time to lighten up and become more childlike, youthful, and innocent?

Fowl (See *Chicken.*)

Fox

Quick Interpretation: Cleverness; solitude; elusiveness

Popular Expressions: Sly as a fox; To outfox someone; Run with the fox and hunt with the hound; Foxy lady

It's interesting how we give animals human character traits. Do foxes really have cunning and deviousness built into their DNA, or do they simply have the same basic traits of any animal: survival and reproduction?

Since we've taken it upon ourselves to label foxes crafty, calculating, and sneaky, ask yourself if that's what the fox in your dream represents.

Perhaps you associate the fox with being endangered, hounded, and hunted for sport. Do *you* feel as if you're being mercilessly hunted by someone or something? Do you think that the odds are stacked against you, that you're outnumbered?

Native Americans often use animal totems to symbolize the "character" of an animal. Do you wish to be more like the fox—for example, more cunning in your business dealings, more acutely aware of yourself in relationships, or better able to nurture and heal yourself? (When a fox is injured, it withdraws to its cave or hole to treat its wounds.)

Was someone you know with the fox in your dream? Is this person not being completely honest with you—that is, are they foxing around?

Today, a sexy person is often referred to as a "fox." Is this how you wish to appear, or is someone you know a real fox and you haven't dared admit it to yourself?

Freckle

Quick Interpretation: Birthmark; true colors; skin deep

Popular Expressions: In your face; Saving face; Put a different face on it

A symbol of youth and innocence, is there anything as cute as freckles? In your dream, do you feel younger than your years, or do you wish to be seen as young at heart? How do you feel when you notice the freckles? Are they your freckles or someone else's? Do you see them as blemishes, as obstacles to perfection, or do they intrigue you and enhance the body's appearance?

Freckles often appear after prolonged exposure to the sun, so ask yourself if, in your dream, they're a symbol of feeling exposed.

Friend

Quick Interpretation: Support; comfort; choice

Popular Expressions: A friend in need is a friend indeed; Friends for life

The most successful way to create a good friendship is to be a good friend. When you see a friend in a dream, it may highlight your empathy for another.

What are you doing with your friend in the dream? Are you giving to the friendship or asking something of it? Describe your friend's characteristics. Do they represent qualities that you wish to emulate?

True friendship is about being able to speak your mind. Does the friend in your dream signify that you want to speak your mind without fear of reprisal or judgment?

Frigidity

Quick Interpretation: Emotional withdrawal; coldness

Popular Expressions: A cold fish; Give someone the cold shoulder

When you feel frigid, it indicates that you're emotionally withdrawn. What don't you feel any warmth toward? Who has left you cold?

Frog

Quick Interpretation: Transformation; major leaps; adaptability

Popular Expressions: A frog in your throat; A big frog in a small pond; From a frog to a prince; Fish out of water; Leap of faith

Frogs symbolize being a fish out of water. They begin life underwater and end up hopping about on land. But ultimately, they hang about waiting for princesses to turn them into princes.

If you see a frog in a dream, consider if you want to be transformed into something greater. Are you waiting for a woman to come along and transform you, or do you wish to get in touch with your feminine side?

Is the frog a symbol of inner beauty? Are you a prince trapped in a frog's body? Another thing to consider is adaptability. Frogs are as comfortable living on water as they are on land. Is there something/someone in your life you want/have to adapt to?

Consider the idea of being camouflaged, too. The frog's ability to camouflage itself is a great survival skill. Is this what you're trying to do—blend into your environment so that no one knows you're there?

Frogs survive on a diet of bugs. If you see a frog munching away in a dream, it may be that you want to get rid of something that's bugging you.

Frogs can also indicate a desire for sudden movement, a need to get out of a situation quickly. A frog can hop out of danger in the blink of an eye. Is there a situation in your life that you want to get out of quickly?

If you hear frogs in your dream, ask yourself if someone you know is dying, or if something in your life is sending you to an early grave.

If you're pondering a big decision, a frog in your dream may indicate a leap of faith—you're jumping from the known into the wild blue yonder. You may be jumping from the frying pan into the fire, or you may be taking a leap of faith that will land you right where you want to be.

As a final consideration, the frog in your dream may indicate the onset of a bad cold or flu—that is, you have a frog in your throat. Or the frog in your throat may mean that you're attempting to disguise your voice or words.

Fruit (Also see *Apple.*)

Quick Interpretation: Abundance; product of your work; protecting yourself

Popular Expressions: Forbidden fruit; The fruits of your labors; To bear fruit; To be fruitful

To dream of fruit is a sure sign of affluence in many contexts. We can be fruitful with our thoughts, our relationships, and our careers. It indicates a time of plenty, a fruitful harvest. What are you enjoying plenty of in your life at the moment? Are you enjoying the fruits of your labors?

Also consider what you're doing with the fruit in your dream. If you're eating it, perhaps it indicates that your body is craving the nutrients the fruit provides. Or if you're apprehensive about the fruit in your dream, is it a warning—a symbol of forbidden fruit?

Take note of the fruit you're eating and ask yourself if it's in or out of season, indicating that you're either in or out of sync with nature.

Fulfillment

Quick Interpretation: Completion; satisfaction

Popular Expressions: Enough is enough; Filled to the brim

When you feel fulfilled, you recognize that enough is enough. What has made you feel complete?

Funeral (Also see *Death.*)

Quick Interpretation: Acknowledgment of change; separation; show of respect

Popular Expression: It's your funeral

Contrary to popular belief, to dream of a funeral can be very positive. From every act of destruction comes an act of creation. Are you at the funeral of someone you know? Has this person recently passed away in real life? Is dreaming of a funeral a way for you to process the grief of loss?

If you're at someone's funeral but you didn't know them directly, then maybe an aspect of your life has died, and the symbol of the funeral indicates that you acknowledge and accept the completion of a cycle. The funeral may be a show of respect for the change that's taking place in your life.

Are you being separated from someone or something in your life at the moment? How do you feel about it?

When we suffer consequences as a result of acting impetuously, we're told that it's our funeral. Perhaps it's time to consider the misgivings you have about the way you're behaving.

Furniture (See *Chair.*)

Galaxy (Also see *Celebrity; Star.*)

Quick Interpretation: Inspiration; limitlessness; exploration

Popular Expressions: Stars in your eyes; Hitch your wagon to a star; Reach for the stars; Out of this world

To see a galaxy in a dream is a powerful symbol indicating infiniteness and vastness. It reminds us that we should never believe we're alone, as there's so much out there in so many different forms.

A galaxy can also symbolize brilliant and notable people meeting in one place. Do you wish to mix with a more enlightened circle of friends, or are you already doing this?

Stars make up a galaxy, and today the word *star* is synonymous with celebrity. Do you want to celebrate life with the stars?

Gambling

Quick Interpretation: Chance; high hopes; obsession

Popular Expressions: A one-horse race; To be at odds with someone/something; Hedge your bets; Don't bet on it; Beginner's luck; A sure thing

The symbol of gambling in a dream is all about taking chances. Do you feel that the odds are stacked against you, or are they in your favor? Are you betting on a sure thing, like whether the sun is going to come up tomorrow? Or are you placing a bet on your favorite sports team winning the big game when they've been undefeated up to this point? (If you follow the same team I do, that's a *real* long shot.)

How do you feel about the wager? Can you afford to lose and are only playing for a bit of fun, or is it imperative that you win? Are you risking it all on a throw of the dice? Are you being compulsive? Look at what's at stake. Are they high stakes and you're gambling with your life, or are you playing a more laid-back game of strip poker where the only thing you're going to lose is your T-shirt? These questions will help you determine whether or not to take a chance on something in your waking life.

Is it time to think about what you're doing? Perhaps you're taking unnecessary risks. Or is your dream telling you it's *time* to get back into the game, take chances, and leave your comfort zone?

Game (Also see *Chess.*)

Quick Interpretation: Escape; childhood; fun

Popular Expressions: A game plan; Give the game away; Ahead of the game; The game of life; Being game to do something

Games are diversions that let us forget about life for a while. Does the game in your dream indicate that it's time for amusement in your life? That it's time to lighten up and play?

What kind of game are you playing in your dream? Is it a board game, a chess game, or a game of hide-and-seek? Depending on how serious the game is, it may be a symbol of childhood innocence and fun. Do you want to return to the days when things seemed a lot more simple?

To be playing a game in your dream may also indicate playing games in real life. Is someone playing dirty in your dream? Do you feel that you're being manipulated, and that everything is underhanded and shady? Or is the game in your dream a symbol of escape? What do you want to escape from? What do you wish did not exist? Ask if the dream is helping you develop a game plan in your life. Do you need to work out a plan of action?

Wild animals are called game when they're hunted? Do you feel that you're being pursued, or are you tracking someone down? The game could also represent a desire for more courage, as you may want to be more game when it comes to pursuing a new career or relationship.

Gang

Quick Interpretation: Protection; strength in numbers; intimidation

Popular Expressions: Gang up on; Walk the gangplank; There's safety in numbers

At one time or another, many of us have wanted to be part of a gang as a way to feel safe and secure. Does the gang in your dream symbolize a desire for group support?

What's the purpose of the gang in your dream? Is it a symbol of exerting your will on others? Or is the gang a symbol of safety in numbers? A way for a minority group to feel protected? Do you think that if you join forces with others, a more powerful outcome will be achieved?

If life is getting you down and you feel overwhelmed by a situation you're in, you may dream of a gang, indicating that things are ganging up on you.

Garage

Quick Interpretation: Clutter; storage; sale

Popular Expressions: The tools of the trade; Jack-of-all-trades

Is the garage in your dream neat and tidy, with the silhouette of every tool painted on the wall and the floor so clean you could eat off it? Or is it so cluttered and messy that you can't even fit your car in? How do you feel about the state of your garage? Do you feel more comfortable in an orderly, organized environment, or do you prefer the clutter? Does this indicate that you either want to be more organized or not so anally retentive?

Is the garage attached to the house or separate? In the past, the stable (which we now call the garage) was usually separate from the house (for obvious reasons). Today, it's more likely to be attached to the house. We want to get to our car more quickly, easily, and effortlessly. If the garage isn't attached to the house, ask yourself if it symbolizes outdated ideas, or reasoning that's no longer valid. Or perhaps you prefer to do things the old way.

If you're in the garage, what are you doing in there? Are you being creative—building, fixing, and enjoying yourself? Or is it your last refuge, a place where you can get away from noise and the hustle and bustle of family pressures? Are you storing things in the garage that will be of value and use to you in the future? Or are you storing junk that you'll never need? Whatever you're doing in the garage, consider it in relation to what's going on in your waking life regarding leisure time and what you choose to store in your memory bank.

What kind of car, if any, is in the garage? Is it one that you own, or one that you aspire to own? If it's the latter, the garage may be a symbol of desire. If you already own it, it may be a symbol of satisfaction. If it's not your car in the garage, how do you feel about someone parking their property in your space?

When we put something in the garage, we want to protect it from the elements. Perhaps you're feeling particularly vulnerable right now and would like to protect yourself from a harsh and merciless environment.

Garbage

Quick Interpretation: Elimination; being wasteful; useless information

Popular Expressions: What a load of garbage; Garbage in, garbage out; One man's trash is another man's treasure

I think it's fair to say that one person's garbage is another person's treasure. What are you judging to be worthless when it may in fact be a valuable resource?

What is being eliminated in your dream? How do you feel about it? Are you glad that it's out of your life, do you feel it's wasteful, or are you indifferent? Your response to the garbage will help you determine your feelings about letting go of what you think is of no further use.

Does disposing of the garbage symbolize getting rid of emotional baggage, or perhaps letting go of toxins? Think about this in relation to what you're doing in your dream and who you're with. Have you recently worked through a personal issue in your life, and the garbage in your dream is a symbol of resolution, of letting go of the crap?

Perhaps the garbage signifies disagreeing with someone else's opinion—that is, you think what they say is a load of garbage.

In our environmentally conscious world, most of our garbage is recycled. Does the garbage in your dream signify that you know you can redefine, rethink, and redevelop aspects of your life that you feel are obsolete?

Garden

Quick Interpretation: Sanctuary; groundedness; weeding things out

Popular Expressions: Lead someone up the garden path; Watch your garden grow; As you sow so shall you reap; A tough row to hoe; Raking up the past; Weed something out

No matter how small our home or apartment is, most of us like to create a garden, even if it's just along the windowsill. To dream of a garden suggests a bountiful time in your life, particularly if the garden is in full bloom, alive, and vibrant. What are you doing in the garden? Are you walking through it leisurely, taking in the sights and sounds? If so, it may indicate that you're enjoying life's bounty at the moment.

Who are you in the garden with? Are you enjoying a prosperous and joyous time with this person/people? If you're weeding a garden, think of it in relation to weeding things out. What are you getting rid of in your life that only gets in the way?

What you sow is what you reap. What is blossoming in your garden?

Garlic

Quick Interpretation: Detoxification; protection; sexual energy

Popular Expressions: Your bark is worse than your bite; Breathing fire

How did we ever come to believe that a string of smelly garlic bulbs could protect us from nighttime demons like vampires? Does the garlic symbolize protection in your dream? What do you feel you need to protect yourself from?

Garlic is also a symbol of detoxification. Do you need to detox? What is toxic—your physical body or emotions? Believe it or not, garlic is said to be an aphrodisiac. Do you want to heighten your sexual energy?

We all know when someone has consumed garlic. Every word spoken pervades the nostrils. Does the garlic in your dream signify that you want people to pay attention to what you say? Do you want your words to have more impact?

Gasoline

Quick Interpretation: Energy; pollution; conversion

Popular Expressions: Run out of gas; Put a tiger in your tank; Running on empty

Dreaming of gasoline may indicate that you want to ignite a situation or add more spark to your life. This smelly liquid gets humans from one place to another. Do you need something to get you going?

Gasoline can signify manipulation. Gas prices seem to go up and down on a whim, even though we've got a seemingly endless supply. Do you feel that someone or something is manipulating your finances?

Gate (Also see *Door.*)

Quick Interpretation: Beginnings; opening up; shutting down

Genitals (Also see *Body Parts; Penis; Vagina; Sex.*)

Quick Interpretation: Reproduction; private parts; release; pleasure

Popular Expressions: Below the belt; Hit you where it hurts; The family jewels

What is all this fuss about our genitalia? Some people may not find the genitals too pretty, but they're very functional!

If you dream of genitals, it's important to first take note of the context of the dream. For example, were you relieving yourself? This may indicate that you need relief from an emotional challenge in your life. Is your dream an indication that it's time to let go of the past? To flush it out of your life?

If you dream of genitals of the opposite sex, ask yourself if you woke up feeling envious or relieved. If envious, then it may indicate that you wish for more of the benefits that you perceive the opposite sex to have. If relieved, then you're clearly quite happy to be your own sex.

Did you dream of genitals of the same sex? If you're a man, did you dream of a larger or smaller penis? If larger, it may indicate a desire to be more potent and desirable in relationships. If it was smaller, then it could signify that you wish to be remembered for your mental capacity and personality rather than your prowess in the bedroom.

If you're a woman and you dream of a vagina, it may indicate a desire to give birth to an idea, or another human being! Do you wish to start a family?

The genitals account for some of life's most pleasurable moments. Is your dream a lusty release? Or are you practicing for when you get lucky?

Genuineness

Quick Interpretation: Authenticity; sincerity; honor

When you feel genuine, it indicates that you're free from pretense; you're authentic and sincere. What do you do in your dream that's so honorable?

Ghost

Quick Interpretation: Spirits; the past; imagination

Popular Expressions: Give up the ghost; Not a ghost of a chance; Lay the ghost to rest; See right through someone

If you're going to dream of a ghost, I'm sure you'd rather it be like Casper than the Headless Horseman. Sometimes ghosts appear in our dreams to show how transparent our actions can be at times. Who is the ghost in your dream? Are its intentions obvious or transparent? Can you see right through them?

How do you feel when you see the ghost in your dream? Are you frightened, surprised, or bemused? Your answer will indicate how you feel about being exposed and/or transparent.

If you're the ghost in your dream, do you wish to be more spiritual? Do you want to be able to maneuver effortlessly within the physical world? Or is it that you just want to scare the hell out of someone?

We often say someone hasn't got a ghost of a chance to imply that they're on an impossible mission. Perhaps the ghost in your dream indicates that a current endeavor or relationship in your life won't succeed.

If you recognize the ghost in your dream as someone you know who's already departed, then clearly you desire to reconnect or resolve a situation with them. What is the purpose of the communication?

If you feel ill at ease because of the encounter, ask yourself if something is haunting you. What do you fear that does not really carry any weight?

Giraffe

Quick Interpretation: High society; tall tales

Popular Expressions: Hard to swallow; Jump down someone's throat; Stick your neck out; Rise above it all

If there was ever a symbol signifying that it's time for you to really stick your neck out, it has to be the giraffe. If you dream of a giraffe, ask yourself if it's time to take chances. Is it time to throw caution to the wind and take a leap of faith?

What is the giraffe in your dream doing? Is it feeding from the highest branches and chewing the best leaves that no other animal can reach? Are you being reminded that when you make an effort to extend yourself, the awards are there?

Has the giraffe got its head in the clouds, indicating that you need to come back down to earth? Or is the giraffe awkwardly trying to eat grass, indicating that being down to earth isn't always practical?

Also consider whether there's something going on in your life that's really hard to swallow. Do you need to think things through before making a decision?

Giraffes get a bird's eye view of the world without leaving the ground. Is this what you wish to be able to do—that is, keep your feet firmly planted on the ground while viewing the horizon clearly?

Glasses (Also see *Sunglasses.*)

Quick Interpretation: Clear vision; observation

Popular Expressions: On the nose; Can't see the forest for the trees; See no evil; Look at life through rose-colored glasses; Out of sight; Keep an eye out; Make a spectacle of oneself

We've all done something that has embarrassed us at some point in our lives. Do you feel that you've made a spectacle of yourself, and that's why you've dreamed of glasses? Consider this if you don't normally wear glasses.

If you often dream of glasses, then I'd recommend that you see an optometrist to get your eyes checked.

We all want to see things more clearly in life. If you're wearing glasses in your dream and you don't normally wear glasses in waking life, then ask yourself if you want to see a situation more clearly. Where are you in your dream? This may indicate the area of your life where you'd like more clarity.

These days, glasses are a fashion statement. Do the glasses in your dream make you feel more or less attractive? Maybe you want to seem more businesslike. Or perhaps you simply want to enjoy the illusions of life—that is, you want to see the world through rose-colored glasses.

Gloominess

Quick Interpretation: Low spirits; despondency

Popular Expressions: Doom and gloom; Down in the dumps

Melancholia and low-spiritedness accompany a feeling of gloom. What makes you feel dispirited in your dream? Is it a reflection of something uncomfortable that's taking place in your working life?

Glove

Quick Interpretation: Protection; elegance; covering

Popular Expressions: The gloves are off; Fit like a glove

I really can't figure out why we say "take the gloves off" when we're ready to fight, when boxers put their gloves *on* to do so. What kind of gloves do you see in your dream? A lacy, delicate pair of gloves may indicate a desire for elegance and refinement, while boxing gloves may indicate that a more aggressive approach is required if you want to deliver a knockout blow.

Today we're accustomed to seeing people wear rubber gloves to protect themselves from germs and bacteria. Are you concerned that someone is trying to infect you with the way they handle things, or do you feel that you could infect others with your way of handling things?

Our fingerprints are unique, and the best way to avoid leaving them behind is to wear gloves. Consider the gloves as a symbol of not wanting to show who you really are or where you've been.

Gluttony (Also see *Food; Feast.*)

Quick Interpretation: Excess; overabundance

Popular Expression: A glutton for punishment

When you feel gluttonous, you want to eat, drink, experience, and endure to excess. What is so irresistible and all-consuming in your dream?

Goat (Also see *Animal.*)

Quick Interpretation: Foolish; hardheaded; having a strong stomach

Popular Expressions: Act the goat; Get someone's goat

Gold

Quick Interpretation: Eternity; value; reward

Popular Expressions: A gold digger; A heart of gold; Worth one's weight in gold; As good as gold; Everything he/she touches turns to gold; The Midas touch

When an individual is invaluable to a project or person, we say they're "worth their weight in gold." Is the gold in your dream a symbol for an individual who's indispensable?

Gold is a precious metal. If you own the gold in your dream, what does it represent that you feel is so precious in your life? Look at where you are and what you're doing to determine what it is. If the gold has been taken from you in your dream, ask yourself if something precious has been taken away from you in your waking life.

Were you given the gold, or were you giving the gold in your dream? Does this signify being valued—that is, that the person giving you the gold values you, or that you value the person you're giving the gold to?

The gold could also signify a reward. If this is the case, what do you feel you're being rewarded for? True kindness and generosity are two things we admire deeply. Is the custodian of the gold in your dream someone with a heart of gold?

Goose (Also see *Animal.*)

Quick Interpretation: Being flustered; golden egg

Popular Expressions: Your goose is cooked; What's good for the goose is good for the gander

Gossip

Quick Interpretation: Rumor mill; sensationalizing intimate detail; source of information

Popular Expressions: Set tongues wagging; Talk with forked tongue; The talk of the town; Spread the word

Have you ever met anyone who doesn't like to hear a little gossip? We all seem to have a good sense of *rumor* (hee-hee)—little titbits that give us insights into what's really going on—at least on the surface. Does the gossip in your dream upset and unnerve you, or does it illuminate you, confirming your suspicions? Who's the gossip about? Is it malicious or trivial?

It's possible and highly probable that a lie can become the truth if enough people repeat it. What untruths do you see in your dream that must be corrected before they become reality?

Graduation (Also see *Academy; School.*)

Quick Interpretation: Acknowledgment; success; completion

Popular Expressions: Old school; Finish what you started

No more teachers, no more books . . . to dream of graduation indicates that it's time to do things for yourself. It's a wonderful symbol for expansion of awareness, prompting the dreamer to acknowledge that they've moved beyond an immediate challenge.

Who's graduating in your dream? Who's getting recognition for their hard work, perseverance, and study? Of course, if you're currently pursuing an academic degree, the graduation is a symbol of wish fulfillment. If you're not studying, then note what you're graduating from. This may indicate an area or aspect of yourself that you feel is important to develop. For example, did you qualify as an academic, technician, or mechanic, indicating that you either need to be thinking more or getting physical.

To dream that you're a graduate may also imply a desire to be seduced by Mrs. Robinson.

If you feel that you haven't been publicly acknowledged or haven't passed the right tests in your career, then you may dream that you're back in school trying to get your diploma.

Granddaughter/Grandfather/Grandmother/ Grandson (See *Family.*)

Grapes (Also see *Fruit.*)

Quick Interpretation: Sensuality; being spoiled; communication

Popular Expressions: Sour grapes; Grapes of wrath; Hear something through the grapevine

Grass (Also see *Marijuana*.)

Quick Interpretation: Informer; getting high; greener pastures

Popular Expressions: The grass is always greener on the other side of the fence; Grass roots; Put someone out to pasture

We always imagine the green, green grass of home to be bountiful. Does the grass in your dream symbolize being homesick and a desire to return to where you felt nurtured, supported, and loved?

What is the grass like in your dream? Fresh and green, or dry and yellow? The state of the grass may indicate how you feel about going back to your grass roots. *Grass* is another word for marijuana. Therefore, perhaps the grass is a symbol of getting high on life, of feeling on top of the world.

The grass in your dream could also be a symbol for thinking that things are better elsewhere—as the saying goes, the grass is always greener on the other side of the fence.

Consider the grass as a symbol of wanting to take things easy and retiring from current endeavors. Perhaps you want to be put out to pasture!

Gratitude

Quick Interpretation: Appreciation; thanks

Popular Expressions: Count your blessings; A blessing in disguise; Thanks for nothing

When you feel grateful, it indicates that you appreciate and give thanks for all that you receive in your life. What blessings have you counted?

If you felt ungrateful in your dream, then it may indicate that you're not counting your blessings. However, no matter how bad the situation, it seems that there's always something to be thankful for.

Grave

Quick Interpretation: Ending; seriousness; going underground

Popular Expressions: Dig your own grave; Turn over in your grave; Dead and buried; A grave situation

Well, it's certainly a place where you can rest in peace—no phone calls, no faxes, no e-mails. It may be frightening and disconcerting to see a grave in your dream, but consider it as a symbol of a final resting place. Who in your dream needs a long rest, and from what?

A grave could also symbolize that it's time to put a situation or challenge behind you and move on—that is, something should be dead and buried. Pay close attention to what's happening at the gravesite. Does it indicate that a grave situation is about to unfold in your life?

Grief

Quick Interpretation: Sorrow; loss

When you grieve, you experience a deep and strong feeling of sorrow caused by loss. What have you lost in your dream? Why is it so difficult to let go?

Groom (See *Bride/Bridegroom.*)

Guard

Quick Interpretation: Protection; imprisonment; alertness

Popular Expressions: Off/on your guard; Catch someone off guard; Lower your guard; Be guarded about something

How times have changed. Today guards are even posted outside discount stores! Guards and feelings of security/insecurity are bedfellows. Who's insecure in your dream? Is the guard a symbol of your own insecurity? What do you feel you need protection from? If you're the guard in your dream, what or who are you protecting? It could be that your unconscious is asking you to be on your guard. Is it time to be a little more cautious than you usually are?

If the guard is a public servant (a warden or sheriff), are you in protective custody, or are you being protected, indicating that you're either in or out of harm's way?

Guilt

Quick Interpretation: Breach of faith; remorse

When you feel guilty, it indicates that you have breached an agreement of conduct you had with yourself and/or society. Whom have you let down? What agreement did you break?

Guitar (Also see *Musical Instrument.*)

Quick Interpretation: Harmony; accompaniment; being plugged in

Popular Expression: With strings attached

Gum (See *Chewing Gum.*)

Gun

Quick Interpretation: Protection; destruction; ambition

Popular Expressions: Going great guns; Jump the gun; Stick to your guns; Gunning for someone; Shoot to kill; Pull the trigger; Fast on the trigger

Who would associate high achievement, success, and abundance with a gun? This is exactly what we do when we say we're "going great guns"! Who has the gun in your dream? Is it your gun or someone else's? What are you, or the person who has the gun, doing with it? Are you using it for protection? What do you feel you must protect yourself against?

Are you being chased by someone with a gun? Why do you feel this person wants to hurt you? What danger do you feel you're trying to escape? The gun is a symbol of destruction. What do you or the person with the gun want to destroy?

Also consider that the gun may be a symbol of tenacity—that is, sticking to your guns. Or it may signify taking off too soon. Do you feel that you've jumped the gun in relation to a recent situation in your life?

Are you acting determinedly in your life and don't want to be diverted from your primary goals? If so, the guns may symbolize a desire to stick to your guns.

Gym (Also see *Aerobics; Exercise.*)

Quick Interpretation: Fitness; vanity; well-being

Popular Expressions: In a sweat; Fit as a fiddle

Why are you at the gym in your dream—to improve your health or to look good? If it's to improve your health, it indicates that it's time to get your muscles working? If it's purely to look good, what part of your body do you want to improve? If you feel the process is a chore, consider that your subconscious may be getting you accustomed to exercise. But if working out is a pleasure and you're already a frequent visitor to the gym, then it may be a dream to encourage you to keep going.

Gypsy

Quick Interpretation: Nomadic; mystical; festive

Popular Expressions: Footloose and fancy free;
Look into a crystal ball

Who among us has not, at some point in our life, wanted to run away and lead a whimsical life of roaming, living off our smarts and hustling our way around the world? Does the gypsy in your dream symbolize a desire to let go of routine and hit the road?

Consider your relationship to the gypsy in your dream to determine how you feel about the idea of being nomadic and unsettled. Are you celebrating and taking part in merrymaking with the gypsy in your dream, or are you wary of the gypsy?

Gypsies are traditionally known to be fortune-tellers. Does the gypsy in your dream signify a desire to look into mystic matters? Do you (or does someone else) want to explore the spiritual world?

An integral part of being a gypsy is belonging to a close-knit group. Is this what you wish for in your life? It is believed that gypsies originally came from Egypt. Could it be that you want to travel to Egypt, sail down the Nile, and delve into the mysteries of the pyramids?

H

Hacker (Also see *Computer.*)

Quick Interpretation: Intruder; virus; mischief making

Popular Expressions: Hack away at something; Breaking and entering

It's amazing how new words creep into our vocabulary. Only since the advent of computers has the word *hacker* been in common use. To dream of a hacker implies that someone or something is breaking into your private and intimate life. What do you want to keep private, or what private information do you feel you have a right to find out? Do you feel the information you've acquired illegally is the truth and therefore you're justified in hacking? Or do you feel violated because someone hacked into your private information?

Do you feel a sense of pride associated with the hacker? Hackers, for the most part, create mischief just for the sake of it. Are you or is someone else on an ego trip?

I always imagined a hacker to be some ax-wielding maniac, chopping and cutting at everything in its path. Is someone or something hacking away at you, inflicting a deep wound that exposes you and makes you feel vulnerable to unseen forces beyond your control?

Hail

Quick Interpretation: Hardened emotions; a greeting; beckoning

Popular Expressions: Rain, hail, or shine; Hail the conquering hero

Why is it that weather people the world over say "hail as big as golf balls"? It's such an overused expression. Is something in your life being overexaggerated by others? Not all hail that falls is the size of golf balls.

The symbol of hail could also imply unexpected danger, as most hailstorms come without warning. But the danger that occurs is usually to property rather than life and limb. Do you feel that your valuables could be susceptible to damage from the elements?

If we accept that water represents emotions, then perhaps the symbol of hail indicates the surfacing of hardened emotions that dissolve as quickly as they arise.

Consider that the hail in your dream may symbolize exultation and respect—that is, you're being hailed by someone.

Hair

Quick Interpretation: Growth; identity; desirability

Popular Expressions: A hair-raising experience; A hair's breadth; Let your hair down; Pull one's hair out; To wig out

When people dream of hair, it's usually the hair on their head. The obvious meaning is grooming and appearance, but on a deeper level, it signifies thought and the conscious mind.

Do you dream about different-colored hair? Is it red and passionate, purple and regal, or gray and old? Is it long and unkempt or short and well groomed? Is it blowing around your eyes and blinding you, or do you feel exhilarated because it's swept back off your face?

Is someone playing with your hair, cutting it, styling it, or dyeing it? Is this person playing around with your thoughts in real life, or are they helping you to relieve tension? The longer your hair is in your dream, the deeper the concerns that are troubling you.

Hair is associated with sexuality. You only have to watch a shampoo ad to realize this. Do you feel desirable? Do you desire someone or something? Are you tying your hair up? Does it represent a desire to hide your sexuality?

If you're cutting or styling someone else's hair, ask if they need your support. A friend dreamed that she was cutting her girlfriend's hair. It turned out that her girlfriend saw her as a mentor because she was helping to relieve her worry.

If you're a woman and dream of underarm hair, it may indicate independence and a desire to disrupt the status quo. If you're a man and dream of chest hair, it may be a sign of virility. If you have an interest in aquatic sports and you dream of being a hairy man or woman, ask if something or someone is slowing you down in life.

I wonder why men often have an abundance of hair growing out of their ears and on their earlobes. Could it be that they're not very good listeners?

Hammer

Quick Interpretation: Strength; power; submission

Popular Expressions: Go at it tooth and nail; Hammer it home; Hit the nail on the head

It was perhaps one of our very first tools, created from the moment we came down from the trees. What point do you want to hammer home? Are you trying to hammer something open? What do you hope to reveal? To hammer away suggests that you or someone else is trying to make a point. Who doesn't want to listen to what you're saying, or who's trying to convince you that they have a valid point? If you're on target and on the right path, you could be hitting the nail on the head.

Hand (Also see *Body Parts.*)

Quick Interpretation: Grip; control; assistance

Popular Expressions: Caught red-handed; Get out of hand; Try your hand at something; Hand it over; From hand to mouth

Handkerchief

Quick Interpretation: Departure; illness; gift

Popular Expressions: Stick your nose into something; Blow your own trumpet; Blow your wad

The advent of tissues has killed the good ol' handkerchief. Does the symbol of the handkerchief imply old customs and ways of doing things? A handkerchief can also symbolize good breeding and manners. Does someone lack this in your dream, or is it something you feel you need more of?

Why is the handkerchief required? Is it due to an illness, indicating a concern about germs being spread? Or are you protecting yourself from airborne bacteria, a symbol for wanting to prevent other people's negativity from invading your space.

A handkerchief can be used to wave good-bye to someone or to attract someone's attention. Is there someone in your life you wish to bid a fond farewell to, or do you want to attract someone's attention?

Harem

Quick Interpretation: Pleasure; service; male fantasy

Popular Expressions: One-man band; An embarrassment of riches

The only job that's no fun in a harem is the eunuch's job. Is the harem in your dream a symbol for wanting to take part in pleasurable pastimes? Or do you feel as if you have to wait in line for some attention?

Originally, the word *harem* literally meant "sanctuary." Do you wish to get away from it all? Relationship obligations in a harem are shared by many. Does this signify that you desire assistance with your everyday commitments?

Is it your harem, indicating that you want a more polygamous lifestyle? Perhaps your dream harem directly represents a fantasy, whereby you're in control of others and they're prepared to satisfy your every whim.

If you're fortunate enough to have a harem in real life, then consider the harem in your dream to be work related!

Harp (Also see *Musical Instrument.*)

Quick Interpretation: Serenity; nagging; being high-strung

Popular Expressions: To harp on something; To string along; On the side of the angels

Hat (Also see *Baseball Cap; Helmet; Hood.*)

Quick Interpretation: Covering; symbol of authority; completion

Popular Expressions: Come out on top; Top something off; Keep it under your hat; Wear many hats; A hat trick

Who'd have thought that wearing a baseball cap back to front would be considered cool! Does it indicate that by turning things around, you can see more clearly?

Who's wearing the hat in your dream? What type of hat is it? What does it say about this person? Does it represent the image they wish to project and what they would have you believe they're like? For example, if they're wearing a beret, do they want to show you that they're romantic and arty?

If you're wearing the hat, how do you feel about it? Is it a covering, a way to protect yourself from ideas or thoughts that are trying to infiltrate your mind? This is certainly worth considering if it's a helmet. If you're wearing a hood, think about it in relation to secrecy and mystery. Has it got anything to do with pulling the hood over someone's eyes? Or if someone else is wearing the hood, are they pulling the hood over your eyes?

Hats also symbolize authority—the military and police wear hats with their uniforms. Is this what the hat symbolizes in your dream? If so, how do you feel about authority in your life? The hat may also signify keeping a secret—that is, to keep it under your hat, or that it's time to take responsibility for your actions and choices—that it's on your head.

A hat can also represent someone who's multitalented and able to perform more than one function at a time. Is the dream telling you that it's possible to don many hats?

Headphones

Quick Interpretation: Privacy; exclusion; being cut off

Popular Expressions: Getting an earful; Music to my ears; I'm all ears

To dream of headphones indicates a desire for personal gratification at the exclusion of others. If you're wearing the headphones in your dream, does it indicate that you wish to have more fun by yourself? If someone else is wearing the headphones, do they want to exclude you from their fun?

If you see headphones lying around in your dream, is your impulse to put them on, indicating a desire to shut out the world? If, instead, you want to get rid of them, is this because you're tired of being excluded from things? See who or what is in the dream with you to determine what you don't want to be excluded from.

What are you listening to? Is it something you must pay close attention to? If you work in the music industry, it may be work related. Are you trying to cut an exclusive deal?

Your hands are free when you wear headphones. This may indicate that even though you want to pay attention to something, you still want to be free enough to handle other things in your life.

Some of the best musicians are able to replicate sound by ear. Do the headphones in your dream signify that you wish to do things relying purely on instinct and memory, and less on theory and knowledge?

Heaven/Hell

Heaven:
Quick Interpretation: Blessedness; contentment; purity

Popular Expressions: Heaven-sent; Move heaven and earth; In seventh heaven

Hell:
Quick Interpretation: Illusion; punishment; retribution

Popular Expressions: All hell breaks loose; For the hell of it; Raise hell

Our images of heaven and hell are as original as our fingerprints. What type of place do you see in your dream? Who deserves to be there? What did they do to get there? Who's being rewarded and who's being punished? What emotions do you feel when you see either heaven or hell? Without heaven there would be no hell. Could the symbol in your dream indicate that heaven awaits you if you accept the hell you're in?

Helmet (Also see *Hat.*)

Quick Interpretation: Protection; war; safety

Popular Expression: In a nutshell

Hiccups

Quick Interpretation: Mistake; indigestion; lust for fear
(a sudden fright gets rid of hiccups)

Popular Expressions: Cough it up; Catch your breath

Has a fright ever stopped hiccups? Do you need to be frightened in order to stop doing whatever it is you're doing? Experiencing hiccups in a dream can indicate that a mistake has occurred. What unforeseen circumstances are stopping you from moving forward in your waking life? A hiccup can also signify sudden inspiration and illumination. Can it be that all you need is a breath of fresh air to get inspired?

Hiding

Quick Interpretation: Ambush; retreat; play

Popular Expressions: A hidden agenda; Hide-and-seek; You can run, but you can't hide

A fox retires to its den to rest and recuperate, and a bear hides out during winter, which suggests that hiding isn't necessarily a clandestine activity.

If you dream that you're hiding, does it indicate that you want time out? Perhaps your subconscious is suggesting that it's time to pull back, find a place that's safe, and take stock of a situation so that when you reemerge you feel stronger.

Who or what are you hiding from? What don't you want others to discover about you? How do you feel? Safe or afraid? If you feel a heightened sense of security, it may indicate that withdrawing from the world or a situation is the best option at this time. If you're afraid, what are you going to lose by being discovered—freedom, health, or credibility?

Upon reflection, you may discover that you are, in fact, hiding from yourself. Are you afraid to expose your "real" self to the world? Why? Are you trying to protect an identity?

If you're hiding from someone else, is it because you fear them, or are you afraid that if they find out what you're really like, they'll lose interest in you?

Hiding can also indicate a desire for a simpler life. When we were children, we played games that seemed meaningless, yet they cultivated our creativity and sense of adventure. When we played hide-and-seek as kids, we believed we were invisible in the most exposed environments. Do you wish you could go back to the days when you were young enough to really believe that anything was possible, and that you could hide from the world simply by curling up in the laundry basket?

Hike

Quick Interpretation: Dismissing someone; communing with nature; setting challenges

Popular Expression: Take a hike

If you're hiking in your dream, does it signify wish fulfillment? Do you want to pack your backpack and get out there in the wide open spaces? Are you about to embark on a hiking trip, and the dream simply represents your anticipation? Or is the hiking in your dream a symbol of setting challenges and getting out there to achieve them?

If someone else is hiking in your dream, how do you feel about it? Are you impressed and wish you had the same love of adventure? Or are you wary and concerned for the person? What does this say about your own attitude toward dealing with challenges?

Also consider whether the hiking symbolizes dismissing someone from your life, or feeling dismissed from someone else's life—that is, telling someone else, or being told, to take a hike.

Hill (Also see *Mountain.*)

Quick Interpretation: Small obstacles; old age; a collection of thoughts

Popular Expressions: Over-the-hill; Making a mountain out of a molehill; A hill of beans; A slippery slope

Hole

Quick Interpretation: Depression; escape; predicament

Popular Expressions: Pick holes in; A hole-in-one; Dig yourself in a hole; A hole in your story

What gets bigger the more you take away from it, and smaller the more you put into it? A hole in the ground! Dreaming of a hole can indicate an impending problem, as you may feel that there's a hole in your thinking. A hole can also symbolize a desire to see the big picture and take a holistic view of things.

If you feel trapped in time, where physical law has no application, then you may dream that you're in a black hole. Of course, if you're at the other end of the spectrum and feel incredibly fortunate, you may see a hole-in-one!

Home (See *House.*)

Honey

Quick Interpretation: Sweet results; perplexing situation; love

Popular Expressions: You catch more flies with honey than with vinegar; A sticky situation; A sticky wicket

Why is it that something so sweet has to be so sticky? Does the honey in your dream indicate that a situation you're in may taste sweet but is in fact sticky? The symbol of honey could also signify that someone wants you to do all the hard work while they sit back and enjoy the fruits of your labors. Perhaps honey is a symbol of someone you love. How palatable is your relationship with them?

If you want to convince someone they should join your cause, or that you're on the right track, then remember that you catch a lot more flies with honey than you do with vinegar.

Honeymoon

Quick Interpretation: Period of harmony; new relationships; consummation

Popular Expressions: The honeymoon period; A labor of love; A love nest

Hood (Also see *Hat*.)

Quick Interpretation: Disguise; reverence; trickery

Popular Expressions: Being hoodwinked; Boys from the hood

Hook (Also see *Fish*.)

Quick Interpretation: Trap; addiction; freedom

Popular Expressions: Off the hook; Get hooked on something; By hook or by crook; Hook, line, and sinker; Hang in there

Seeing a hook in a dream could indicate success or that you've finally found someone's hot button—that is, you've worked out the hook that finally makes your scheme work.

Does the hook in your dream symbolize being trapped—are you getting hooked in? Are you trying to get someone (or is someone trying to get you) to do something they (or you) don't want to do? How do you feel about it? Do you just accept it, or do you feel resentful?

The hook may also symbolize addiction. Is this what your dream is trying to draw your attention to? Who's addicted?

To be let off the hook suggests being set free. Are you or is someone else in your dream removing something from a hook, suggesting that you (or they) are being set free? The hook is also a great symbol for perseverance. Perhaps it's telling you to hang in there?

If you dream of a fishhook, what are you trying to catch? Or is the hook in your dream a symbol of seduction, indicating that you have taken the bait?

If you feel you've been taken for a ride, then you might dream of a hook, as it can indicate that you're gone—hook, line, and sinker!

Hooker (See *Prostitute*.)

Horizon

Quick Interpretation: Illumination; unattainable quests; meeting place (sky and earth)

Popular Expressions: On the horizon; New horizons; The sky's the limit

If there's one thing in this world that's impossible to reach, it's the horizon. Does the horizon in your dream indicate that some things should be admired from a distance, and there's no need to get up close? The horizon symbolizes new opportunities and the realization of expectations, indicating that something joyful is coming up—that it's on the horizon. It may also signify that things are coming together for you and that you're able to integrate the most difficult challenges in your life—as the horizon is where heaven meets earth.

Horse (Also see *Animal.*)

Quick Interpretation: Transportation; race; unexpected success

Popular Expressions: Dark horse; Back the wrong horse; Get on your high horse; Right from the horse's mouth; A horse of a different color; Horse around; Back in the saddle

Horses revolutionized human endeavor. They allowed us to travel more quickly and decisively. On the day they were domesticated, humans became better hunters and fighters.

A horse is a symbol of freedom, strength, and power. A person on horseback is in a more dominant position than one on foot. Are you in a powerful position? Is someone exerting power/influence over you?

Consider the emotions/feelings that come up for you in the dream. Are you in control of the horse, or is the horse taking you for a ride? Also, consider what type of horse it is. Is it a racing horse or a working horse? The horse may represent where you are in life. For example, a friend dreamed that she was plodding across a field on a Clydesdale. She was frustrated because she wanted to move more quickly. The symbol indicated that she needed to slow down.

If you work with or own a horse, the significance may be specific to your situation. For example, if you dream of riding across a meadow on your horse, it may signify exercise, whereas if you don't own a horse, it may represent a desire to get away.

In a lot of cultures, the horseshoe is a symbol of good luck. If the horseshoe comes off the horse in a dream, it may mean that you need to protect your possessions or your territory. Remember the saying "If you lose one nail, you lose a horseshoe, then a horse, then the army, and finally the kingdom"? Maybe it's time to nail things down, either in a material sense or in the sense of marking your place.

If you're a gardener, the horse symbolizes growth—that is, the horse is associated with manure.

Hospital (Also see *Doctor.*)

Quick Interpretation: Recuperation; life support; attention

Popular Expressions: No quick fix; Just what the doctor ordered; Blood, sweat, and tears

I know why hospital food tastes so bad—it's an attempt to make the medicine taste so good! What's going on in the hospital in your dream? Are you working in the hospital or visiting? Is someone close to you in hospital, or are you a patient? How do you feel about the hospital? Does it symbolize recuperation after a tough time? Or is it a symbol of dependence—for example, you (or someone else) needs the hospital for life support?

Hospitals are also associated with awareness. Is your unconscious drawing your awareness to a physical problem in your life that needs your attention? Of course, if you work in a hospital, to dream of one may indicate work-related concerns.

Also consider if there's something in your life that needs repairing or maintaining.

Hotel (Also see *Accommodations.*)

Quick Interpretation: Rest; pampering; hospitality

Popular Expressions: An open house; Be my guest

House (Also see *Apartment.*)

Quick Interpretation: Security; comfort; government

Popular Expressions: Bring the house down; A house divided cannot stand; Get on like a house on fire; There's no place like home; Home is where the heart is

Houses relate directly to the body. Often a dream about a house will feature different levels to represent the higher self, the physical self, and the subconscious.

Where are you in the dream? What are you doing? If you're playing in the attic, it may indicate a time of contemplation. If you're working in the basement, you may wish to unmask a message from the subconscious. What light do you want to bring to this "secret" part of yourself? If the lounge room or living area is messy, look at your physical body. Do you feel run down? Are you ill?

Become the house and ask yourself questions such as "Am I in disrepair?" "Am I attractive?" "Am I open and easy to get into?" or "Am I closed and impenetrable?"

People sometimes dream of the family home or a house that symbolizes care and peace—such as a grandparent's or mate's house. This may suggest a time of calm, of feeling looked after.

Dreaming of a funhouse may signify a desire to live it up and party. Perhaps you or someone else is trapped in a tedious environment.

It's important to consider what you're doing in the house and how you feel about doing it. If you dream that you're cleaning up the kitchen or the fridge, ask yourself if you've been overindulging. If the cupboards are barren and bare, do you feel that your life is lacking in some area? If you're home alone, do you feel abandoned or at peace with yourself?

Wherever you are in the house, ask what that place represents to you and how you feel about being there. If you're in the kitchen, maybe it's time to focus on nourishment. Is your house cluttered or ordered? Is it bare or spacious?

The important thing to remember is that there's no place like home—it can tell us so much about ourselves.

Husband (See *Family.*)

Hypnotism

Quick Interpretation: Control; planting seeds; illusions

Popular Expressions: To be spellbound; Cast a spell on someone; Mind over matter; See eye-to-eye

Without realizing it, we hypnotize ourselves every day in order to do what we feel adds more meaning to our lives. Are you the hypnotist in your dream, indicating that you want to exercise more control over your own mind or the way you think? If someone else is the hypnotist, does it indicate that someone is trying to control you unfairly? Consider hypnotism as a symbol of wanting to change someone's mind, or that someone wants you to think differently. The symbol also suggests that things can return to normal in the blink of an eye.

Ice

Quick Interpretation: Frozen emotions; feeling refreshed; cooling things off; trapped in time; noncaring

Popular Expressions: As cold as ice; Break the ice; Put something on ice; Ice maiden; Frozen in time; Freeze assets; Stuck in your ways

Being frozen means that you're sealed in time. The rest of the world moves on, but you're as stiff as a board. Do you feel frozen in your dream, or is someone or something else locked in an icy envelope? What wants to stand still? What are the benefits of not progressing any further? Seeing something or someone frozen can symbolize caution or a need to slow down. It can also indicate an unwillingness to move forward and change with the times, and suggests frozen and heavy emotions.

In life, we often freeze someone's assets to protect our investment. Perhaps the symbol in your dream has a financial meaning, indicating caution with money.

Some foods that we like to eat, such as sorbet and ice cream, only taste good if they're frozen. Ask yourself if something is more palatable and digestible when frozen.

Ice Cream

Quick Interpretation: Treat; variety; sweetness

Popular Expressions: Lick something into shape; Lick a problem; Couldn't melt in your mouth

I'd like to think that dreaming of ice cream indicates that you're licking a problem you're currently dealing with before it gets too sticky. If you're enjoying the ice cream in your dream, is it time to treat yourself to something pleasurable? And remember, it's in your hands. If you're not enjoying the ice cream, is what you feel you should have worked out, with sweet results now going sour?

Ice cream is supposed to be sweet, so if someone hands you ice cream in a dream and it's sour, does this mean they're not as sweet as they seem? If someone else is eating the ice cream and you desire it, then perhaps your subconscious is telling you that you want more sweetness and variety in your life. Or if the ice cream is sticky and runny in your dream, it may mean that if you don't focus on the situation at hand, it could turn out to be a real mess.

If you want to get on top of everyone else, you want to scoop 'em. How many scoops of ice cream are on your cone?

Ignorance

Quick Interpretation: Feeling uninformed; out of the loop

Popular Expression: Ignorance is bliss

When you feel ignorant, it indicates that you lack knowledge or feel uninformed. What baffled you in your dream? What don't you want to acknowledge?

Impatience

Quick Interpretation: Restlessness; intolerance

Popular Expression: Patience is a virtue

Feeling impatient is the experience of intolerance or restlessness when you're delayed, whether it be on a project, or when a friend or associate is late. What do you want to complete quickly in your dream? What made you feel that you were running out of time?

Infant (See *Baby.*)

Infection (Also see *Body Parts.*)

Quick Interpretation: Invasion; parasites; dissemination of ideas

Popular Expressions: Add insult to injury; To have itchy feet

If things or people are bugging you, you may dream of having an infection. What or who is bothering you? Could that result to the infection in your dream?

What is actually infected in your dream? Is it part of your body or someone else's? Perhaps it's time to make an appointment with a health professional to get it checked out.

How do you respond to the infection? Do you ignore it and let it get worse, or do you attend to it right away? How you respond may indicate how you react to things that demand your immediate attention.

Is the infection in your dream a symbol of invasion? Look at the body part that's being invaded and think about it in relation to how you perceive that part. For example, if your hand is infected, do you feel that someone else is trying to handle things for you?

Consider the infection as a symbol of disseminating ideas—that is, you either intentionally or unintentionally want to infect anyone you come in contact with, with your ideas.

We all know that laugher is very infectious, so perhaps the infection in your dream indicates that it's time to loosen up and not take yourself so seriously. Is it time to have a good laugh about your situation?

Infinity

Quick Interpretation: Lack of restrictions; limitlessness

When you feel infinite, it indicates that you feel unrestricted. Anything is possible. What has made you feel limitless?

Injury (Also see *Body Parts.*)

Quick Interpretation: Slowing down; challenges; taking offense

Popular Expressions: The first cut is the deepest; The injured party

Most of the time, an injury in a dream indicates wounded pride. Is it a time for more empathy and understanding?
What is injured in your dream? If it's a part of the body, consider the injury in relation to the body part. For example, if your (or someone else's) back is injured, does it indicate that you don't feel supported? Is the injury a warning that you should slow down, or that your life is particularly challenging at the moment and it's time to take care of yourself?

To feel injured is also to take offense. Is this what the injury in your dream signifies? Have you offended someone, or has someone offended you?

When we think we've been dealt an injustice, we feel injured. Who do you feel has misjudged you and therefore treated you unfairly?

Innocence

Quick Interpretation: Lack of guilt; integrity

Feeling innocent indicates that you always act with integrity. What has made you feel guilt free?

Insect

Quick Interpretation: Feeling annoyed; being pesky; variety

Popular Expressions: A fly in the ointment; Wouldn't harm a fly; Don't bug me

Some people can be real pests. They bother you just when you're about to relax. Do the insects in your dream symbolize people in your life who are getting under your skin?

Insects are notoriously known to cause discomfort. Are the insects in your dream annoying you? Where are you, and who are you with? What does this say about what's troubling you in your waking life?

What type of insects are in your dream? Mosquitoes, indicating that someone or something in your life is feeding off you, sucking your energy? Ants, suggesting that you're perhaps feeling overwhelmed because of a buildup of frustration? Grasshoppers, signifying a desire to hop away? Think about the insects in your dream and determine your unique associations with them.

Do the insects in your dream symbolize variety? How do you respond? Are you excited by so much choice, or do you find it confusing?

The symbol of insects could also indicate paranoia. Do you feel that people are listening in on your conversations, following you around, and perhaps even bugging your phone?

Insensitivity

Quick Interpretation: Lack of feelings; being thick-skinned

When you feel insensitive, it indicates a lack of feeling toward others. Why are you so heavy-handed in your dream? What has caused your lack of empathy?

Inspiration

Quick Interpretation: Creativity; imagination

Popular Expression: Genius is 1 percent inspiration and 99 percent perspiration

When you feel inspired, you're in the spirit of creativity. What has sparked your imagination?

Internet (Also see *Computer.*)

Quick Interpretation: Knowledge; checking things out; information overload

Popular Expressions: A web of intrigue; What a tangled web we weave

The Internet reminds us that each of us is a part of a global community. How do you feel about surfing the Net in your dream? Do you feel that everything you could possibly desire is there for the taking, that you have the whole world at your feet? Or do you feel overwhelmed, lost, and overloaded with information, not knowing where to start?

The way you feel about the Internet in your dream will indicate how you feel about the incredible times we live in, where information on any given subject is available instantly.

Are you looking at a specific Web page in your dream? What information are you looking for? Does it have anything to do with careers, romance, or current affairs? How does it relate to your current circumstances? For example, if you're using the Internet at work, does your dream relate to career, co-workers, and commercial aspirations? Do you wish to climb the corporate ladder, and do you feel that how far you get depends on how savvy you are with this new and evolving medium?

If you dream that you're in an Internet chat room, then it probably has more to do with relationships. The Internet allows you to have a relationship with any number of people worldwide, and to discuss the most intimate details of your life with them while remaining anonymous. There's something liberating about developing a relationship that doesn't rely on physical appearance or animal magnetism, but instead on the way you string words together.

Do you feel that the Internet is the domain of the young, and that the technology is way beyond you and too difficult to comprehend? Does this indicate that you're afraid of change and new things? Or do you see yourself using the Net effortlessly even though you've never turned on a computer in your life? Does this mean that you're not frightened of change and new challenges?

Of course, if you really need a vacation and you want to get out there, surf, and relax, then perhaps surfing the Net symbolizes doing just that!

Interrogation (Also see *Torture.*)

Quick Interpretation: Duress; exposure; distrust

Popular Expressions: Getting the third degree; In the spotlight; Spilling the beans

It's not always necessary to answer every question when you're put under pressure. Does the interrogation in your dream indicate that it's time to practice sacred silence?

Who's being interrogated in your dream? Are you doing the interrogating, or is someone else? What are you (or the person doing the interrogating) trying to find out?

If you're being interrogated, do you feel that you're under duress, like you're being given the third degree? How do you respond? Who's interrogating you? Is this person trying to get you to share something about yourself that you don't want to disclose? Why is it so important that you keep this information to yourself?

If you're doing the interrogating, what are you trying to expose? Perhaps you're interrogating someone you know, indicating a lack of trust. Is this lack of trust valid?

Do you feel that your every move is being put into question? Is the inquisition you're facing appropriate, or are the inquisitors acting outside their jurisdiction?

Intoxication (See *Drunkenness.*)

Intuition

Quick Interpretation: Inner knowing; gut feeling

Popular Expression: Woman's intuition

When you feel intuitive, it indicates that you have a sense of knowing without reason. What is it that can't be explained with logic but is nevertheless valid?

Investment

Quick Interpretation: Commitment to the future; forethought; value judgments

Popular Expressions: Putting your money where your mouth is; Save for a rainy day

Life is far more enjoyable when we can rely on our investments to support us rather than having to go out and support ourselves. Is the investment in your dream a symbol of looking for someone or something else to provide you with security?

What kind of investment are you making in your dream? Is it a good investment or a bad one? Of course, the first thing to consider is whether it relates to an investment you've made or are thinking of making in your waking life. The dream may be putting you in touch with how you really feel about it.

To dream of an investment may also indicate that you want to make a commitment to the future, not necessarily a monetary investment, but an investment in a relationship or career. The circumstances of your dream will, of course, help you to determine what you wish to invest.

Perhaps the investment symbolizes forethought. Do you, or does someone else in your dream, have forethought about an issue or situation? Or are you or they making value judgments about something?

We all want interest from our investments. Could the investment in your dream symbolize a desire to become more interested in your personal affairs?

Invincibility

Quick Interpretation: Overcoming obstacles; feeling unbeatable

When you feel invincible, it indicates that you know you can overcome all obstacles or challenges. What has prompted you to move beyond your limitations?

Invitation

Quick Interpretation: Being a guest; socializing; surprise

Popular Expressions: Flavor of the month; Meeting of the minds; Ask and you shall receive

We all want to be included. We have a desire to be part of things, and above all we want to be *asked* to be part of things. Does the invitation in your dream indicate that others find you desirable or that you wish to be desirable?

Who receives the invitation in your dream? How does the person feel about getting it? Is the invitation a symbol of being social? If you're sending out invitations in your dream, does it indicate a desire to *be* social? An invitation also symbolizes acknowledgment. Who's being acknowledged in your dream? Are you acknowledging someone, or is someone acknowledging you?

It's important to remember that an invitation can signify having options, as it's your choice whether you want to RSVP or not.

Irrationality

Quick Interpretation: Lack of clarity; unreasonableness

When you feel irrational, it indicates that you lack clarity and aren't thinking things through. What has transpired in your dream that needs clarification? Has someone behaved unreasonably?

Irritation

Quick Interpretation: Annoyance, impatience

Feeling irritated is the experience of annoyance, impatience, or displeasure toward a situation. What annoyed you in your dream? Who's rubbing you the wrong way?

Island

Quick Interpretation: Solitude; retreat; being surrounded

Popular Expressions: On island time; No man is an island

On an island, life is simple. It's less stressful than living on a large continent. Do you want to downsize and simplify your life? The most important thing to note is whether the island in your dream symbolizes getting away for fun, or for solitude and the hermit's life.

Ivory

Quick Interpretation: Beauty; immortality; music

Popular Expressions: An ivory tower; Long in the tooth

Ivory can be a symbol of disgusting waste. A whole animal is discarded for two teeth! What is it in your life that you feel is a deplorable waste of your talents, ability, or love?

Jackpot

Quick Interpretation: Good fortune; accumulated success; unexpected advantage

Popular Expressions: Hit the jackpot; Hit pay dirt

We'd all love to strike pay dirt with the minimum amount of sweat. Does the jackpot in your dream symbolize an increase in wealth, or a breakthrough such as finding the solution to a challenge?

Jaguar (Also see *Animal.*)

Quick Interpretation: Stealth; stalking

Popular Expression: Like a wildcat

Jail

Quick Interpretation: Confinement; punishment; supervision

Popular Expressions: In a jam; Get out of jail free; Jailbird; A prison of one's own making

The jail warden usually serves the longest sentence. When you dream of being in jail, don't jump to the conclusion that it's punishment. It could signify that you'll be paid to look after and rehabilitate someone.

Who is in jail in your dream? Are you the one who's being confined? Why do you feel that you need to be punished? Do you feel that you've committed an act of wrongdoing? Or do you feel you're being punished for something that isn't your fault? Are you trying to escape from jail? Think about this in relation to wanting to escape from something in your life. Is a job, relationship, or uncomfortable situation making you feel enclosed and trapped?

If someone else is in jail, what are they doing in there? Do you feel they deserve to be there, or are you trying to get them out? Does this person represent an aspect of yourself that you either want to confine or let loose?

Jar

Quick Interpretation: Containment; protection; being shaken

Popular Expression: Get caught with your hand in the cookie jar

Where would we be without jars? Up to our knees in mess, that's where. The important thing to focus on first is what type of jar is in your dream. Then ask yourself what's inside. Are the contents bitter, sweet, valuable . . . or is the jar empty?

Jealousy

Quick Interpretation: Resentment; insecurity

Popular Expressions: The green-eyed monster; Hell hath no fury like a woman scorned; Green with envy

When you feel jealous, it indicates that you're resentful of a perceived rival or of a perceived advantage you feel the rival has. What causes you to feel insecure in your dream? Why are you suspicious?

Jet (Also see *Airplane.*)

Quick Interpretation: Speed; being propelled forward; intensity

Popular Expressions: A jet-setter; Faster than a speeding bullet; Jet off somewhere; Cool your jets

Jewelry (Also see *Diamond.*)

Quick Interpretation: Adornment; pretension; investment

Popular Expressions: Jewel in the crown; Diamond in the rough; Diamonds are a girl's best friend

Diamonds are a girl's best friend, and true friends are really *hard* to come by. Is your dream about friendship and the difficulty of maintaining it?

Are you wearing the jewelry in your dream, or is someone else? Is it for show or adornment? Do you (or the person wearing the jewelry) want to show the world how rich and well off you are? Does this truly represent how you (or they) feel, or is it pretense, the jewels being only for show?

What is the jewelry like? Is it valuable, or cheap and tawdry? Does the jewelry reflect your self-esteem?

Is a particular piece of jewelry featured in your dream? Consider the piece in relation to the part of the body you (or someone else) wear it on. For example, if it's a necklace, how does it reflect the way you communicate, or if it's earrings, how do they reflect your (or someone else's) ability to listen?

Also consider that the jewelry may symbolize an investment. Are you thinking of investing, or, depending on the value of the jewelry, does the dream represent an investment you just made?

If you're wearing the jewelry in your dream, does it represent a desire to come across as the jewel in the crown?

Jockey

Quick Interpretation: Taking a chance; lightweight; teamwork

Popular Expression: Jockeying for position

Dreaming of a jockey signifies teamwork. The jockey and the horse work as one to get past the finish line. This is a powerful symbol indicating that it's time to be a team player so you can get the inside track to success.

Joke

Quick Interpretation: Making light of matters; loosening up; jesting

Popular Expressions: You must be joking; The joker's wild

It's always good to have a joker on the team, as it's impossible to stay angry at people when they put a smile on your face. Is it time to let go and laugh even though life can be serious at times?

Who's making the joke in your dream? Is it funny, or aren't you amused? To be laughing at a joke in your dream indicates that you're experiencing a time of lightness and joy in your life. If you're not amused, then ask yourself why. Have you lost your sense of humor, or do you think the joke is in bad taste?

Do you feel that the joke in your dream symbolizes making light of matters? Who is doing so? How do you feel about it? Or do you feel that the joke indicates loosening up, that it's time to not be so serious about life?

Also consider whether something in your life has been pushed to the limits—that is, is beyond a joke. Or perhaps the joke is a symbol of incredulity, a message from your unconscious telling you that you must be joking!

The saying "Loosen up, no one gets out alive" is so true. After all, the best remedy for life's challenges is a good old-fashioned joke.

Joy

Quick Interpretation: Light in spirit; good fortune

Feeling joyful indicates that you're full of spirit and delight, that you're enjoying good fortune. What is making you feel exhilarated?

Judge (Also see *Trial.*)

Quick Interpretation: Authority; verdict; official course of action

Popular Expressions: Don't judge a book by its cover; Pass sentence; Sit in judgment; Acting as judge and jury

Why is it that some of us get paid to judge, and the rest of us spend our whole lives trying not to? What or who is being judged in your dream? Are you doing the judging, or is someone judging you? How do you feel about it? Is it an unfair judgement, or is it appropriate?

Is the judge in your dream a symbol of authority? If so, how you respond to the judge is a great indicator of how you respond to authority in your waking life. Perhaps you're the judge in your dream, indicating that you have authority over someone or something in your life. What are you passing sentence on?

Perhaps the judge represents taking an official course of action in your life regarding a present concern. Do you feel that you need to act officially to bring an issue or concern to completion in your waking life?

The judge may also symbolize reaching a verdict. Have you decided on a course of action you're going to take regarding an important issue or concern? Or has someone decided on a course of action for you? How do you feel about it?

Perhaps the dream is reminding you to be more observant, to reserve your judgment until you have a clear understanding of your situation.

Juggler (Also see *Accountant.*)

Quick Interpretation: Balance; timing; dexterity

Popular Expressions: Keep your eye on the ball; Juggle the books

If you have to juggle the books to avoid a penalty, then you could expect to see a juggler in your dream rather than an account-ant. Is it that no matter what it takes, you want things to balance out in your favor?

Who's the juggler in your dream? If it's you, do you feel that you have a thousand and one things going on at once in your life? Is the juggler a reminder that you need to establish a balance between your relationships, career, and social life in order to make life fulfilling?

If someone else is juggling, do you admire that person for being able to keep so many things going at once? Or are you concerned that they're doing too much?

Does the juggling symbolize frustration—that is, you feel that too many things are up in the air and nothing is coming to fruition? Does every situation in your life seem to be going around in circles?

What are you juggling in your dream? Is it harmless objects, indicating that it doesn't matter if you make a mistake and drop something, as no harm will come to you? Or is it dangerous items like lit torches, indicating that you should be careful or you may get burned?

Life moves so fast that we now eat, watch television, and con-duct a conversation at the same time. Perhaps the juggler signi-fies that we have to be multitalented and be able to do a number of tasks at once to keep things up in the air.

Jungle (Also see *Forest.*)

Quick Interpretation: Organized chaos; biodiversity; competition

Popular Expressions: Law of the jungle; It's a jungle out there; A concrete jungle; Survival of the fittest

The jungle is nature's metropolis; everything co-existing in divine disarray. How do you feel about being in the jungle? Do you feel you're stuck in an impenetrable, tangled mass, or is the jungle a symbol of beauty and richness?

The jungle as a symbol of coexistence indicates that everything inhabiting the one area is complementary and rich in biodiversity. Does this represent your life? How do you feel about it? Do you believe that it's a matter of survival of the fittest and no one can be trusted because predators may be camouflaged? Or do you feel supported, an intricate part of the web of life?

There's a lot of imagined fear associated with the jungle. You never know what's crawling around beside you, and you can't be sure that you aren't going to be ambushed from above. Are you preoccupied with imagined fears in your waking life that keep you from enjoying the beauty that surrounds you?

Are you lost in the jungle, overwhelmed by its density and confused about your options? The jungle may also indicate that you can't see a clear path ahead. Do you feel the journey you're on at the moment is full of unseen dangers and pitfalls? Are you afraid that you may not see them before it's too late?

The jungle may also signify that it's time to excel. The jungle is less daunting when you look at it from above. The higher up you're perched in the jungle, the less frightening it is. From a higher viewpoint, you can see exactly where you are and what direction you have to go in. You can make clear decisions. Does the jungle in your dream indicate that it's time to rise above limitations?

Junk (See *Garbage*.)

Kangaroo (Also see *Animal.*)

Quick Interpretation: Acting quickly; success; determination

Popular Expressions: Jump at the chance; A hop, skip, and a jump; It's in the bag; Spring into action; With a spring in your step

Karaoke

Quick Interpretation: Fantasy; attention; loss of inhibition

Popular Expressions: Out of tune; A tongue-lashing; Playing the fool

Karaoke is a magical experience. Three drinks and a microphone and suddenly you're a pop star. Is it a symbol of hidden talent waiting to be discovered, or does it reveal an absence of talent? Is the karaoke singer able to carry it off, or is someone acting the fool by masquerading as someone with talent?

Karate

Quick Interpretation: Self-defense; being focused; a sudden blow

Popular Expression: A swift kick (to some body part)

Karate is a symbol of inner power and self-defense, but with the advent of action movies, it's become a means to beating up the bad guys—20 of 'em all at once. Does this indicate that the original purpose of a journey has been corrupted?

Kettle

Quick Interpretation: Refreshment; announcement; being overheated

Popular Expressions: The pot calling the kettle black; Ma and Pa Kettle

Dreaming of a kettle symbolizes letting off steam, particularly if you've bottled things up inside. The beautiful thing is, after you turn off the heat, you end up with something that's warm and stimulating.

Key

Quick Interpretation: Opening; opportunity; answer

Popular Expressions: Under lock and key; The key to your heart; All keyed up; Off-key; When one door closes, another one opens

Where would we be without keys? Quite clearly, locked out! Keys are a status symbol—that is, the number of keys you have on a key ring, as well as the shapes, colors and sizes, all say something about you.

In your dream, are there lots of keys on a key ring or just one key? Do you find the keys or lose them? Are they your keys or someone else's?

Keys can be used to lock things up and keep them safe, providing a sense of security. They can also be used to unlock things to give you access and freedom. They can open doors.

If you see one key in a dream, it may suggest that you have an answer to a question that's currently concerning you, a simple and quick solution that will open the door and clear the way. If you see a bunch of keys, it may indicate that there are many solutions to a current concern. This is important, because it reminds us that there are many ways to solve a problem.

Is the key old and antique-looking, a reminder of the stability of the past? Newer keys are often mass produced and easy to copy, tending to indicate quick solutions.

Where are the keys? Are they at home or in the office? Perhaps the solutions or explanations for your dilemmas can be found where you located your keys. What mysteries need to be unlocked in these areas of your life?

Does someone else lose keys in your dream? Do you feel that you're walking out of step with them, or that you're not compatible and that your relationship is out of key—that is, not harmonious? Consider this carefully, particularly if the person is blaming you for losing the keys.

Does someone have your keys in the dream? Do you feel that they control you? Or are the keys really and truly yours, suggesting that you're in control of your own destiny?

Kindergarten

Quick Interpretation: Being carefree; beginnings; playfulness

Popular Expressions: Handle with kid gloves; Back to the drawing board; Chalk it up; Back to basics

Life was so simple and carefree in kindergarten. Does your dream of kindergarten represent a desire to go back to the days when you weren't put through any major tests? You could play for half a day and sleep through the rest. Do you want to get back to basics? If you have any children in kindergarten, the interpretation may be more specific. Think about your dream in relation to how you feel about your children going off to school.

King (Also see *Monarchy; Palace; Queen.*)

Quick Interpretation: Elevation; power; control

Popular Expressions: Live like a king; A king's ransom; Long live the king

To dream of kings and queens today is more about figure-heads and tradition than power. Does the king in your dream signify a desire to have more pomp and ceremony in your life?

Who is the king in your dream? If it's someone you know, do you feel that they rule your life? How do you respond to their rule? If you're the king, what are you ruling over? How do you feel about such a responsibility?

If the king is a stranger in your dream, how are you relating? Is the king an aspect of yourself that's ruling your life? Or is the king a symbol of elevation, something you aspire to?

In times past, the king was a symbol of power and control. Think of this in relation to how the king appears in your dream. Who has the power and control? You or someone else? How do you feel that this relates to your waking life? Do you feel empowered or disempowered? Do you want people to value your opinions a lot more?

Kiss

Quick Interpretation: Pleasure; intimacy; acceptance

Popular Expressions: Kiss and make up; Kiss-and-tell; Kiss up to someone; Kiss someone's feet; Give lip service; On everyone's lips; With a stiff upper lip; Pucker up

Kissing is one of the most intimate forms of communication and can be shared in so many different ways, depending on the message you wish to convey.

Is the kiss in your dream a peck on the cheek—that is, a form of gratitude or acknowledgment? Is it on the hand, as a mark of respect and subservience? Is it on the feet, indicating unconditional devotion, or that you or someone else in your dream is begging for forgiveness? Or is it a passionate and sensual kiss?

The type of kiss you experience will indicate what you either want to receive from or give to the person you kissed. For example, if you dream that you kiss a work colleague whom you're not physically attracted to, then it may be a display of respect for one another's work. But if you dream that you kiss the same person on the feet, then it may signify that you're in awe of the way they get things done—or that you're bowing down to this person.

Where you place the kiss, or where the kiss is placed on you, is also important. Planting a kiss on someone's forehead isn't as intimate as passionately placing a kiss on their lips. One is a sign of brotherly/sisterly love, the other a sign of lust.

How do you feel about the kiss? Most relationships begin with a kiss—does it symbolize new romance? Or do you feel it's a kiss good-bye?

If, in the dream, you're passionately kissing someone you know (whom you aren't romantically involved with), then it may indicate unfulfilled desire. The dream kiss may be more than enough, or it may be your subconscious instructing you to go for it. The only way to know is if the dream recurs.

If you're passionately kissing a stranger, try to get a sense of what attracted you to them. Whatever the individual symbolizes indicates what you want more of in your life. For example, if you're kissing a person from a particular ethnic group, perhaps you want to travel to wherever they're from, or you want to adopt their particular lifestyle.

Of course, if someone plants a kiss on your backside in a dream, it symbolizes that they're agreeing with you to gain favor. So, beware of being lured into a false sense of security.

Kitchen

Quick Interpretation: Entertainment; creativity; sustenance

Popular Expressions: Everything but the kitchen sink; If you can't take the heat, get out of the kitchen; Too many cooks spoil the broth; What's cooking?

Where would you be without a kitchen? Hungry! Is the kitchen in your dream a place of warmth and nourishment, or is it really hot and stressful—that is, you can't stand the heat and must get out of the kitchen?

Do you feel overjoyed at the thought of preparing a meal for others, or is it a burden, a chore you wish you didn't have to do? Does this reflect your attitude toward life at the moment?

Is the kitchen a symbol of resourcefulness? Do you feel that you're able to make something out of nothing, whip up a feast from leftover odds and ends? Or don't the ingredients mix well together, and no matter how closely you follow a recipe, it doesn't taste good, indicating that you're disappointed with something in your life.

Cooking is a word we often use when we want things to happen (to get things cooking), or when we feel things are moving along at a desirable pace (it's cooking). How are things cooking in your kitchen?

Kite

Quick Interpretation: High aspirations; lofty ideas; flying high

Popular Expressions: Let's go fly a kite; High as a kite; Lift your spirits; Rise above it all

It's amazing how things evolve. To be as high as a kite no longer simply means to be excited; it also means to be intoxicated. Does the kite in your dream indicate that it's time to lift your spirits?

Who's flying the kite in your dream? Does it symbolize high aspirations, a desire to reach for the stars? Or does it symbolize lofty ideas that need to be grounded in order for you to bring them to fruition?

The kite also symbolizes flying high. Are things going particularly well for you at the moment? Perhaps you feel as though you've just made it through a rough patch and it's a time of lightness.

If the kite isn't being flown in your dream, does it symbolize lying low, that you don't have the energy to fly right now? It may indicate that you need to take the time to think things through before you go out there and fly.

Also consider whether the kite is a symbol of airing an idea or opinion—that is, you fly a kite to determine the public's response.

Kitten (Also see *Cat.*)

Quick Interpretation: Being carefree; boundless energy; playfulness

Popular Expression: Don't have a kitten over it

Knife

Quick Interpretation: Separation; straight to the point; sharpness

Popular Expressions: Like a hot knife through butter; Put the knife in; You could cut the atmosphere with a knife; Cut to the bone; Sharpen your skills

Words can often be more agonizing and hurtful than the sharpest blade. Does the knife in your dream indicate that unkind words have been spoken, cutting you to the bone?

Consider whether the knife symbolizes separation. If you're holding the knife in your dream, what are you doing with it? What do you want to separate from? Or if someone else is holding the knife in your dream, do they want to separate from you?

Is the knife being used as a weapon? What are you trying to protect yourself from? If someone is attacking you with a knife, are they attacking an aspect of yourself? Look at where you are in the dream and who's attacking you to determine what aspect it might be. Perhaps it's something about yourself that you're refusing to face.

The knife may also symbolize getting right to the point of something. Again, you have to consider what you're doing in the dream and how you feel about it to determine whether this is what the dream is telling you.

Also consider the sharpness of the knife. Is it time to really be on your toes? Should you be sharpening your skills?

Knight

Quick Interpretation: Chivalry; being rescued; quests

Popular Expressions: A knight in shining armor;
Throw down the gauntlet

Knights are associated with heroism, dedication, and quests. Does the knight in your dream indicate that you want to rescue someone or that you want to be rescued? Knights protect their soft centers with hard armor. Do you want to protect your vulnerability with a bulletproof vest?

Labyrinth (See *Maze.*)

Lack

Quick Interpretation: Deficiency; not having enough

When you feel a lack, you believe you're deficient, that you don't have enough. What do you feel is missing from your life? What do you need more of?

Ladder (Also see *Climbing; Fall.*)

Quick Interpretation: Success; shifting fortunes; progression

Popular Expressions: Move up in the world; Ladder of success

The ladder is the perfect symbol of success unless you suffer from vertigo! Are you climbing the ladder of success in your life, perhaps the corporate ladder? Do you have an idea of where you want it to take you?

If someone else is climbing the ladder in your dream, how do you feel about it? Do you believe they're getting ahead in life and you're not? Or are you holding the ladder for them, helping them to get ahead?

What condition is the ladder in? Old and rickety, indicating that your climb to the top is precarious? Or strong and solid, signifying an easy climb to the top? Maybe the ladder isn't being used at all in your dream, or you're working out how you can use it. Think about what you're doing with the ladder in relation to success and ambition.

Perhaps you're climbing down the ladder in your dream, indicating a change in direction. Have you enjoyed a time of success in your life and now you're coming down from your perch? If so, look around and see if anyone has been supporting you while you've been at the top. Is it time for a little gratitude?

Lake (Also see *Water.*)

Quick Interpretation: Sanctuary; vacation; reflection

Popular Expression: Go jump in a lake

Lamb (Also see *Animal; Sheep.*)

Quick Interpretation: Youth; gentleness; being easily deceived

Popular Expression: Like lambs to the slaughter

Lamp (Also see *Light.*)

Quick Interpretation: Illumination; being healed; showing the way ahead

Popular Expression: Shed light on something

If the lamp is on, then it may indicate a desire to shed light on something. If it's off, you may have enough light but know that if things need clarity, there's a resource close at hand. Dreaming of a lamp indicates that illumination is at your fingertips.

Lane

Quick Interpretation: Mystery; hidden danger; shortcuts

Popular Expressions: The fast/slow lane; Lovers' lane; The road less traveled; Off the beaten track

Why would you create a lane when you could build a road? Is the lane in your dream a symbol of bad planning? Lovers' lanes are legendary for romance. Does the lane in your dream symbolize your desire to seduce someone?

Laughter

Quick Interpretation: Feeling uplifted; loosening up; light-heartedness

Popular Expressions: Laughter is the best medicine; No laughing matter; Have the last laugh

Laughter is a wonderful dream symbol that leaves you feeling lighthearted and uplifted when you awaken—unless of course someone is laughing at you in your dream! So the first thing to consider is how you feel about the laughter. Are you laughing, or is someone else laughing at your expense?

If you're laughing, does it symbolize loosening up? What has happened in your life to lighten the load? Perhaps you're refusing to take your life too seriously and you feel that laugher is the best medicine.

Is someone else laughing in your dream? What are they laughing at? Perhaps it's at something you feel is no laughing matter. What in your life do you feel others aren't taking seriously?

Of course, laughter can also mean that success is at hand and that you get to have the last laugh.

Lawyer (Also see *Judge; Trial.*)

Quick Interpretation: One-sided arguments; being counseled; deliberations

Popular Expressions: Lay down the law; Take the law into your own hands; A law unto yourself; And justice for all

What's happening in your life that's made you dream that someone is on your case, or that there's a need for justice? Are you the lawyer in the dream, indicating a desire to take the law into your own hands? What is the lawyer doing in your dream? Is he or she defending or persecuting you? How do you feel about it? Did you know that the oldest man who ever lived was a lawyer? When they added up all the hours he billed his clients, he turned out to be 250. Do you feel that you're being over-charged for something?

Laziness

Quick Interpretation: Idleness; indifference; lack of motivation

Popular Expression: The quick brown fox jumps over the lazy dog; A lazy, hazy day

Feeling lazy in a dream indicates that you feel idle and indifferent to activity. Why aren't you motivated to act?

Leaf (Also see *Tree.*)

Quick Interpretation: Detachment; rebirth; falling away

Popular Expressions: Take a leaf out of someone's book; Turn over a new leaf

Lecture

Quick Interpretation: Acquisition of knowledge; reprimand; guidance

Popular Expressions: Speak your mind; Speaks volumes

The only time we want to be lectured is when we're trying to acquire knowledge or learn something. At any other time, we think people should mind their own business. Is the information you're hearing in your dream bothersome or informative?

Leech

Quick Interpretation: Reducing pressure; being healed; freeloader

Popular Expressions: After your blood; Make your blood run cold; Bloodsucker

The first thing that comes to mind when one thinks of a leech is that someone or something is trying to suck your life blood and drain your energy. However, leeches have also been used for medicinal purposes. Decide whether the leech in your dream is helping or hindering you.

Leg (Also see *Body Parts.*)

Quick Interpretation: Movement; sensuality; good luck

Popular Expressions: Don't have a leg to stand on; On your last legs; Give someone a leg up; Break a leg

Lemon (Also see *Fruit.*)

Quick Interpretation: Bitterness; refreshment; defective

Popular Expressions: A real lemon; Leaves a sour taste in your mouth; Sourpuss

Lesson

Quick Interpretation: Learning; being instructed; breakthroughs

Popular Expressions: Learn your lessons well; That'll teach you

Everything we do has a lesson. Big or small, it's stored in our memory banks and we learn a little more about what makes us tick. Is the lesson in your dream interesting, boring, worth remembering, or simply drivel that clogs up your gray matter? It's important to notice who's giving the lesson. How do you feel about it?

Lethargy

Quick Interpretation: Sluggishness; laziness; inactivity

Popular Expression: Slow as molasses

When you feel lethargic, you experience a state of sluggish indifference. What is the cause of your aversion to activity?

Letter (Also see *Envelope; Post Office.*)

Quick Interpretation: News; reaching out; expression

Popular Expressions: A dead letter; The letter of the law; To the letter; Poison-pen letter

Not too many things are more exciting than having a full mailbox. Do you receive a letter in your dream? Who is it from? Why do you feel that this person needs to communicate from afar? Perhaps they're overseas, or maybe the dream represents your desire to hear from them.

Are you writing a letter in your dream? Whom are you writing it to? What do you want this person to know?

A letter symbolizes receiving or sharing news. Do you have some news you'd like to share? Perhaps you're receiving news about an important event.

Also consider that the letter may signify expression. Maybe you're looking for the perfect words to communicate an important event in your life.

The letter may also indicate that you shouldn't believe or accept everything that's written down in front of you, as some things aren't worth the paper they're printed on.

Liberation

Quick Interpretation: Freedom; lack of constraints

Popular Expression: As free as a bird

When you feel liberated, it indicates that you've risen above limitations. What constraints have been removed that previously impeded your progress?

Library (Also see *Book.*)

Quick Interpretation: Acquiring knowledge; silence; collection of ideas/thoughts

Popular Expressions: Hit the books; Cooking the books; Throw the book at someone; Knowledge is power

Light (Also see *Candle; Fire; Lamp.*)

Quick Interpretation: Exposure; illumination; not heavy

Popular Expressions: Bring to light; Light at the end of the tunnel; See the light

In his song "Here Comes the Sun," George Harrison wrote some of the most beautiful lyrics ever put to music. The sun's little beams of light have the extraordinary ability to make us feel empowered. Does the light in your dream symbolize that the worst is over and that there's light at the end of the tunnel?

If you're experiencing challenging times in your life, is it time to think outside the square you live in and throw some new light on the way you're thinking? Light in a dream can also indicate that the best way to get rid of low self-esteem is to reignite the light inside of you. By staying strong, bright, and warm, every moth in town will be attracted to you.

Lighthouse

Quick Interpretation: Beacon; direction; warning

Popular Expressions: Pave the way; Shine a light on things

When you see a lighthouse, it usually means the seasickness is over. Is the lighthouse in your dream warning you of impending danger, or is it beckoning you with open arms to a safe shelter? Are you in the lighthouse, shining the light for others, or is someone else in the lighthouse, shining the light for you?

Lightning (Also see *Storm.*)

Quick Interpretation: Message; clarity; illumination

Popular Expressions: Lightning never strikes twice; Lightning fast; A bolt out of the blue; Lighten up; Gone in a flash

Lightning isn't only a complex symbol; it's also free electricity. The first association is that it's a powerful symbol of indestructible, immeasurable energy, coming straight at us from the heavens.

Lightning is a visual display of power. How do you feel when you see lightning in your dream? Do you run from it, or are you inspired? Like a bolt out of the blue, it illuminates you.

Are you concerned because you believe that lightning only strikes the same place once? Perhaps you're experiencing a sense of loss because of a memory you know will never be repeated.

The lightning may symbolize a special moment in your life that came and went in a flash. Do you wish to revisit the experience? Do you feel vulnerable? Or have you recently found out a shocking truth—that is, you've been struck down by lightning. People who are religious may feel that if they don't get back on the straight and narrow, they'll be struck by lightning.

Lightning may be coupled with a feeling of desire. The dreamer is either searching for something to spark their imagination, or is enjoying the undertakings of a new project. Lightning may also symbolize motivation and illumination. If a relationship, or your career, is in a gridlock, you might see lightning in a dream to shock you out of a humdrum situation.

After lightning strikes, clarity is experienced. It may be time to lighten up, or begin a spiritual journey toward enlightenment.

If someone is struck by lightning in your dream, would you like them to be more involved in your life? Perhaps they need to be "shot" out of your life.

Lily (Also see *Flower.*)

Quick Interpretation: Femininity; tranquility; purity

Popular Expressions: To gild the lily; Lily-white

Limousine

Quick Interpretation: Extension; affluence; fame

Popular Expressions: No one gets a free ride; Ride in style

You always know there's no celebrity in the back of a limousine when the windows are down. Are you trying to attract attention to yourself, or is someone trying to get your attention? If the windows are turned up, do you feel excluded because you don't know who's there? Do you see the limousine as a status symbol for the rich and famous, a desire you have for yourself? Or are you unimpressed, believing that a limousine ride is a waste of money?

Line

Quick Interpretation: Being on time; taking your place; patience

Popular Expressions: Toe the line; Line up; Wait your turn

To dream of a line of some sort indicates patience, and waiting for your turn in an orderly fashion. People run around as though they haven't got a minute to waste. Is it time to slow down and smell the roses?

Lion (Also see *Animal; Cat.*)

Quick Interpretation: Power; kingdom; danger

Popular Expressions: Fight like a lion; Throw someone to the lions; King of the jungle

The words *majestic* and *powerful* immediately come to mind when thinking of the lion as a dream symbol. Lions are also associated with a desire to be right, and are at the top of the food chain. When you're at the top, you feel that no one is going to hunt you and that you're master of your realm.

If you're a woman, your association with the lion may be different. The lion may symbolize your partner, whom you feel you have to run around after and feed while also raising the children. Do you associate a feeling of subservience or slavery with the lion in your dream? How do you feel around the lion in your dream? Is it a symbol of being dominated? Or wanting to dominate?

Lion dreams are common among people who are about to embark on new careers or jobs. If this applies to you, the lion symbol indicates that you may have a strong tendency to impose your ideas and ways in the new environment or situation. A new, dominant lion will destroy all cubs he has not sired once he has taken over the pride. Are you attempting to claim the dominant position?

To dream of a lioness may signify a strong desire to foster teamwork. Lionesses only hunt in packs. Do you prefer to work in a group?

There's an air of snobbery associated with a pride. Are you being a social snob? Or do you feel excluded by a particular social group? Do you have to compromise yourself to be accepted? Or are you part of a tight clique that doesn't allow any new ideas or concepts to penetrate?

Lips (Also see *Body Parts; Kiss.*)

Quick Interpretation: Sensuality; insincerity; talking back

Popular Expressions: Button your lip; A stiff upper lip; Pay lip service to something; Give someone lip; Read my lips; Kiss someone off

Lipstick (Also see *Cosmetics.*)

Quick Interpretation: Seduction; accentuate; exaggerate

Popular Expressions: On someone's lips; Read my lips

Anytime you want to emphasize a point, you highlight it. Does the lipstick in your dream symbolize a desire to emphasize your words? Do you feel more attractive after you apply the lipstick? Who are you trying to attract, and to what end? Is there an erotic undertone to the lipstick, or is it purely window dressing?

Lodging (See *Accommodations.*)

Loneliness

Quick Interpretation: Isolation; craving attention

Popular Expressions: A lone wolf; Lonely but not alone

Feeling lonely indicates that you believe you're isolated from others. Whose attention do you crave? Why do you feel removed from others?

Loss

Quick Interpretation: Doubt; disorientation

Popular Expression: At a loss for words

When you feel at a loss, it indicates that you're unable to see your way forward and you feel uneasy. What is responsible for the doubt in your dream? Why do you feel disoriented?

Lover (Also see *Sex.*)

Quick Interpretation: Desire for intimacy; self-love; familiarity

Popular Expressions: Put something to bed; Lover's lane; Dream lover

The safest sex you could ever have is with a dream lover, especially when you understand that there's no such thing as thought crime. Do you wish to have more intimacy in your life? What are your dream lover's attributes or features, and are they aspects of yourself that you'd like to develop? Does the dream signify wish fulfillment, perhaps?

Do you recognize the individual you're making love to, or is it a stranger? If it's someone you had a relationship with whom you no longer see or think about, are you trying to resolve issues in order to bury the relationship, or do you have a desire to reconnect? If it's a stranger, do you wish to make your sex life more exciting?

If the lover is a family member, it may indicate that you hope for a stronger bond with this family member—a desire to get closer to them.

Scientists often say that we're no more than walking, talking, organic pharmacies, manufacturing the most incredible chemical concoctions. Your dream lover could be the by-product of testosterone, progesterone, and androgens running through your body, sparking the imagination to make love.

Luck

Quick Interpretation: Good fortune; an open door

Popular Expressions: Opportunity knocks; The luck of the draw; Good-luck charm; The luck of the Irish

When you feel lucky, it indicates that you're ready and waiting to open the door when opportunity knocks. How would you describe your good fortune? Did you have to work for it, or is it an unexpected windfall?

If you dream that you're unlucky, you feel that opportunity has knocked and you didn't hear it. Why do you feel that you have failed? What is the cause of your misfortune or dissatisfaction?

Luggage

Quick Interpretation: Vacation; holding on; a load

Popular Expressions: Comes with baggage; Pack your bags; Left holding the bag

In the past, if you said you were carrying luggage, you meant a couple of suitcases full of personal items. Today it indicates that you're carrying around a lot of past issues with you that haven't been dealt with, which are affecting your ability to move on. Does the symbol of luggage in your dream indicate that you're carrying around too much of the past and it's time to stop worrying about the future? Remember, it's the present that's the gift.

Lust

Quick Interpretation: Desire; passion

Popular Expression: Lust for life

When you feel lustful, you experience intense or unbridled desires. What is the focus of your passions in your dream? What must you have at all costs?

Mafia

Quick Interpretation: Close family ties; secrecy; corruption

Popular Expressions: A nose for crime; Law unto yourself; Mob mentality

To dream of the Mafia may indicate that you feel that organized crimes have been perpetrated against you. The symbol may also indicate a desire to be part of a family that sticks together through thick and thin, a family that would kill for one another.

Mail (See *Envelope; Letter; Post Office.*)

Makeup (See *Cosmetics.*)

Mannequin

Quick Interpretation: Static beauty; attention seeking; being on display

Popular Expressions: A model pupil; A role model; Model behavior; A living doll; Pretty is as pretty does

Why is it that when we see someone undressing a mannequin in a shop window, we look the other way? Does the mannequin in your dream symbolize a desire to be a living doll? Perhaps there are individuals around you who pretend they're beautiful people but really have no spirit.

Mantra

Quick Interpretation: Inner journey; seeking solitude; tuning in

Popular Expressions: In the lap of God; Mind games

Mantras are magical words that open pathways to greater self-awareness and enlightenment. If you see or hear a word in your dream that you believe could be a mantra, I suggest you use it.

Marathon

Quick Interpretation: Great distances traveled; endurance; steady pace

Popular Expressions: In the long run; Run for your life

Marathon runners are much more fortunate than hundred-meter sprinters. Imagine . . . your whole Olympic experience over in under ten seconds! Dreaming of a marathon may indicate that even if the road is long and arduous, by completing it you're a winner.

Mardi Gras

Quick Interpretation: Celebration; exuberance; lack of inhibitions

Popular Expressions: Dance as if there's no tomorrow; Dance until the cows come home; Party till dawn; Let your hair down

A Mardi Gras is a joyous celebration where everyone in the community lets their hair down and acts more outrageously than normal. Do you wish to cut loose and celebrate, and all you need is a good excuse?

Marijuana (Also see *Grass.*)

Quick Interpretation: Natural high; dope; joint venture

Popular Expressions: Get a buzz on; Snake in the grass; High as a kite; Living the high life

There was a time when you went down the street for a joint and came back with a leg of lamb under your arm. These days it refers to altering your state of consciousness. Ask yourself, do you think the person smoking the marijuana in your dream is a dope, or that you are? Or does the marijuana symbolize a desire to be social—that is, the custom of passing a joint around as a bonding ritual?

To dream of marijuana may also suggest a desire to escape or step away from the world around you. Is this your way of reminding yourself to practice detachment?

Do you feel guilty in your dream because you're smoking something prohibited? If so, it may indicate that you feel that a momentary high isn't worth the risk.

Does someone in your dream offend you by smoking marijuana in front of you? Or do you feel concerned for this person? If you're a parent, perhaps you're concerned that your child is smoking marijuana.

If you're offended, who's smoking the marijuana? What do they represent to you? Do you fear that aspect of them within yourself? For example, if the person smoking the marijuana in your dream is wearing something low-cut and see-through, perhaps you fear losing control if you become intoxicated and let your guard down.

On the other hand, you may admire the person smoking the marijuana and want to share in their experience.

Marketplace

Quick Interpretation: Commercial gathering; bargains; provisions

Popular Expressions: On the market; Pay the price

If you want to find a bargain, then the marketplace is the place to go. Ask yourself, do you enjoy haggling with others? Or do you feel uncomfortable because the price isn't fixed? Are you trying to sell someone something, or do you want to buy? Are you satisfied with the price you pay for what you want?

Marriage (Also see *Bride/Bridegroom.*)

Quick Interpretation: Agreements; commitment; union

Popular Expressions: Meet your match; Stand on ceremony; Till death do us part; Wedded to a concept; Tying the knot

Marriage is a three-ring circus: a wedding ring, an engagement ring, and surrender-ring. Does the marriage in your dream symbolize that you're willing to let go of your independence and commit to another?

You may dream of marriage if you're preparing for the big day in your waking life. Are you about to get married? How do you feel about it? If you're not about to get married, and no one close to you is about to get married, think of it in relation to making a commitment. Are you thinking about making a commitment to someone or something? How do you feel about it? Your dream will let you know (without a shadow of a doubt) whether you should go through with the commitment or not.

Marriage is also a symbol of agreements. Is the marriage in your dream symbolic of making an agreement with yourself, or with someone else? What is this agreement?

Also consider that marriage is a union. Who or what are you about to unite with? Is this union productive? Are you about to unite with an aspect of yourself?

Perhaps the marriage in your dream indicates that you've finally found someone or something that's your equal—you've met your match. Or does the marriage signify that you or someone else in your life is being excessively formal or polite—that is, standing on ceremony?

If you're not married and have no desire to tie the knot, then maybe the marriage in your dream symbolizes a union between you and your shadow. The question is, how will you consummate it?

Mask

Quick Interpretation: Deception; disguise; defense

Popular Expressions: Hidden agenda; Lose face; Two-faced; Hide one's face in shame; Mask one's desires

Is there anything more liberating than going to a ball or a party where everyone is wearing a mask? The mask allows you to act differently, to be another person. The mask in your dream could signify that you want to unmask hidden desires.

Who's wearing the mask in your dream? If it's you, do you want to cover something up, or does it indicate that you want to show a different face to the world? If the mask symbolizes covering up, what do you want to hide—an aspect of yourself or a physical handicap? Why do you feel you need to cover it up? If you want to show a different face to the world, what kind of face do you want to show? Perhaps you're sad and wish to show a happy face.

If someone else is wearing the mask, is it a disguise? What do you feel they're trying to hide from you? Or are they trying to show you a different face, one that perhaps you haven't noticed before?

A mask is also a symbol of defense. Is there someone or something in your life that you want to defend yourself from? Also consider the power that can come when you put a mask on and become the person or character that the masks represents. If you feel empowered wearing the mask in your dream, think about what it represents to you. How can you adopt these characteristics or traits into your own life to feel more empowered?

265

If you're at a masquerade ball in your dream, do you feel that people aren't showing their true colors? Or do you enjoy not seeing people for who they really are?

Massacre

Quick Interpretation: Termination; inhumanity; helplessness

Popular Expressions: Get away with murder; Armed to the teeth; A killing spree

While seeing a massacre in a dream can feel horrific and unsettling, it can also have the exact opposite meaning, as after every act of destruction comes an act of creation. What do you feel will be born from the turmoil?

To dream of a massacre can also symbolize termination. Who or what is being massacred in your dream? Perhaps the massacre is a strong reminder that a situation or relationship has come to an end in your life and it's time to move on.

A massacre is also a symbol of an inhumane act. Are you massacring or being massacred? If you're massacring, why do you feel you have to act this way? Do you feel that violence is the only way to escape a situation you're in? If you're being massacred, who is the perpetrator? Do you feel that this person takes advantage of people's vulnerability?

The massacre may also represent a time in your life when you feel you're getting away with murder—or someone else is!

Mattress (Also see *Bed.*)

Quick Interpretation: Support; rest; hidden wealth

Popular Expressions: On top of things; Right on the money; Make your bed and lie in it

Maze

Quick Interpretation: Confusion; challenge; puzzle

Popular Expressions: Talking in riddles; Light at the end of the tunnel; No way out

Don't you think it's strange that something that's so orderly, precise, and manicured can be confusing? If you're in a maze in your dream, does it indicate that you feel challenged or confused about a certain situation in your life at the moment? How do you feel about being in the maze, and how do you respond to being in there?

Perhaps you're watching someone else in the maze. Does this person represent you? Does the dream indicate that although you feel like you're stuck in a maze right now, you only need to wait, and trust that everything will work out as it's supposed to?

When you get to a point in life when you're tired of dead ends in relationships or careers, the maze that you're in becomes solvable and you find the exit.

Meadow

Quick Interpretation: Being carefree and natural; liberation; playfulness

Popular Expressions: Take a hike; Field of dreams; A new playing field; Put something out to pasture

Does the symbol of a meadow indicate that it's time to put something out to pasture? For example, is it a good time to retire and take it easy? Or does the meadow symbolize your desire to get out in nature with friends or family and celebrate a beautiful summer's day?

Meat (Also see *Food.*)

Quick Interpretation: Sustenance; butchery; domestication

Popular Expressions: Dead meat; One man's meat is another man's poison; The meat of the matter; A meaty subject; A meat market

When we're under pressure or stuck between two opposing points of view, we may feel like the meat in the sandwich. Who or what is forcing you to take sides and make decisions?

Meat can also symbolize personal taste, and the fact that everyone has a right to their own opinion. Your dream may be reminding you that one person's meat is another person's poison.

If you're a vegetarian and dream of meat, consider whether your body is experiencing withdrawal symptoms. The meat in your dream may represent a desire for protein.

Also consider the literal connotations. Is your unconscious telling you that you need more protein in your diet?

Medal

Quick Interpretation: Respect; achievement; interference

Popular Expressions: Hero worship; A medal of honor

Everyone loves to worship a hero. How do you spot one? By the medals adorning their chest. Does the medal in your dream indicate that you want to be publicly acknowledged for your deeds?

If you're receiving a medal in your dream, is someone showing you respect and honor for a recent achievement? Or are you honoring someone else? What are you or they being honored for? How do you feel about it?

Think about what you're doing with the medal in your dream. It may signify how you think and feel about being rewarded, or about other people being rewarded.

If you receive a medal from someone you don't respect in your dream, do you feel they're meddling in your affairs, pinning something on you that you don't deserve?

Medicine

Quick Interpretation: Relief; healing; trust

Popular Expression: A dose of your own medicine

Even more significant than the medicine itself is the reason why it's being administered. Is it used as a salvation or to simply get you back on your feet? Are you receiving the medicine or giving it? Does it do the trick, or does it leave a sour taste in your mouth? Is the medicine a placebo? If so, this may indicate that it's time to put mind over matter.

Memory Loss (See *Amnesia.*)

Mermaid

Quick Interpretation: Duality; warning; seduction

Popular Expressions: Fish out of water; Tall tales; Best of both worlds

The mermaid is a symbol of desire. In your dream, do you wish to live in two worlds? Or perhaps you want to make the best of both worlds. Do you want to be tempted, but only in fantasy? Or do you want to tell tall tales in the hope that someone will believe you? The mermaid may also indicate that there's something in your life that you want, but it's going to take a lot of faith to get it.

Meteor

Quick Interpretation: Outside forces; collision; obstinate beliefs

Popular Expressions: Hit rock bottom; Down-to-earth; Come crashing down; A meteoric rise; Collision course

With so many meteor films around, it's no wonder that we dream of them. Does the meteor in your dream indicate that you feel circumstances in your life, that are beyond your control are going to have a massive impact on you?

Military (Also see *Soldier; War.*)

Quick *Interpretation:* Discipline; enforced rule; obeying commands

Popular Expressions: Armed intervention; Join forces; Fight for a cause

It's wonderful to see the cavalry appearing over the hill in a dream, because it indicates that relief, reinforcement, and help is on the way. The sounding of the trumpet signifies that the nightmare is over.

What are the soldiers doing in your dream? Are they enforcing the law or protecting national security? Are you enforcing something in life (a rule of conduct or morality), or protecting it?

If you're a part of the military in your dream (but not in real life), then perhaps it indicates a desire to achieve more in your life, the military being a symbol of discipline and organization.

The military also symbolizes obeying commands. Are you forcing others to obey your commands, or are they forcing you to obey theirs?

What in your life do you feel needs armed intervention in order to resolve it? Does the military symbolize a desire to join forces, indicating that you feel more empowered as part of a group?

If you're feeling indecisive, especially about important life-and-death issues, and you dream of the military, it may indicate that you prefer to have a foot in both camps to ensure that whatever you decide, the outcome won't be devastating.

Milk

Quick Interpretation: Kindness; sustenance; being ripped off (milked)

Popular Expressions: The milk of human kindness; To milk it for all it's worth; Crying over spilled milk; The land of milk and honey

Milk is a symbol of letting go. How many times have we been told not to cry over spilled milk? What are you hanging on to that you can't do anything about? It's in the past, it's gone, but it's still occupying your thoughts.

Milk is also a symbol of plenty, as we've all thought about going to the land of milk and honey.

Millionaire

Quick Interpretation: Affluence; accumulation of wealth; desire

Popular Expressions: One in a million; Feel/look like a million dollars

When you're facing mighty challenges, are going against the tide, and feeling as though you have one chance in a million, dreaming of a millionaire represents a desire to increase your luck.

Who is the millionaire in your dream? If it's you (and you're not a millionaire in real life), then it may simply be wish fulfillment, or it could signify great wealth and richness in your life. Are you enjoying good fortune at the moment?

If someone else is the millionaire, how do you feel about it? Think of this person as an aspect of yourself; how you respond to them may indicate how you feel about wealth.

Also consider whether the millionaire symbolizes the accumulation of wealth. What are you doing with these riches? Why do you need to accumulate them?

Most of us can remember a day when everything worked: It was a good hair day, the outfit fit perfectly, our skin was smooth, and we looked like a million dollars. Is your dream reminding you how great you can look with a little effort?

Mime

Quick Interpretation: Silent expression; accentuating inner feelings; overdramatization

Popular Expressions: Put thought into action; Mum's the word; Actions speak louder than words; My lips are sealed

To dream of a mime signifies that it's time for someone to put their nose to the grindstone and get some work done; after all, as we all know, actions speak louder than words.

Minister (See *Priest.*)

Mirror

Quick Interpretation: Reversal; observation; vanity

Popular Expressions: Mirror image; See things back to front; Smoke and mirrors

You can tell a lot about yourself if you dream of a mirror, especially if you see your reflection. It indicates that you want to take a closer look at yourself. It screams: Look at what I've become! It also reminds you to look at a situation or circumstance from a different perspective.

A mirror image is a reflection. Is there a situation in your life that you need to reflect upon? Does it suggest that you're the type of person to "face" issues? Or does it represent your outward appearance only and has to do with how you think people perceive you?

It's important to be aware of any emotions you experienced in your dream. Do you like what you see in the mirror? Are you embarrassed or uncomfortable? Does the image annoy or please you? Your reactions are a great barometer of how you feel about yourself.

Is your mirror image younger than your present age, or older? If the image is younger, it may indicate that you feel fit and healthy, or that you wish to be fit and healthy. If it's an older image, it may signify that you wish to be more mature or learned, or perhaps you feel you are.

If you see someone else's reflection in the mirror, is it someone you emulate? What is it in the mirror that you wish to become, or which characteristics of that person do you wish you had?

The mirror was the gateway Alice entered in *Through the Looking Glass*. Do you want adventure in your life? Do you want to escape from a mundane existence and explore a world where anything is possible?

Miser (See *Stinginess*.)

Mist (See *Fog*.)

Mistletoe (Also see *Christmas; Kiss*.)

Quick Interpretation: Celebration; intimacy; decoration

Popular Expressions: Kiss-and-tell; Furtive kisses

How strange that we should use a tree parasite (mistletoe is a parasitic plant) as an excuse to kiss someone! Does the mistletoe in your dream symbolize that you need an excuse or permission to show your affection to someone else?

Mobile Phone (See *Cell Phone*.)

Moderation

Quick Interpretation: Sensible behavior; balance

When you choose to live a moderate life, it indicates that you like to avoid extreme behavior. You take care not to step beyond sensible limits. What brings balance to the situation in your dream?

Modesty

Quick Interpretation: Moderation; humility

When you feel modest, it indicates that you have a moderate opinion of yourself, and reasonable expectations of your skills and talents. What is it that's inappropriate to show off or make a big fuss over in your dream?

Monarchy (Also see *King; Queen.*)

Quick Interpretation: Power of the hierarchy; sovereignty; tradition

Popular Expressions: King of the castle; Queen for a day; Getting the royal treatment

Monastery

Quick Interpretation: Dedication; reclusiveness; abstinence

Popular Expression: A safe haven

If you're experiencing a time in your life when you'd like to be in a relationship with individuals who think like you, look like you, and do the same things as you, then you may dream of a monastery. In a monastery, everything is so rigid and programmed, but no one wants to escape. You feel safe knowing that everyone around you is on the same path.

Money

Quick Interpretation: Abundance; desire; energy

Popular Expressions: Right on the money; Put your money where your mouth is; Money talks; Money burns a hole in your pocket; Cash in hand; Spend like there's no tomorrow; Making change

Bingo! You've just won the lottery in a dream and you're feeling on top of the world. In a dream, money is often an instant manifestation. You don't have to earn it, it just "pops" up.

When you dream about money, it's important to determine how you feel about it. Do you feel deserving, guilty, generous, or happy?

Money is only a piece of paper or plastic; it's our association with money that's important. The way a person handles money can tell you a lot about them. How do you handle the money in your dream? Are you receiving it or giving it away? It may signify a gain or a loss in your life.

Look at the money you're receiving. A person I know saw Italian lire in a dream and it turned out that he had a desire to travel to Italy. Someone else I know dreamed about British pounds, only to be presented with the opportunity to travel to London soon after.

How new is the money in your dream? Is it crisp and shiny, or dirty and out of circulation? This will give you insight into the money or abundance that's in your life . . . or coming into your life. For example, you may dream of money that's old and torn. This can signify the sale of a house you bought 25 years ago.

Money can also signify choice. A person I know once dreamed that he wanted to buy a pie from a pie shop but had no money. Sometime later he walked past a pie shop and, like in his dream, felt the urge to buy a pie. He had a pocketful of money but chose not to buy one because he knew he would be eating at home. It was the same outcome as the dream—no pie, but the dreamer realized there was one significant difference: choice.

Monkey (Also see *Animal; Baboon.*)

Quick Interpretation: Mischief; copycat; having fun

Popular Expressions: Monkeying around; Monkey business; Monkeying with something; A monkey on your back; Going ape

Moon

Quick Interpretation: Feminine aspects; high spirits; being influenced

Popular Expressions: Once in a blue moon; Over the moon; Promise someone the moon; Mooning at someone (or mooning someone)

Why does the full moon bring out weirdness in people? Does the moon in your dream indicate that you want to act out of character or be a little crazy?

To dream of the moon can signify that you're experiencing a transformational time in your life, as the moon is associated with the unconscious. How does the moon appear in your dream, and how do you feel when you see it? Is it a glowing full moon, indicating fullness and intensity; or is it a crescent moon, indicating new beginnings?

The moon is also a symbol of the feminine, of woman. Think about the feminine influences in your life. How do you feel about femininity? Consider this in relation to how the moon appears in your dream.

We know that the moon influences the tides, and it's also said to influence our emotions. Do you feel that someone or something in your life is pushing you around emotionally?

The moon can also symbolize ecstatic joy (being over the moon), or maybe it indicates a rare occurrence, as in once in a blue moon. If so, perhaps it's time to put on your party shoes and dance until sunrise.

Mortgage (Also see *Debt.*)

Quick Interpretation: Debt; commitment; ownership

Popular Expressions: Stake a claim; Mortgaged to the hilt; A day late and a dollar short

A mortgage is a magical symbol. It has the ability to make a month feel so short but a year feel so long. Whom do you feel it's necessary to borrow from so you can achieve your goal? How secure do you feel about the transaction? Can you repay the debt effortlessly, or could you be in over your head and lose it all? This dream symbol takes on very personal meanings if, in your waking life, you're paying off a mortgage, about to embark on a mortgage debt, or have people around you who are affected by their mortgage payments. If any or all of these options are the case, ask yourself one simple question: How do I feel when I hear the word *mortgage?*

Mosquito (Also see *Insect.*)

Quick Interpretation: Intrusion; pest; attack

Popular Expressions: Bloodsucker; Bite more than you can chew; Get a buzz on

Moth (Also see *Insect.*)

Quick Interpretation: Transformation; habitual searching (looking for the light); fragility

Popular Expression: Like a moth to a flame

Mother (See *Family.*)

Mother-in-law (See *Family.*)

Motivation

Quick Interpretation: Excitement; enthusiasm

When you're motivated, it indicates a desire to act with enthusiasm. What are you excited about?

Motorcycle

Quick Interpretation: Freedom; escape; rebellion

Popular Expressions: Kick-start; Get in gear; Rebel without a cause

If there was ever a symbol that indicates you want to take things into your own hands and put matters under your personal control, then it's the motorcycle. Do you want to be more rebellious, or more of an individual? If you use a motorcycle as your normal means of transportation, then the meaning of your dream is a lot more personal and may be an extension of your own experience. If someone else is on the bike in your dream, are you concerned about their safety and think it's an inappropriate means of travel, or do you want to hop on, too, and create two rebels without a cause?

Mountain (Also see *Climbing*.)

Quick Interpretation: Dramatization; high expectations; miracles

Popular Expressions: Faith will move mountains; Make a mountain out of a molehill

Why did the ancients believe that the gods lived up in the mountains? It's so cold and bleak up there that if you were a god, wouldn't you live in the Bahamas?

Climbing a mountain in a dream suggests wanting to move to higher ground. How big is the mountain, and how is the climb up? Is it an easy climb, or is it littered with obstacles? If it's difficult, what must you overcome? What's stopping you from reaching the top? If you're only climbing a hill in your dream, does it symbolize modest ambitions?

A mountain can also symbolize high expectations. Do you have high expectations of yourself or someone else, or does someone have high expectations of you? How you move up or down the mountain in your dream will clearly indicate how you respond to high expectations—your own or others.

Also consider that the mountain may symbolize dramatization. Are you overdramatizing something in your life? Or does the mountain signify miracles, as if you can move mountains?

To see mountains in a dream can also indicate a change in attitude or a change in how you do things, because if Mohammed can't go to the mountain, the mountain must come to him.

Mouse (Also see *Animal.*)

Quick Interpretation: Experimentation; timidity; stealth

Popular Expressions: Timid as a mouse; A cat-and-mouse game; While the cat's away . . .

Mouth (Also see *Body Parts.*)

Quick Interpretation: Expression; an opening; disrespect

Popular Expressions: A loudmouth; Mouth off; Word-of-mouth

Movie (See *Film.*)

Movie Theater (See *Cinema; Film.*)

Mud

Quick Interpretation: Down to earth; camouflage; in trouble (big mouth)

Popular Expressions: Stick-in-the-mud; Your name is mud; Sling mud at; Here's mud in your eye

If you're bogged down, or prevented from moving forward in your relationships or business, then you may dream of mud. It can also indicate that you're not understanding something that everyone around you thinks you should. Basically, your perception is clouded and murky.

Mug

Quick Interpretation: Face; refreshment; replenishment

Popular Expressions: Not your cup of tea; Mug shot; Getting mugged

A mug, as opposed to a cup, conveys a sense of wanting more. What do you want a lot more of in life? Are you drinking from the mug in your dream, or is someone else?

The word *mug* is also slang for *face*. What does the mug in your dream look like, and how does this relate to the way you see yourself or someone else? For example, if you dream that the mug you're drinking from is covered in advertising, do you feel over-commercialized? If someone else is drinking from or holding a mug with a peace symbol on it, does it signify that you should make up with them? Ask yourself what's written all over your face, or someone else's, as evidenced by the mug.

A mug shot refers to a photograph taken as a result of being caught doing something wrong. Is the mug in your dream an expression of feeling guilty about something?

What's in the mug? Is it a stimulant like coffee, or a relaxant like herbal tea? Is your dream telling you to get your butt into action, or is it telling you to just relax?

Mule (Also see *Animal.*)

Quick Interpretation: Hard work; stubbornness; crossbreeding

Popular Expression: As stubborn as a mule

Murder (Also see *Death; Massacre.*)

Quick Interpretation: Termination; loss of control; excessive display of force

Popular Expressions: Scream bloody murder; Get away with murder; Put the fear of death into someone

To see or commit a murder in a dream symbolizes termination. Who's murdered? What has been abruptly taken away from you? If you're the murderer, does the murder signify that you're getting rid of an aspect of yourself that you don't like? Why do you feel that you have to display excessive force?

Perhaps the murder symbolizes loss of control. Who has lost control? What is so drastic in your life that you had to take this course of action?

Mushroom (Also see *Food.*)

Quick Interpretation: Food; parasite; caution

Popular Expressions: Keep in the dark; To cap something off

Music

Quick Interpretation: Inspiration; good news; responsibility

Popular Expressions: Face the music; Music to my ears

Music soothes the savage beast. If you hear music in a dream, what are you annoyed about that you want relief from? The symbol of music can also indicate that you want more harmony in your relationships. Of course, if you're a musician, your dream may relate to your craft.

Musical Instrument

Quick Interpretation: Expression; dedication; entertainment

Popular Expressions: Play to your own tune; Blow your own trumpet; Fiddle around; Dance to your own drummer

Good news is on the way—something is like music to your ears. What type of musical instrument are you playing or listening to in your dream? Do you play this instrument in your waking life, or is it an instrument you'd like to play? If it's an instrument you play, is your dream an extension of your obsession with music, a way to perhaps work through a tune or composition? If it's an instrument you don't play, maybe it's time you started? Perhaps it's an appropriate way for you to express yourself.

Each musical instrument has a different effect on the emotions. Does the musical instrument in your dream affect the way you feel? In what way? If someone else is playing the instrument, how do you feel about it? Is it entertaining or annoying?

To dream of a musical instrument also suggests dedication. Are you ready to dedicate yourself to something in your life? Or do you want to goof off and just fiddle around?

Mustache

Quick Interpretation: Masculinity; vanity; inner strength

Popular Expressions: Right under your nose; A hair's breadth away; A stiff upper lip; Put on a brave face

Whether you're male or female, dreaming of a mustache signifies that there's something right under your nose that you're being made aware of.

Nail

Quick Interpretation: Being cornered getting results; crucified

Popular Expressions: Hit the nail on the head; Nail down; Another nail in the coffin

The questions to ask here are: Who's doing the hammering, and what needs to be nailed down?

Naked

Quick Interpretation: Bareness; exposure; without defenses

Popular Expressions: The naked truth; Bare one's soul; Stripped to the bone

A friend who was about to become a radio announcer dreamed that she was at a nightclub dancing naked on a podium. She expressed embarrassment at having had such a dream, but what else would you dream about when you're about to expose yourself to the world?

Nudity in a dream signifies a desire to show your true colors. If you're naked at work, it may indicate a fear of being exposed in some way—perhaps you feel that you're incapable of fulfilling your job requirements. If you've been dishonest, it may indicate a fear of being found out.

If you feel as though you're often misjudged or misunderstood, you may have a dream of partial exposure. For example, you may find yourself at a board meeting without your shirt on.

How do you feel about being naked? Are you excited, or do you try to cover up? Is someone looking at you? Are you at work? Is it a special event? Do you feel exposed? A person may dream of being naked if they find out that someone has read their diary or passed around private e-mails without their permission.

Sometimes you may see someone else naked in a dream. A woman called me once because she dreamed that she saw the Dalai Lama naked and felt it was sacrilegious. However, it more likely symbolized a desire to show the world her spiritual side. If you see someone else naked in a dream, ask yourself what that person symbolizes.

When all is said and done, though, my practical side always likes to have the last say. Your dream of nudity may simply indicate that you need a new set of clothes.

Navy (Also see *Military*.)

Quick Interpretation: Foreign shores; escape; confinement

Popular Expressions: At sea; Between the devil and the deep blue sea; Ship out

Neck (Also see *Body Parts*.)

Quick Interpretation: Support; risk; pain

Popular Expressions: Pain in the neck; Breathe down someone's neck; Stick your neck out

Needle (Also see *Syringe*.)

Quick Interpretation: Bring together; patch things up; annoy

Popular Expressions: Like looking for a needle in a haystack; Being needled by someone; Hard to pin down

We all get annoyed or needled from time to time by people and situations. It's interesting that you should dream of an item that fastens things together to indicate that you're annoyed. Perhaps you should consider "getting together" with what has annoyed you to understand where the aggravation is coming from.

Negativity

Quick Interpretation: Criticism; unpleasantness

When you're feeling negative or behaving in a negative way, observe any debilitating thoughts that may be occupying your mind. What are you critical of in your dream? Do you feel as though someone is criticizing you?

Negligence

Quick Interpretation: Lack of attention; being ignored

When you feel neglected, it may indicate that you believe someone is paying you insufficient attention or respect. You feel disregarded. Why do you feel ignored in your dream? Whom do you crave more attention from?

Nephew (See *Family.*)

Nest

Quick Interpretation: Home; commitment; comfort

Popular Expressions: Feather your nest; A nest egg; Empty-nest syndrome; Return to the nest; Fly the coop; Hatch an idea

When birds build a nest, it's tailor-made to their breeding habits. A nest is specially built for the occupier by the occupier, and as such, is personal and individual. The nest not only offers incubation, but also safety from predators, protection from the elements, and comfort.

What kind of nest do you see in your dream? Tiny birds can build the most intricate nests that are engineering feats and the epitome of security. Do you desire a nest like this? Do you want to be secure, grounded, well established, and protected?

What kind of animal do you think lives in the nest? Is it a predator or a bird of paradise? Do you feel that you're living with or surrounded by predators? Perhaps the nest has been built by a peacock, indicating a desire to cultivate an artistic and creative environment. The nest may also symbolize your desire to nest—that is, enter a relationship and build a home.

If you want to leave the "nest" (a common feeling among teenagers), a symbol of a nest and leaving it may appear in a dream. As an adult, it may mean that you want to sever a relationship or change your area code.

Where the nest is placed can be telling. Is it wobbling precariously on the end of a branch that's about to break, indicating that you feel you're on shaky ground? Is it high in a tree, or on the ground? The height of the nest may indicate where you think your sanctuary is. Is it in the intellect, or more grounded and down-to-earth? Are chicks or eggs in the nest? Eggs can signify aspirations and desires, and chicks often symbolize commitment, work, and dedication.

Are you being fed in the nest, indicating that you're looking for support and nourishment from someone else? Or are you constantly returning to the nest with food, indicating that you feel you're the provider and others are dependent on you for survival?

Is there something in your waking life that you'd like to incubate? What ideas or concepts would you like to hatch and bring into the world?

Net

Quick Interpretation: Being caught; profit; communication

Popular Expressions: Cast a wide net; Slip through the net; Surf the Net

In this day and age, you don't need a board or wet suit to surf, just a computer and an Internet account. Does the net in your dream symbolize a desire to access mountains of information or communicate freely?

What are you doing with the net in your dream? Are you using it to catch something? What you're trying to catch may symbolize what you wish you had more of in your life. For example, if you're trying to catch a fish, you may wish for more flow in your life. If someone else is using the net in your dream, what are they trying to catch? Is your life caught up in theirs? How do you feel about it?

A net may also symbolize profit. Are you enjoying a profitable time at the moment, or is someone else? Perhaps you wish to take stock of a situation, either in business or in a relationship—that is, you want to see the net effects of your actions.

Newspaper

Quick Interpretation: Deadlines; information; sensationalism

Popular Expressions: Not worth the paper it's printed on; It's news to me; Front-page news; Stop the presses

It's more important to see what has been printed in the newspaper than the newspaper itself. What is the message? What do you need to learn, or what has to be dismissed? Is the information not worth the paper it's printed on, or is it front-page news?

Niece (See *Family.*)

Nose (Also see *Body Parts.*)

Quick Interpretation: Inquisitiveness; good sense of smell

Popular Expressions: Keep your nose out of it; Nosing around; Follow your nose; Sniffing around; The smell of success

Nurse

Quick Interpretation: Comfort; support; recovery

Popular Expressions: Nurse back to health; A wet nurse

The first thing that comes to mind when I think of a nurse is noble service, someone who puts their own health at risk for the benefit of others. Nurses signify hard work, dedication, and support. Who's nursing whom back to health in your dream? Is it an act of love, or does it look/feel like an overwhelming chore?

A couple of important questions to ask when you dream of a nurse are: "What needs to be healed in my own life?" and "How do I go about doing it?" Do you want to become a healer? Are you nursing someone in the dream? Does it represent a situation in your life that needs to be healed?

Is someone nursing you? Do you recognize the person who's nursing you? Do you want to heal or make up with them, or do they have an answer for you? If you're the nurse, perhaps you need to consider whether you should be more caring.

Look at the era you're in, too. Is the nurse in a modern-day setting, or is she a Florence Nightingale character? If the dream has an old-fashioned feel to it, maybe you're looking for a more natural way to heal. If it has a modern feel, perhaps you want to adopt a more scientific approach.

Does your dream signify that someone is mothering you too much, trying to be a wet nurse who brings forth mother's milk but not to her own child?

Also consider if you or someone else is being a martyr. Nursing involves self-sacrifice, and nurses are often the unsung heroes. Are you sacrificing your dreams for another purpose? Are you happy to do so, or do you feel bitter and resentful?

Nymph

Quick Interpretation: Seduction; play; elusiveness

Popular Expressions: Play into someone's hands;
In temptation's way

Seduction plays a part in all our fantasies. The nymph in your dream may symbolize giving into or being tempted by seductive creatures, but knowing it's safe, as they only exist in your imagination.

Oar

Quick Interpretation: Movement; exercise; leverage

Popular Expressions: Row, row, row your boat; Doesn't have both oars in the water

Whenever you know you really have to put effort into something, the oar may appear in a dream. It can also show up when you're acting irrationally or if people around you are a little bit nuts. Boats only go around in circles when one oar is out of the water!

Obsession

Quick Interpretation: Preoccupation; fixation

When you're obsessed, it clearly indicates that you're preoccupied with a thought, feeling, or activity. In your dream, who or what do you believe you can't live without? What is the cause of your fixation?

Obstinance (See *Stubbornness*.)

Ocean (Also see *Beach; Water.*)

Quick Interpretation: Enormity; delving deep into your emotions; being surrounded by high emotion

Popular Expressions: A drop in the ocean; Oceans apart

Most of us have felt, at one time or another, that our efforts are insignificant; we feel like a drop in the ocean. Do you wish to have a greater effect on others?

How do you see the ocean in your dream? Is it gentle or rough? If the ocean represents your emotions, how do you feel? Do you see tidal waves, indicating that you're overwhelmed? How are you interacting with the ocean? Are you playing in it or running away from it? Perhaps you're plumbing its depths, indicating that you're delving deeply into your emotions? If other people you know are playing in the ocean, think about how you relate to them emotionally.

The ocean is also a symbol of enormity. What do you feel knows no limits in your life? Is this particularly true of your outlook on relationships—that is, you know that there are plenty of fish in the sea?

Octopus (Also see *Animal.*)

Quick Interpretation: Ambidextrous; being sucked in (tricked); networking

Popular Expressions: Not a leg to stand on; To spread your tentacles

Office (Also see *Work.*)

Quick Interpretation: Work; dedication; duty

Popular Expressions: Bring home the bacon; To hold office; Another day at the office

These days we spend more time at work or in the office than we do at home. Does the office in your dream indicate that you mean business in your career? What are you doing in the office? Is it the office where you work? If it is, take particular note of how you're feeling. Perhaps it's time to reassess your job, or what you want from your career.

An office in a dream is clearly a symbol of work. How do you perceive your working life? What you're doing in the office and whom you're with will help you determine your perception of work.

An office can also symbolize dedication and duty. Are you dedicated to your work, or do you feel that duty binds you to things you'd prefer not to do? Can it be that you have political aspirations or delusions of grandeur and you desire to hold high office?

Oil

Quick Interpretation: Wealth; pollution; inspiration

Popular Expressions: Burning the midnight oil; Like oil and water; Strike oil

This is a paradoxical symbol that can either mean black gold and wealth or pollution and devastation.

Old Age (Also see *Aging*.)

Quick Interpretation: Feeling worn out

Popular Expressions: Over-the-hill; No spring chicken

Dreaming that you feel old or are old clearly indicates that you feel aged, tired, or worn out. Do you believe your ideas are outdated? What is wearing you out in your dream?

Olive

Quick Interpretation: Peace; underlying creativity (hidden seeds); resilience

Popular Expression: An olive branch

If someone around you projects a soft exterior but you know they're really hard inside, you may dream of an olive.

The olive is such a versatile food. It can be used for everything from an appetizer to an oil. Perhaps you're looking for more versatility in your life.

Operation (Also see *Body Parts.*)

Quick Interpretation: Getting to the core of the matter; understanding; planning ahead

Popular Expressions: Quick fix; Cut to the bone; Just what the doctor ordered

When you feel successful in life, you may dream of a smooth operation. Is something in your life that you thought would be extremely perilous to handle working out well and running more smoothly than you thought?

What is being operated on in your dream? Is it a part of your body? How do you feel about the operation? Do you feel it's necessary because it's going to fix a long-term problem? What problem do you believe it will make better? If you're about to be operated on in your waking life, think of the dream as a way to work through and process your emotions.

If someone else is being operated on in your dream, how do you feel about it? What part of the anatomy is being operated on? An operation can also symbolize planning ahead—that is, like an army operation. Do you feel a need to prepare for the future? What needs a plan of attack?

If someone is mean, judgmental, and has no empathy for others, then you may dream of open-heart surgery.

Optimism

Quick Interpretation: Positive outcomes; bright future

Popular Expressions: All's well that ends well; The future looks bright; Happy days are here again

Feeling optimistic in a dream indicates that you're anticipating a favorable outcome to a situation or event. Why is the future so bright?

Orchard

Quick Interpretation: Abundance; getting back to nature; being picked on

Popular Expressions: Bear fruits; Fruits of your labors

An orchard is a place of plenty. The only problem is, it's plenty of the same thing. Perhaps you're getting too much of a good thing and it will turn sour if you're not careful.

Orchestra (Also see *Music; Musical Instrument.*)

Quick Interpretation: Cooperation; being in tune; under someone else's command

Popular Expressions: Overplay your hand; Sing the same tune; Conduct yourself properly

If you finally feel as though things are coming together and everyone is marching to the same tune, dreaming of an orchestra is a great sign. It can also indicate that you want everything to come together. It's important to observe who the conductor is.

Orthodontist (See *Dentist.*)

Oven (Also see *Kitchen*.)

Quick Interpretation: Fertility; bringing ideas together; heating things up

Popular Expressions: Bun in the oven; Half-baked idea; Cook your goose; Turn up the heat

Owl

Quick Interpretation: Wisdom; healing; predator

Popular Expressions: Wisecrack; A night owl; Words of wisdom; A real hoot

An owl is a complex symbol. To work out its meaning in a dream, first consider your ethnic background. If you're Caucasian, an owl often symbolizes wisdom and knowledge. If you're Mediterranean, it symbolizes healing. In Etruscan and Roman times, the medical establishment used the owl as a sign to let people know where to come for medical aid. In Eastern and Native American traditions, the owl is viewed as a predator.

The owl can see in the dark, which suggests soul searching. In a dream, it may indicate that if you look hard enough at an issue, all will be revealed. Are you in the dark about something? The owl can also represent your shadow side. It may appear in a dream when you're finally able to see and accept something about yourself that you previously refused to acknowledge.

It's important to consider the motif of the dream—which is often revealed through its location. Are you in a place of learning? Perhaps contemplation and learning are appropriate for you at this time.

Does the owl land on someone in your dream? For example, if you see an owl land on your crazy Aunt Josephine, whom you haven't seen for ten years, it may suggest that some type of healing is about to take place between the two of you. If the owl lands on a part of your body, consider whether it needs treatment.

If you feel scared in the dream (maybe you're running away from the owl or being attacked by it), consider whether someone in your life is preying on your thoughts or your creativity.

Owls also kill rats and in this way can be seen as pest exterminators. If you see the owl land on someone in your dream, ask if that person is a pest in your life—someone you need to get rid of.

The owl may also represent a desire to be alone. It's a solitary creature, and its solitude is what makes it so mysterious.

Oyster

Quick Interpretation: Hidden treasure; hard exterior; good fortune; lust

Popular Expressions: The world is your oyster; Pearls of wisdom

We get told repeatedly that we should never judge a book by its cover. Dreaming of an oyster is a very powerful reminder of this. It looks pretty ugly and rough on the outside, but on the inside you may find a pearl or even an aphrodisiac!

Package

Quick Interpretation: Surprise; consolidation; completion

Popular Expressions: Wrap things up; Part and parcel;
Good things come in small packages

It's said that good things come in small packages. If you see a small package in your dream, it may be a reminder that even the small things you do in life can have a great effect on others.

What kind of package do you see in your dream? Is it a surprise package, indicating surprises in your life? Who is the package for? Maybe you're giving the package to someone. Do you have a surprise for them? Or is someone giving *you* the package, perhaps indicating that they're about to spring a surprise on you?

Dreaming of a package can also symbolize consolidation. Is something being consolidated in your life? Have you reached a firm resolution about a situation or person?

The package may also signify completion—that is, wrapping things up. Or perhaps it indicates that you've handled an issue successfully.

Pain (Also see *Ache.*)

Quick Interpretation: Suffering; distress

Popular Expressions: No pain, no gain; Sticks and stones may break my bones . . .

The experience of pain indicates that you feel distress or suffering in your body or mind. Who or what has inflicted suffering in your dream? What is the cause of your distress?

Paint (Also see *House.*)

Quick Interpretation: Camouflage; decoration; rejuvenation

Popular Expressions: Paint the town red; Like watching paint dry; Paint someone into a corner

It's amazing what a fresh coat of paint can do. It can convert the most drab room into one that's bright and new. Does the paint in your dream symbolize a desire to take a fresh look at things?

What are you painting? Are you trying to camouflage something or decorate and beautify it? If the painting is an attempt to camouflage, what don't you want other people to see? Think about the object you're trying to camouflage in relation to yourself. If you're painting a house, for example, see the house as a symbol of yourself to determine what you're trying to camouflage. It may be that you want to decorate or rejuvenate this aspect of yourself.

Perhaps you're painting a picture in your dream. What is it a picture of? You may want to reproduce it now in your waking life. How do you feel about it? Is it picture perfect, or are you trying to make something picture perfect? Who or what is in the picture? Is it an indication of what you've chosen to include in your life right now—meaning that someone or something is in the picture?

To dream you're painting may also indicate that you must concentrate on the situation at hand, as you don't want to end up painting yourself into a corner.

Palace (Also see *King; Queen.*)

Quick Interpretation: Aspirations; tradition; opulence

Popular Expressions: Building castles in the air; Queen for a day; Long live the king

How times have changed. Today, we refer to the presidential palace more often than we do the palace of kings and queens. Do you feel that the only worthwhile things in life are those you work hard for, rather than those that are handed to you on a platter? Also, your palace is your home. Perhaps the palace in your dream indicates that it's time to count your blessings.

Panther (Also see *Animal*.)

Quick Interpretation: Shadow; stealth; seduction

Popular Expressions: On the prowl; Darken my doorstep

Parachute

Quick Interpretation: High flyer; need to slow down; preparation

Popular Expressions: Happy landings; Taking a hard fall; Down-to-earth

If it's time to focus on self-sufficiency and self-support, then you may see a parachute in a dream. It's a reminder that you need to rely on your own ability to land on your feet.

Parade

Quick Interpretation: Celebration; being on show; having fun

Popular Expressions: On display; Rain on someone's parade; Show off

Whenever we want to display who we really are or what we believe in, we put it on parade. Are you showing off in the parade, or are you watching someone else who's trying to get your attention? It's important to note what kind of parade it is. Is it a party or celebration, indicating that it's time to get away from hard work and let your hair down because it's the festive season? Or is it a military parade, either indicating a show of force and strength or a show of respect and admiration?

Paramedic (See *Ambulance*.)

Paranoia

Quick Interpretation: Suspicion; mistrust

Popular Expressions: Danger up ahead; The worst is yet to come; Even paranoiacs have enemies

When you feel paranoid, you perceive the world in an extremely suspicious or fearful way. What or whom don't you trust in your dream? What imagined danger have you magnified?

Park

Quick Interpretation: Respite; playfulness; high maintenance

Popular Expressions: Playing on a level field; A walk in the park

No matter which way you look at it, the park is a place of rest and recreation (except for the gardeners). Parks are often sanctuaries in the middle of concrete jungles that help us get back to nature. Do you need rest and recuperation?

Passenger (Also see *Driving*.)

Quick Interpretation: Taking it easy; switching off

Popular Expressions: A passing acquaintance; Not pulling your weight; Taken for a ride

Passion

Quick Interpretation: Strong and/or amorous feelings

Popular Expression: A passion play

When you feel passionate in a dream, it indicates that you have intense feelings for something or someone. What are you so passionate about?

Passport

Quick Interpretation: Freedom; rite of passage; identification

Popular Expressions: Passport to freedom; Show your true colors

A passport gives you a sense of belonging to a larger group. It also represents freedom, as it allows you to cross borders and move around the world.

If you're about to embark on an overseas trip, or someone you know is about to leave, then of course the passport in your dream has a different connotation. It symbolizes what you need to do to get the journey started. Also consider that it could signify wish fulfillment. We all want to get away to exotic destinations from time to time, so the passport in your dream may indicate that you've given yourself permission to go.

Patience

Quick Interpretation: Something worth waiting for; being even-tempered

Popular Expressions: Patience is a virtue; Slow and steady wins the race; Wait your turn; Good things are worth the wait

When you're patient, it indicates that you're able to handle difficult or tedious situations without losing your temper or getting upset. What is worth waiting for?

Pea (Also see *Food.*)

Quick Interpretation: Similarity; inner nourishment; seed

Popular Expression: Like two peas in a pod; Pea brain

Peace

Quick Interpretation: Calmness; relaxation

Popular Expressions: Peace and quiet; The calm before the storm

When you feel peaceful, it indicates an experience of calm or quiet. You feel safe and secure. What has influenced this state of tranquillity?

Pearl (Also see *Jewelry; Oyster.*)

Quick Interpretation: Classic style; hidden treasure; bright ideas

Popular Expressions: Pearls of wisdom; Cast pearls before swine

Pen

Quick Interpretation: Power of words; expression; confinement (pen in)

Popular Expression: The pen is mightier than the sword

If you want to make sure that you don't forget something, you put it in ink. Does the pen in your dream indicate that you're ready to commit to something?

What are you doing with the pen in your dream? If you're writing with it, what do you wish to express? Or does the pen symbolize feeling confined or being penned in?

Most of us would love to have a wider circle of friends. Can it be that you're looking for a pen pal?

Pendulum

Quick Interpretation: Indecision; procrastination; precision

Popular Expression: The pendulum swings both ways

The pendulum is a karmic symbol. You know that what swings away will come back. It also symbolizes indecision because it keeps rocking back and forth. Consider that the pendulum may also indicate that you want to keep in time and not be out of step with others.

Penis (Also see *Genitals; Sex.*)

Quick Interpretation: Maleness; pleasure; jealousy

Popular Expression: Penis envy

Perfume

Quick Interpretation: Gift; attraction; covering up

Popular Expressions: Come up smelling like roses; On the scent; Follow your nose

When sweat is generated, we do everything we can to camouflage it with perfumes, aftershaves, and deodorants. In your dream, does the perfume symbolize a desire to hide your true self from others? Do you want to camouflage the way you feel? Do you want to convince people that everything is roses even though you don't feel that way inside?

What are you doing with the perfume in your dream? Are you putting it on yourself, is someone else putting it on you, or are you giving or receiving the perfume? Your answer will help you determine who's trying to camouflage whom.

Perfume can also signify desire and attraction. If you're splashing it on yourself in a dream, it may mean that you wish to break out of your shell, that you want your reputation to precede you *and* leave a mark. What fragrance do you use? If it's one you don't use in your waking life, perhaps you should try it.

Perfumes are usually precious, expensive liquids that have been bottled. Do you feel that you're full of precious, creative ides that are bottled up, and used only at the whim of others?

Pessimism

Quick Interpretation: Bad outcomes; hopelessness

Popular Expression: The worst is yet to come

When you feel pessimistic in a dream, you expect a situation (or situations) in your life to have the worst possible outcome. What do you feel you can't overcome? What has left you devoid of hope?

Petroleum (See *Gasoline.*)

Petticoat (See *Slip.*)

Photograph (Also see *Camera.*)

Quick Interpretation: Memories; moments in time; celebration

Popular Expressions: A photo finish; A photo opportunity; Picture this; The picture of health; Let's see what develops; A developing situation; Something that's negative

Check out who and what is in the photograph. This may be what you want to freeze in time and remember forever. Also consider whether you're seeing things clearly. If the photo is out of focus, it may indicate that your judgment is cloudy. If you see loved ones you miss or people from foreign shores in the photo, it may indicate a desire to reconnect or travel.

Physician (See *Doctor.*)

Piano (Also see *Music; Musical Instrument.*)

Quick Interpretation: Tolerance (ebony and ivory); being in tune; strung out

Popular Expressions: Off-key; Out of tune; Tickle the ivories

Picnic

Quick Interpretation: Outing; natural setting; feeling carefree

Popular Expressions: It's no picnic; One sandwich short of a picnic

Dreaming of a picnic symbolizes a desire to get out and enjoy nature. Do you need to get away from it all? In your dream, are you enjoying a picnic with family and friends, or strangers? This may indicate that you want to have fun with people you know or with new people.

To dream of a picnic also indicates feeling carefree. Do you feel free and unencumbered in your life at the moment, or is someone in your dream feeling that way? How do you respond?

Picture (See *Photograph.*)

Pig (Also see *Animal.*)

Quick Interpretation: Something forbidden; stubbornness; self-acceptance

Popular Expressions: Happy as a pig in mud; When pigs fly; Don't be a pig; Pig out; To hog something; Go hog-wild

Pill

Quick Interpretation: Relief; safety (contraception); illusion (placebo)

Popular Expressions: A bitter pill to swallow; Don't be a pill

We have pills to help treat everything today. Dreaming of a pill symbolizes a desire for a quick fix. What do you want a quick fix for—weight loss, financial success, or love? Is something being forced on you that you don't want to accept? Is it a bitter pill to swallow? Or perhaps your dream has something to do with your fertility, and your desire to get on or off the Pill.

Pillow

Quick Interpretation: Rest; comfort; playfulness (pillow fight)

Popular Expressions: Pillow talk; Sleep on it

Rest, taking it easy, and comfort are associated with this dream symbol. When you see a pillow in a dream, it may signify that you want a rest from dreaming! Some say that pillow talk is an enjoyable pastime. Whom do you want to share your pillow with so they can dream on it, too?

Piranha

Quick Interpretation: Strength in numbers; hidden danger; being bothered

Popular Expressions: Something eating away at you; Do a number on someone; Bite off more than you can chew

Why is it that in all the piranha films, everyone manages to fall overboard! Does the piranha in your dream signify that something is eating away at you, and if you don't do anything about it, you'll be totally consumed by it?

What are the piranhas doing in your dream? Are they attacking you or someone else? Do you feel that they're a symbol of hidden danger? That something is lurking behind the scenes ready to pounce? Are you the piranha, or is someone else?

The piranha is also a symbol of strength in numbers. Do you feel that you need the strength of a group behind you to get where you need to go, and that you must be vicious to get there? Or perhaps you feel you're being attacked by a group of people or situations—viciously!

We've all bitten off more than we can chew at times in our lives, and the only way out is to get our friends to lend a hand. The piranha is a great symbol of teamwork.

Pity

Quick Interpretation: Feeling like a victim; regret

Popular Expressions: Let's have a pity party; A town without pity

When you feel pity, it indicates that you see others or yourself as victims of circumstance. Whose circumstances are you judging in your dream? Do you feel that someone deserves better?

Pizza (Also see *Food.*)

Quick Interpretation: Eating on the run; variety; appetite

Popular Expressions: Eat humble pie; Pie in the sky; Pie in your eye; Slice of life; On the sauce; Something that's cheesy

The humble pizza has taken the world by storm. It started out as a means to put leftovers to good use, and ended up as fast food *and* a gourmand's delight. If you're making a pizza in your dream, it may symbolize a need to be resourceful and enterprising with your tools and talents. Is it a reminder that you can make something out of nothing?

If someone else is making the pizza, is that individual—or what they represent to you—a source of sustenance for body and mind? Is the pizza overflowing with delicious toppings, or is it quite modest with a scraping of sauce and a dash of cheese, indicating either abundance or lack? Perhaps the pizza represents a desire for a richer, more sumptuous experience over a modest, ascetic one.

Is your pizza cut into neat segments, or do you need to tear it apart with your hands? This may indicate a desire for structure, or a belief that the only way to solve a dilemma is to roll up your sleeves and dive right in.

Do you gobble up the pizza in your dream and get indigestion, or do you only eat a few pieces, well aware of the consequences if you eat too much? This is a great barometer of your intuition. It can also reveal the strength of your willpower. Are you resisting the temptation to eat a succulent pizza because you're on a diet?

Finally, what type of pizza is it? What do you think it indicates? For example, if you dream of a pizza with the works, does it mean that you're looking for an all-encompassing experience? If the pizza is delivered, who brought it to you?

Plastic Surgery (See *Cosmetic Surgery.*)

Play (Also see *Toy.*)

Quick Interpretation: Acting up; escapism; rehearsal

Popular Expressions: Act the part; Get in on the act; Play hard to get

If you don't want to give in too easy or be too available, you play hard to get. Perhaps you need to be less accessible.

Are you playing in your dream, or do you dream of a play? Clearly, if you're playing in your dream, it indicates a joyful and uplifting (light) time in your life. Rejoice! If someone else is playing in your dream, how do you feel about it? Do you feel light and carefree, or do you get frustrated, wishing they would stop fooling around and get serious?

Are you watching a play in your dream, or are you part of a play? If you're watching a play, who are the characters? Are they people you know? Do you feel that they're acting up? If you dream you're in a play, does it symbolize a desire for escapism, or is it a rehearsal for a play you must act in, in your waking life? Is your subconscious asking you to act the part?

Dreaming of a play may also indicate that you want to take part in a new project or adventure—that is, get in on the act. Or perhaps you don't want to and you'd prefer to play it safe.

Pleasure

Quick Interpretation: Gratification; enjoyment

Popular Expressions: No pleasure without pain; It's my pleasure

When you experience pleasure in a dream, it indicates that your senses are gratified. What is the source of your gratification?

Poem

Quick Interpretation: Expression; metaphors; something thought-provoking

Popular Expressions: Without rhyme or reason; Chapter and verse

Traditional poems are so tight and bright, so neat and tidy. They symbolize a desire to articulate your feelings. Do you need to express yourself differently? Are you looking for some rhyme and reason to what you say or to what people are telling you?

Poison

Quick Interpretation: Termination; pollution; gossip (poisoned thoughts)

Popular Expressions: Name your poison; One man's meat is another man's poison; Poison-pen letters; A bitter pill to swallow

Dreaming of poison indicates that you should take care with what you swallow. Does the poison signify that you don't want to accept things with blind faith?

There are poison-pen letters and poisonous sentiments. The symbol of poison may indicate that you should take care with your words.

Poker (Also see *Cards; Gambling.*)

Quick Interpretation: Chance; hidden feelings; good fortune

Popular Expressions: A poker face; As stiff as a poker; Taking a gamble; Not in the cards; Not the sharpest card in the deck; To ace something; Jack-of-all-trades; Diamond in the rough; Being dealt a good hand; Hands down; Calling a spade a spade; Let's make a deal

Police

Quick Interpretation: Dropping the ball; Being on guard; something outlawed; security

Popular Expressions: Cop a feel; Cop out; His word is law; Law and order; To the letter of the law

This symbol requires a book all its own. It's a subject bigger than *Ben Hur,* because our feelings about people in authority are subject to constant change, day to day, situation to situation.

When you're in danger or stuck in a predicament, seeing a person in a police uniform is a blessing. But when you're traveling ten miles over the speed limit and talking on your cell phone without your seat belt on, the last thing you want to see is a police car pulling up behind you.

How do you respond to the person in uniform in your dream? Do you feel safe and protected, or are you frightened or intimidated?

Is your freedom in jeopardy? Are you the police officer in your dream, indicating a desire to command more respect—or a need to visibly display your authority and officially announce that you hold a position of power?

Is someone you know in a police uniform? Do they have power or authority over you? Is this person a hindrance or a help?

What is the police officer doing in your dream? Making your life easier? Or unnecessarily holding you up—holding you hostage for something that has nothing to do with you?

Of course, if you're a member of that honorable profession, or related to someone who is, then there's a whole different set of questions you need to ask. The symbol takes on an immediate and personal significance, and you must consider the dangers and stress associated with the job.

When they grow up, a lot of kids want to be police officers, to have a car that can go through red lights, to speed down the highway with the siren blasting, and to carry a gun. Does the police officer in your dream signify that you wish to break all the rules and get paid for it?

Politician (Also see *Election.*)

Quick Interpretation: Lust for power; expediency; being voted in

Popular Expressions: Vote of confidence; Old windbag; Power play; Elect to do something

The worst thing about politicians is that they get elected! What is the politician doing in your dream? Is it someone you know? How do you feel about the politician? Are they giving you advice on a particular issue, indicating trust, or are they annoying you with rhetoric? If it's a politician you know, what do they represent to you? Look at the context of the dream to determine how you feel and what you think about such character traits.

A politician can symbolize a lust for power. Is this what the politician represents in your dream? Are you or is someone else in your dream lusting for power, indicating a desire for respect and acknowledgment?

If someone is in a situation that you believe is cut-and-dried but they won't give you a straight answer, then the politician may indicate that they're playing politics with you.

Pollution (Also see *Fog; Smog.*)

Quick Interpretation: Damage; spoilage; creating awareness

Popular Expressions: Where there's smoke, there's fire; Smell a rat

We are the only animals that pollute. Every other creature that inhabits this planet leaves a mess, but there's always something that benefits from it. Does the pollution in your dream indicate that you've created a mess? Or are you living in the mess that someone else has created? Is the dream a message—that is, can the mess be avoided if people think more consciously? Who is being thoughtless? Is someone in your space, or are you in someone else's space?

If you live in a big city and dream of pollution, is it time to get out of the city and into nature for a breath of fresh air?

If you already live in the country, the pollution may be a warning, particularly if you're considering a business venture. If you are, consider what the cost on the natural environment could be.

We all need to be environmentally conscious. Is your dream telling you to get out there and join a "green" group?

Pornography (See *Sex; X-Rated.*)

Positive Feelings

Quick Interpretation: Confidence; happy state of mind

Popular Expressions: Happy days are here again; The best is yet to come

When you feel positive in a dream, it indicates a confident and favorable state of mind. What has removed the doubt from your mind?

Post Office (Also see *Envelope; Letter.*)

Quick Interpretation: Message; networking

Popular Expressions: Play post office; The letter of the law; Red-letter day; The check is in the mail; Stamp of approval; Put a stamp on it; To stamp something out

With the advent of e-mail, the number of personal letters to go via snail mail has decreased. Is the post office in your dream a symbol of changing times and changing needs?

The post office in your dream may also indicate a desire to network. You may have something to offer other people, and you trust the post office to deliver your message professionally.

If you need to sort things out in your life—that is, put them where they belong, then you may dream of a post office, as each item that goes through that facility is individually sorted.

Often things can get out of hand when you share a good idea with others. Before you realize it, others have taken over and you're left out in the cold. If you want to put a stamp on your original thoughts, then there's no better place to do it than in a post office.

Pot (See *Grass; Marijuana.*)

Potato (Also see *Food.*)

Quick Interpretation: Beneath the surface; versatility

Popular Expressions: Drop something like a hot potato; Couch potato; Go underground

Poverty (Also see *Slum*.)

Quick Interpretation: Lack; unfortunate circumstances; relinquishing material wealth

Popular Expressions: Beg to differ; From rags to riches; Poor little rich boy (or girl)

There's always someone worse off than you. Dreaming of poverty may remind you to count your blessings. Think of all the things you have in your life to be grateful for.

Praise

Quick Interpretation: Favorable traits; compliments

Popular Expressions: Being showered with praise; Praise the Lord; Damned with faint praise

When people shower you with praise, it indicates that your most favorable aspects or traits are recognized by others. People think highly of you. Do you need compliments to feel good about yourself, or is it water off a duck's back?

Pregnancy (Also see *Birth*.)

Quick Interpretation: Giving birth to ideas; opportunity; harboring desires

Popular Expressions: A pregnant pause; The mother lode; Full of life; Born again

You can't be half pregnant. It's all or nothing. Therefore, dreaming of pregnancy signifies commitment to a situation once the first step has been taken.

If you dream you're pregnant, ask yourself if it's wish fulfillment. Are you hoping to get pregnant? Or does it symbolize a desire to give birth to a creative project? Are you putting lots of time and energy into a project at the moment? How you feel about the pregnancy will help you determine how you feel about the project.

The pregnancy may also represent an aspect of yourself that you hope to give birth to. Look at where you are and who you're with in the dream to determine what aspect this may be.

Pregnancy is also a symbol of opportunity. Are new opportunities presenting themselves in your life? Or if you dream that someone else is pregnant, do you feel that it represents a new opportunity opening up in their life?

If you know in your heart how a situation is going to work out, or you're aware of how things are going to unfold for you, then you may see yourself or the individual you're working with pregnant—basically, you can see the shape of things to come.

Priest

Quick Interpretation: Authority; being an intermediary; dedication

Popular Expressions: In the lap of God; For heaven's sake; A man of the cloth; To minister to someone; A vow of silence

Whatever your interpretation or feelings about priests, it's accepted that they're in the business of promoting religion. Do you want to promote your spiritual beliefs?

What is the priest doing in your dream? Is he a symbol of authority, perhaps indicating a desire for direction in your life at the moment? What are you being told to do or take notice of?

A priest can also signify mediation. Who's the priest in your dream? Is it you? Who are you mediating between? How do you feel about it? If someone else is the priest, is he mediating for you? Perhaps you feel you need someone to help you solve a pressing problem in your life.

To be a priest, you must take certain vows. Therefore, is the priest in your dream a symbol of upholding certain values?

We've all been guilty of taking things for granted at times. Does the priest in your dream indicate that it's time to count your blessings and be grateful for where you are?

Prison (See *Jail.*)

Prostitute

Quick Interpretation: Desire; lust; personal choice

Popular Expressions: Put something to bed; No free rides; Make your bed and lie in it; Call girl; A woman of ill repute

It's the oldest profession of all—and the operative word is *profession*, the act of hiring an individual to provide a service.

Are you the prostitute, or is the prostitute in the dream a representation of you? Explore any emotions or feelings that come up. Do you feel desirable, attractive, and sensual? Do you feel joy because someone is willing to pay a price to be intimate with you?

If the experience isn't enjoyable, does it indicate that you feel limited? Do you feel that you're in a position where you're forced to undertake certain tasks that you don't really want to do, but have to in order to survive?

Is someone else the prostitute? Do you feel that this person can be bought? Can you trust this person? Do you feel that they may betray you to the highest bidder? Do you approve of the person's choice to be a prostitute, perhaps signifying a desire you have for that person to explore their most intimate talents? Do you encourage them to get out there and take risks?

Do you pay a prostitute to service you in your dream? Do you feel that you have to pay someone to give you attention? Do you believe that people will only associate with you if you give them something in return? Or can it be that you simply want to have a good time with someone without committing to a long-term relationship?

If you have a huge desire to complete tasks that are 90 percent done, you may see a lady of the night in your dreams, as you know it's time to put things to bed.

Protection

Quick Interpretation: Safety; shield

Popular Expressions: Safety in numbers; Angel on my shoulder

When you feel protected in a dream, you know you're shielded from adversity. What has made you feel invulnerable?

Protest (Also see *Activist; Riot.*)

Quick Interpretation: Resistance against the status quo; feeling insulted; self-righteousness

Popular Expressions: Being read the riot act; Protest too much; Protest march

It seems that no matter what you do, someone will protest against it. Even the quest to save beautiful and lush rain forests has its protestors. This symbol clearly suggests that there are always two sides to even the most righteous cause. Should you be considering someone else's feelings even though you know you're right?

What are you (or someone else) protesting in your dream? Is it the status quo, indicating a desire to overthrow existing conditions? Or are you protesting *for* something such as peace or equal rights?

Does the protest in your dream signify that you feel insulted? Who or what has offended you? Or is someone protesting against a perceived offense of yours?

Protesting can also symbolize self-righteousness. What do you feel that you (or the person protesting in your dream) are in the right about? Are you becoming zealous or fanatical about something?

It may also symbolize hidden guilt. What are you protesting too loudly about?

Psychic

Quick Interpretation: Looking into the future; trust in the opinion of others; impatience

Popular Expressions: Heaven sent; The slings and arrows of outrageous fortune; Read someone's mind

There aren't too many people who haven't consulted a psychic just to check on how things are going to end up. Who is the person in your dream you believe will have an answer for you? Is the answer profound and easy to understand, or is it in parables that require the nose of Sherlock Holmes and the brain of Agatha Christie to work out? Do you like what you're told about your future, or are you frightened by it? Is the outcome something you know in your heart, with the dream simply reinforcing this knowledge?

What divination tool does the psychic use—a crystal ball, bumps on your head or lines on your hands, Tarot cards? Perhaps this form of divination has some interesting answers for you if you care to find out more about it.

Seeing a psychic can also signify wish fulfillment. Have you been pondering whether or not to seek out a medium to gain insights that will help you determine a direction for your future? You may even be looking for a mentor.

Puppet

Quick Interpretation: Control; lack of will; entertainment

Popular Expressions: Like a puppet on a string; Holding the strings; Left hanging

Is there anything worse than waiting for someone to make up their mind? You've done the hard work, put in the effort, and all you want is a decision. Does the puppet in your dream symbolize that you've been left hanging?

What are you doing with the puppet in your dream? Is it a symbol of control? Consider the type of puppet it is to determine what you want to control in your life. The puppet may be you. Who's pulling your strings? Perhaps it suggests a lack of will. Do you let other people run your life? How do you feel about it?

If the puppet represents someone else, do you feel that you have too much control over this person's life? Do you treat this person like a puppet on a string? The puppet may also symbolize entertainment. Are you being entertained in your dream, or is someone entertaining you?

Can it be that you feel someone is setting a trap for you, or would you like to ambush someone you're suspicious of? The puppet in your dream may indicate that they're giving you (or you're giving them) enough rope to hang yourself (or them) on?

Purse (Also see *Wallet.*)

Quick Interpretation: Transformation; winnings; generosity (open purse)

Popular Expressions: You can't make a silk purse from a sow's ear; Hold the purse strings; Tighten/loosen the purse strings

Puzzle

Quick Interpretation: Not obvious; uncertain; complicated

Popular Expressions: Don't miss a trick; Brainteaser; Something that's puzzling

Aren't dreams puzzling enough? Why would you want to dream of a puzzle? Is your desire to work things out piece by piece in your life taking up too much of your time?

What kind of puzzle do you dream of—a jigsaw puzzle, a crossword puzzle, or a brainteaser? Who's trying to solve the puzzle? Perhaps it's a symbol of uncertainty, and the dream indicates that you're working through it. It may also indicate that something in your life isn't obvious, that it needs to be thought through before you can determine its meaning.

Dreaming of a puzzle also suggests dealing with something that's complicated. How do you feel about the puzzle in your dream? Are you up for the challenge, or do you feel overwhelmed? If someone else is working through the puzzle in your dream, is it your puzzle or theirs? If they're working through your puzzle, this may be the person who can help you sort through a complicated issue in your life. You may believe that they have the final piece of the puzzle.

Pyramid

Quick Interpretation: Mystery; great achievements; timelessness

Popular Expressions: Old as the hills; If only the walls could speak

How did they build the pyramids? No matter how many documentaries have been made, no one knows how the Egyptians did it.

Pyramids symbolize extraordinary creative feats. Is the pyramid in your dream new and fully functional, or is it ravaged by the passage of time? If new, it may indicate that you need to go back in time to unravel a mystery that you're presently dealing with. If it's old and ravaged, it could signify that outward appearances aren't important, your true self is what counts, and what you believe in will stand the test of time.

If you feel that the symbol is work related, do you feel that you're being treated like a slave—that is, even though your contribution is enormous, you're not being acknowledged?

The pyramids are steeped in mystery. Does the pyramid in your dream symbolize a desire to develop your mystical side, enabling you to get in touch with your immortality? For women, it may relate to a desire to become more fertile—a desire to become a "mummy"!

When you climb a pyramid, you recognize that the farther up you get, the less of it there is. Perhaps the pyramid in your dream signifies that the further you get on your spiritual path, the more isolated it becomes—and ultimately it's just you.

Quarrel (Also see *Fight.*)

Quick Interpretation: Inner debates; difference of opinion; letting off steam

Popular Expressions: Breathe fire; Come out fighting

Queen (Also see *King; Monarchy; Palace.*)

Quick Interpretation: Regalness; duty; fertility

Popular Expressions: To live like a queen; Queen for a day

Most of us would like to live like royalty, but perhaps just for one day, given the pressure and focus on royal families. Could it be that you want all the privileges associated with being a queen without the responsibility?

Who is the queen in your dream? Is it you or someone you know? If it's you, do you feel regal? Or do you think the person who's the queen is regal? What have you (or the other person) done in your (or their) life to deserve such recognition? What do you feel you (or they) are being recognized for?

Queen is also a widely used word for a gay male. Do you need to expose the feminine side of yourself? Or is it time for you to come out of the closest?

A queen is expected to bear a lot of responsibility. What do you feel you must bear responsibility for in your life? Or do you feel that the person who's the queen is responsible for your life? How do you feel about it?

Do you see the queen as a symbol for having to keep up appearances? Would you like to be more like this in your own life, or do you feel there isn't anything worse than having to watch everything you do and say? Also consider the queen as a symbol of fertility. Are things in your life conducive to growth right now? Is it time to get productive?

Perhaps the queen and what her reign represents indicates how you want to live your life. For example, if you dream of Queen Victoria, do you wish to live a life of high morals and prudish behavior? Or if you dream of Elizabeth I, are you more interested in a life of courage and expansion?

Quicksand

Quick Interpretation: Unsupported; going under; feeling suffocated

Popular Expressions: Stick-in-the-mud; Sink or swim

If you ever felt that you were being stifled, suffocated, or swallowed up by circumstances, then quicksand is the perfect symbol to illustrate this. Also consider that you may feel unsupported and ungrounded at the moment, so it's time to build solid foundations.

Quilt

Quick Interpretation: Warmth; kinship; bonding

Popular Expressions: All sewn up; A patchwork quilt; Quilting bee

Quiz (Also see *Examination.*)

Quick Interpretation: Being tested; investigation; distrust

Popular Expressions: Call into question; In the spotlight; Under the gun; Test one's mettle; Put to the test

Race

Quick Interpretation: Competition; ethnic background; athleticism

Popular Expressions: The rat race; One-horse race; Race against time; A race to the finish; Race relations; Run for your life

Why is it that we spend lots of time doing the things we least like doing? Does the race in your dream symbolize that it's time to get out of the rat race?

What kind of race is it, and who are you racing against? Why do you feel you have to compete with this person? Are you winning or losing the race? This may indicate how you feel about a competitive situation in your life at present.

If you're not running the race, who is? Are you backing a particular player? Whom are you backing? Think about the race in relation to ethnic background. Is there a war of the "races" taking place?

A race also symbolizes athleticism. Do you feel athletic? Or is someone in your dream inspiring you to be so?

If you dream of a running race, a marathon in particular, does it symbolize patience—that is, you know that everything will work out in the long run? Or do you dream of a 100-meter sprint, perhaps indicating that you want to get things over and done with quickly.

Radio

Quick Interpretation: Broadcasting; need to listen; entertainment

Popular Expressions: In tune; On the same wavelength; Make waves

What are you listening to on the radio? What do you need to hear? Whom do you want to be in tune with? Or maybe it's time to switch off from outside influences.

Raffle (Also see *Gambling.*)

Quick Interpretation: Taking chances; fund-raising

Popular Expressions: A guessing game; Fall into your lap; The luck of the draw

Rain (Also see *Storm.*)

Quick Interpretation: Relief; release; disappointment

Popular Expressions: As right as rain; Rain or shine; Rain on someone's parade; You're all wet; Shower someone with gifts or praise

Why is that humans only want to get wet when they're half naked? Put on a swimsuit and we don't care how wet we get, but if we're fully clothed, we scurry around as though bricks are falling from the sky. Does the rain in your dream make you feel vulnerable, as though you've been caught unprepared and exposed to the elements? Or is the rain a metaphor for tears, and you wake up feeling refreshed and at ease, as though it has helped you release the grief associated with past pain?

Is someone else caught in the rain in your dream? Are they unprepared, or do they have an umbrella and raincoat with them, indicating that they're forward thinkers?

The rain may also indicate that you should be saving more money and preparing for a rainy day. Do you have to be more organized for the future?

If a lot of people are caught in a downpour in your dream, does this symbolize that others are raining on your parade? Do you often feel that your ideas and/or moments of adulation and attention are ripped away by others?

Rain may also be a symbol for sweat. What task is so arduous that it's making you perspire?

Rainbow

Quick Interpretation: Good fortune; enlightenment; celebration

Popular Expressions: A pot of gold at the end of a rainbow; Seeing someone's true colors

I haven't met anyone who doesn't feel uplifted and charged after a rainbow dream.

The rainbow symbolizes showing your true colors, experiencing life as you really are. Do you want people to see your true colors? Do you want to see the world's, or someone else's, true colors?

Dreaming of a rainbow may signify the end of a dark, stormy period, and the beginning of something new that's calm and sunny. The rainbow may be a bridge between what was and what is.

Do you associate the rainbow in your dream with a feeling of abundance after a lot of hard work and dedication? Are you determined to find the pot of gold at the end of the rainbow? A rainbow can also indicate promise; if you reach the end of a rainbow (solve a problem), your reward is a pot of gold.

There are many songs about rainbows, and one of the most popular speaks of utopia, a place where your dreams come true. Does the rainbow in your dream represent a desire to be somewhere that's calm and serene, where you can meet your highest aspirations?

Scientists may have a rational explanation for rainbows, but the dreamer in us knows there's much more to this exquisite show of color.

Rat

Quick Interpretation: Deception; survival; peskiness

Popular Expressions: Rat on someone; Smell a rat; Rat race

It's funny—wherever humans go, rats follow. Six rats even took part in one of the space-shuttle missions. Add a furry tail to a rat's body and you get a squirrel. But because the rat has a long, slimy tail, spreads disease, and lives in squalor rather than trees, we dislike it.

If you see a rat in a dream, perhaps someone in your life is acting dishonorably and without integrity. Why is this person behaving like a rat? Is it because of circumstance or environment?

Rats spread disease only because they live in sewers. Similarly, the person who represents a rat in your dream may not be acting with integrity because they simply don't know any better. Perhaps you need to explain to them how you feel about what they're doing to you.

Does the rat signify adaptability? Rats can survive anywhere, and within a few generations they become immune to most poisons. The rat in your dream may suggest that you, too, will overcome all obstacles in your path. If someone you know represents the rat, perhaps they have character traits that you need to adopt to survive. For example, if you dream of someone who's notoriously tight with money and they're with a rat, perhaps you want to be more like this person and spend less money.

You may dream of rats if you feel someone is betraying you or gossiping about you—in essence, the person is "ratting" on you.

Rats are used for testing in most laboratories; they (along with mice) are the creatures most experimented on in the world. Do you feel that you're under a microscope? Is someone pushing your buttons and playing with your feelings and emotions just to see how you'll react?

Rationality

Quick Interpretation: Reason; understanding

When you're in a rational state of mind, it indicates that you're acting or thinking with reason or understanding. Why do things seem so logical to you?

Reassurance

Quick Interpretation: Confidence; relief

When you're reassured, it indicates that your confidence has been restored; you're relieved of anxiety and/or worry. What or who has made you feel supported?

Refugee

Quick Interpretation: Eviction; survival; seeking acceptance

Popular Expressions: Voting with your feet; Fresh pastures; Man without a country

On the surface, a refugee appears to be a sad and arduous symbol. However, it can also signify that it's time to leave everything that represented who you were to move on to another experience. The symbol indicates that drastic steps need to be taken and everything abandoned for you to reinvent your life.

Relaxation

Quick Interpretation: Peace; ease

Popular Expressions: Peace and quiet; Cool, calm, and collected

When you feel relaxed, it indicates that you're at ease and feel unrestricted. Why do you feel so cool, calm, and collected?

Religion (See *Worship.*)

Reptile (See *Alligator; Anaconda; Snake.*)

Resentment

Quick Interpretation: Ill feelings; lack of forgiveness

Popular Expressions: Talk behind someone's back; Ill will

Feeling resentful indicates that you harbor ill feelings toward someone or something due to insult or injury. Who offended you in your dream? What do you feel can't be forgiven?

Respectability

Quick Interpretation: High esteem; Impeccability

To feel respected indicates that you feel highly regarded. What is it about yourself that you feel deserves respect?

Rest Room (See *Toilet.*)

Retirement

Quick Interpretation: Reward; redundancy; withdrawal

Popular Expressions: Time to call it a day; Out of circulation; Over-the-hill; The end of the road; Being put out to pasture

Why is it that when we finally get our acts together and know everything about our professions, we're put out to pasture? Dreaming of retirement may indicate that you have so much to offer but can't get anyone's attention. It may also signify that it's time for a well-earned rest. It's important to explore the emotions associated with the dream. Are you joyful or sad about the retirement?

Reunion (Also see *School.*)

Quick Interpretation: Reconnection; reuniting; celebration

Popular Expressions: The old school; School of hard knocks; Having a ball

Don't you wish you were someone who wrote down and kept phone numbers? It would make reunions so much easier. How do you feel about the reunion in your dream? Do you feel apprehensive or excited about meeting people from your past? Or do you feel proud because you know that you look better and have achieved more than anyone else in your class? Or is it the opposite, and it makes you feel like a failure, as you believe that you've underachieved.

When you dream of a reunion, it's important to ask yourself whom you would like to see from your past. What is it about your past that you want to experience again?

Ribbon

Quick Interpretation: Prize; decoration; reminder

Popular Expressions: Win a gold ribbon; Show your true colors

Ribbons represent your feelings. The brighter the ribbon, the happier the mind. The ribbon can also be a symbol of achievement or acknowledgment. If you're wearing a ribbon on your lapel, it may symbolize what you believe in and who you support. Does it indicate a desire to be more involved in social issues?

Rice (See *Food.*)

Rifle (Also see *Gun.*)

Quick Interpretation: Protect; attack; search

Popular Expressions: Rifle through something; The big guns; Shoot to kill; A killing spree; Aim and fire; Set your sights on something

Ring (Also see *Bride/Bridegroom; Marriage.*)

Quick Interpretation: Commitment; ownership; calling someone up

Popular Expressions: Call into question; Till death do us part

A ring publicly announces that you're committed in some way. Perhaps dreaming of a ring indicates that you want a commitment from someone.

Riot (Also see *Protest.*)

Quick Interpretation: Uncontrollable emotion; overthrowing oppression; disregard for law and order

Popular Expressions: Read the riot act; A laugh riot

The big question is, what caused the riot? The answer to this may be more important than the riot itself, as riots don't occur without a reason. Who's rioting in your dream? Are you taking part in the riots or standing back watching? If you're involved, why do you need to take such desperate action? Is something in your life being thwarted by uncontrollable emotion?

A riot also symbolizes overthrowing oppression. Are you overthrowing something or someone that you feel has had an oppressive influence on your life?

If other people are rioting in your dream, what are they rioting about, and how do you feel about it? Rioting is an act of defiance. Is it time to take things into your own hands regarding a certain matter in your life, or do you feel that taking things into your own hands will only make matters worse?

The worst thing about a riot is being an innocent bystander while one is taking place. Do you feel that you're caught up in situations or events that have nothing to do with you?

Ritual

Quick Interpretation: Tradition; commemoration

Popular Expressions: Habit-forming; Old habits die hard

A ritual is something we use to protect ourselves or to create something for ourselves. Does the ritual in your dream indicate that you're becoming superstitious, or are you hedging your bet and doing it just in case it might work?

River (Also see *Water.*)

Quick Interpretation: Transformation; flow; source

Popular Expressions: Sell someone down the river; Cry me a river; Bank on something

Robot

Quick Interpretation: Control; repetition; efficiency

Popular Expressions: Slave labor; Doing something by rote

Wouldn't it be wonderful if you could really get a robot to do everything for you? Chores would be a thing of the past. Does the robot in your dream symbolize freedom from the mundane tasks that you have to perform day to day?

To dream of a robot suggests control. Are you controlling or trying to control the robot in your dream? If the robot represents your life, how well do you feel you're controlling your life at the moment. If someone else is controlling the robot, do you feel that they're controlling your life?

A robot is also associated with repetition. What about your life do you feel is robotic and predictable? Or does the robot symbolize efficiency—getting things done mechanically and in an orderly fashion?

Perhaps the robot in your dream signifies that you have no passion for the tasks or activities you're involved in; you're just going through the motions.

Rock

Quick Interpretation: Strength; reliability; being disturbed

Popular Expressions: Solid as a rock; On the rocks; Between a rock and a hard place

There isn't anything like standing on a rock to make you feel secure, as you have something solid under your feet. Are you looking for strong foundations or something powerful to build upon?

Rocket

Quick Interpretation: Inspiration; exploration; probing

Popular Expressions: Put a rocket under someone; It's not rocket science; Out of this world

How many times in life have individuals taken a simple task or concept and turned it into a complicated situation? Does the rocket in your dream indicate that it need not be rocket science in order to work properly?

Are you on a rocket that's about to blast off in your dream, perhaps indicating that something in your life is about to take off? What project or endeavor do you hope will make a big hit?

Dreaming of a rocket also suggests inspiration. If you're *in* the rocket, do you feel inspired, or if you're looking at the rocket, do you feel that the inspiration is outside you? Look at who is in the rocket to determine who or what inspires you.

A rocket also signifies exploration and extending your boundaries. Is it time to explore a job or relationship and step outside your comfort zone?

Also consider whether the rocket symbolizes something in your life that looks difficult and needs to be recalculated so you can work out a new angle on it.

Roller Coaster

Quick Interpretation: Extreme behavior (highs and lows); amusement; finding pleasure in fear

Popular Expressions: On the up-and-up; Go along for the ride; A bumpy ride

Why is it that we pay to go on roller coasters, but when life is like a roller coaster, all we want to do is get off? Does the roller coaster in your dream indicate that you don't mind the ups and downs as long as you know they'll be short lived?

Roof (Also see *House.*)

Quick Interpretation: Protection; summit; capping things off

Popular Expressions: Hit the roof; Raise the roof; It's on the house; Blow your top; Get on top of things

We mere humans often experience anger, and for some reason this is referred to as "hitting the roof." What has caused you to blow your top? Dreaming of a roof may also mean that you want to get on top of things and see things from a different perspective with no walls to bind you.

Rooster (Also see *Animal; Bird.*)

Quick Interpretation: Virility; wake-up call; alarm

Popular Expressions: Something to crow about; Rule the roost

Rope

Quick Interpretation: Binding; security; being twisted

Popular Expressions: At the end of your rope; Know the ropes; Show someone the ropes

If the rope in your dream anchors you, it may symbolize strength and security. Or perhaps you hope someone will fail because you've given them enough rope to hang themselves with.

Rose (Also see *Flower.*)

Quick Interpretation: Affection; feeling uplifted; cheerful situations

Popular Expressions: Life is a bed of roses; Stop and smell the roses; The last rose of summer

Rubbish (See *Garbage.*)

Rug (Also see *Blanket; Carpet.*)

Quick Interpretation: Covering; toupee; warmth

Popular Expressions: Pull the rug out from under you; Lie like a rug; Cut the rug

Run (Also see *Chase; Race.*)

Quick Interpretation: Exercise; escape; endurance

Popular Expressions: On the run; Run the show

Saddle

Quick Interpretation: Control; burden; pressure

Popular Expressions: Back in the saddle; Be saddled with; Get off your high horse

When you're in the saddle, you mean business. Does the saddle in your dream symbolize that it's time to get things started, to move forward in your life?

Or have you been a bit uppity lately? Is it time to get off your high horse?

Sadness

Quick Interpretation: Loss; lack

Popular Expressions: Sad sack; Turn that frown around; Down in the dumps

When you feel sad, it invariably indicates that you're focused on loss in your life and feel less spirited. What didn't you want to lose in your dream? Do you feel that there's something missing from your life?

Safety

Quick Interpretation: Protection; security

Popular Expression: Safety in numbers; Rather be safe than sorry

When you feel safe, it indicates that you feel secure and nothing can ruffle your feathers. What gives you the feeling that you have the resources to handle all challenges?

Sailing (Also see *Boat; Ship; Yacht.*)

Quick Interpretation: Freedom; being blown away; ease of movement

Popular Expressions: Make sail; That ship has sailed; Smooth sailing; Get wind of something

Sailing implies freedom and buoyancy. What do you want to sail away from? What do you want to get wind of? Are you experiencing rough seas, or is it smooth sailing? Think about this in relation to your state of mind.

Sale (See *Auction.*)

Sales (See *Selling.*)

Salt

Quick Interpretation: Dependability; spicing things up; aggravation

Popular Expressions: Salt of the earth; Take it with a grain of salt; To salt something away

Although salt is critical for survival, too much salt can kill you. Does the salt in your dream indicate that you're overindulging without considering the consequences? Is it time for you to be more charitable and understanding, as you know you can be the salt of the earth?

Sand (Also see *Beach; Quicksand.*)

Quick Interpretation: Passing of time; impermanence; being worn down

Popular Expressions: The sands of time; Sand something down; Bury your head in the sand

When things move and shift in your life, it's not uncommon to see sand in a dream. Sand symbolizes the nomadic spirit. Is someone in your dream burying his or her head in the sand, refusing to take notice of what's going on around them? Or is the sand symbolic of a challenging situation at hand, where things have to be smoothed out and "sanded"?

Scale

Quick Interpretation: Balance; something fishy; repetitive

Popular Expressions: In the balance; Strike a balance; Tip the scales

We're all searching for balance in our lives. We don't want to be too hot or too cold, too passionate or too indifferent. Dreaming of scales may signify a desire to get on an even keel. Scales may also indicate that you want to climb up and achieve, perhaps scale a mountain or a wall. Also consider that you may want to put something into its true perspective in relation to its surroundings—meaning that you're measuring everything to scale.

Scar

Quick Interpretation: Healing; permanent reminder; isolation

Popular Expressions: Make your mark; Leave a lasting impression

If you're constantly manufacturing new skin, and the birthday suit you wore yesterday is different from the one you have on today, why do scars persist? The memory of what caused the scar must be so powerful. Does the scar in your dream indicate that although the past has gone, for some reason you don't want to let go? Instead, perhaps you want a constant reminder of what happened.

Scent (See *Aromatherapy; Perfume.*)

School (Also see *Academy; Graduation; Reunion.*)

Quick Interpretation: Knowledge; conformity; friendship

Popular Expressions: The old school; The school of hard knocks; Live and learn; Can't teach an old dog new tricks

If you asked 1,000 people what this symbol means, you'd get 1,000 different responses. What are your memories of school? Are they happy-go-lucky? Were you a successful jock who excelled at sports, a genius in the classroom, and in with the right crowd? Or were you bullied from the first day, last in every race, and could never recall what year Columbus stumbled across America?

Your school-day memories are important because they may help you understand why the symbol of school appears in your dream. Is something happening in your life that's reminiscent of your school days? Or are you reliving an incident from those times that had a huge impact on you?

If you're a teacher, it may symbolize challenge and dedication, or indifference, depending on whether you see your job as a vocation or a means to an end. But the most obvious association is that school is a place of learning. Are you learning something new in life?

If you're back at school with people you didn't attend school with but who are in your life now, is there anything you'd like them to learn from you, or are they teaching you something?

Is there a teacher in your dream? Who is the teacher and whom are they teaching? Do you get the feeling that it's time to check the facts and circumstances of your life? Is there a situation in your life that requires further study or investigation before you jump in?

If you're the teacher in the dream, what do you want others to learn from you, see in you, or understand about you? If you're not the teacher, who's sharing information with you? Does it empower or offend you?

What are you being taught? Are you traveling the world in a geography class? Are you moving through the ages in a history class? Or are you totally confused in an algebra class?

The symbol of school may also suggest that it's time for you to stop collecting information about the world and simply live in it.

Scissors

Quick Interpretation: Severance; ceremony; creativity

Popular Expressions: Cut corners; Can't cut it; Cut-and-dried; Cut a rug; A cutting remark; Be snippy with someone

There's no better way to separate something than with a pair of scissors. What do you want to cut free from your life?

What are you doing with the scissors in your dream? Are you using them to cut something? What do you want to cut? If the scissors symbolize severance to you, then what you're cutting is what you want to sever from your life.

Scissors also imply ceremony. Do the scissors in your dream signify the opening of something new in your life, or do they symbolize the completion of a creative project? Scissors may also represent creativity. Are you creating something with the scissors in your dream?

There are times when we all want to take shortcuts and cut corners to complete a task. Do the scissors in your dream indicate that you feel you haven't got a minute to waste, or that you must complete a task at all costs?

Scrapbook

Quick Interpretation: Preservation of memories; private mementos; acknowledgment

Popular Expression: To scrap something

We keep scrapbooks to remind us of achievements or a series of events. Is someone in your dream living in the past? Are you or is someone else proud of the book?

Perhaps the scrapbook indicates that you're over a situation and it's time to let go—in other words, it's time to scrap it.

Sculpture

Quick Interpretation: Artistic; permanent; seeing things from all angles

Popular Expressions: A chip off the old block; To chip away at something; Mold someone in your image

If there was ever a symbol of one's ability to make something out of nothing, it would be a sculpture. Imagine the rock that became the Venus de Milo. Wouldn't you have loved to have seen that hunk of marble?

What type of sculpture do you see in your dream? Whatever the sculpture is of, think of it in relation to wanting to keep something in a static state. A sculpture can symbolize a desire to capture a moment in time. What do you wish to capture in the hopes that you can keep it with you permanently?

A sculpture also suggests being able to see things from all angles. What do you want to get close to so you can observe its intricate detail?

Does the sculpture symbolize self-esteem? On the surface it might look like a cold hunk of nothing, yet by chipping away at it and working on it, you discover its true beauty.

Secret

Quick Interpretation: Protection; mystery

Popular Expression: Close to the vest

When you feel secretive, it indicates that you're not openly expressing true feelings or pain. What do you want to protect in your dream? Would exposure be too painful?

Secret Agent (See *Spy.*)

Seed

Quick Interpretation: Potential; impregnated with thoughts/ideas; pecking order (seeding in sport)

Popular Expressions: As you sow so shall you reap; Gone to seed; Bad seed; Sow your wild oats

What a marvelous thing a seed is. Inside each and every one is the promise of a field or forest. Perhaps the seed in your dream is a poignant symbol indicating that so much can come from so little. One small random act of kindness may affect an entire life. One courageous act can change the course of humankind.

Selfishness

Quick Interpretation: Egotism; self-serving feelings

Popular Expressions: Looking out for number one;
Me, myself, and I

When you feel selfish, you display excessive concern for yourself and your desires. Who's putting their needs above everybody else's? Are you being egotistical or self-serving?

Self-Pity

Quick Interpretation: Self-indulgence; victimization

Popular Expression: Poor, poor pitiful me

Experiencing self-pity indicates that you're dwelling self-indulgently on your sorrows or misfortunes. Why do you feel so sorry for yourself in your dream? Are you fishing for sympathy?

Selling

Quick Interpretation: Closure; increased wealth; convincing arguments

Popular Expressions: Sell someone short; Sell your soul;
Sell someone down the river

It's said that you should only buy from people you like. If you see a salesperson in a dream, does it indicate that you want to be liked more or surrounded by people you favor?

Are you trying to sell something in your dream, or is someone trying to sell you something? What do you want to sell, and how do you feel about selling it? Think of whatever it is you're trying to sell in relation to yourself. Is this how you wish to sell yourself to others?

If someone is trying to sell you something, are you buying it? In other words, how do you feel about what they're trying to sell you, and how do you respond? Selling is all about delivering convincing arguments. Do the arguments sound convincing to you? Think about how this relates to your waking life. Is someone trying to convince you to do something that you don't want to do? Are they trying to convince you to sell your soul?

Serenity

Quick Interpretation: Calmness; peace

Popular Expression: Peace and quiet

When you feel serene, you experience a state of mind that's free from disturbance; you're unruffled. What is the source of your inner peace?

Servant

Quick Interpretation: Loyalty; pampering; public service

Popular Expressions: Cannot serve two masters; Being a slave to something; Slaving over something; At your service; At your beck and call

Wouldn't it be wonderful to have a butler cleaning up after you and pampering you? Can dreaming of a servant indicate that you require a little tender loving care to get you through a challenge?

Who is the servant in your dream? If it's you, how do you feel about it? Are you at someone's beck and call? Is it a role you enjoy playing? If someone is waiting on you, think about it as a symbol of being pampered. Is it time to drop the reigns of your life and let someone else look after you for a while?

Is the servant in your dream a public servant, indicating security? Do you like the security of the job, or is it time to leave and take a risk in the commercial world?

Sex (Also see *Genitals; Lover; Penis; Vagina; X-Rated*)

Quick Interpretation: Creation; desire; lust

Popular Expressions: Hot to trot; Screw around; Labor of love; Make love, not war; The fair sex; Sex symbol

One thing's for sure: The safest sex you're ever going to have is in your dream state. If you dream of sex, the first thing to ask yourself is: "How did I feel?" Were you exhilarated? Repulsed? Was it enjoyable? How you felt about the sex in your dream is a strong indicator of how you feel about it in your waking life.

Who are you having sex with? Do you desire and lust after this person? Or would you like to adopt more of this person's characteristics?

If you see yourself or your partner having sex with other people, are you living out your worst fear? Or are you suspicious of your partner? What has caused your distrust? Is it your fear and insecurity, or their infidelity?

As disturbing as it may seem, we may dream of having sex with a family member. This indicates a desire to bond and become more intimate with the person, rather than sexual desire.

Raunchy or pornographic sex in a dream can be quite healthy. Don't feel guilty about it. It may simply indicate that you wish to explore new horizons. And what better place to experiment with that than in your dream state!

Shadow

Quick Interpretation: Being followed; inseparable companion; feeling overpowered

Popular Expressions: Cast a long shadow; Without a shadow of a doubt; Walking in someone's shadow

You can get rid of almost anything in your life except your shadow. The shadow is a wonderful symbol of love and self-acceptance because the light and dark side of anything is part of the whole. And no matter how big or small your shadow side is, it's important to remember that shadows wouldn't exist without light.

Shark

Quick Interpretation: Predator; scavenger; strength

Popular Expressions: A real shark; Loan shark; In the jaws of death; Get your teeth into something

If any fish has a rotten press secretary, it's the shark. Does the shark in your dream symbolize exaggerated danger, unfounded fear, and paranoia? Is something in your life causing anxiety? Could it be that whatever it is, it's all hype and no bite?

Sharks are the scavengers and vultures of the deep sea. They'll eat anything. Does the shark in your dream indicate that you're surrounded by scavengers and opportunists who want to overpower and consume you in your waking life?

A whole heap of inedible objects have been found in sharks' stomachs, including spare tires and hubcaps. Do people expect you to swallow and accept whatever they dish out? Do they expect you to digest what's unpalatable?

If you're attacked by a shark in your dream (and you haven't survived a shark attack in your waking life), is it a surprise attack? Are you innocently frolicking in the surf and minding your own business when it happens, or are you already in deep water when the shark attacks? If the former is the case, do you feel that you have to pay for things that aren't your doing? Or do you need to watch out and take stock of a situation that has you stuck in deep and dangerous waters? How did you end up in the shark-infested waters? Who or what led you there? Why are you in this predicament?

Perhaps you're the shark in the dream, and you want to get your teeth into something or someone, or is the shark someone who wants to get their teeth into you? Do you know any man-eaters?

Shaving

Quick Interpretation: Unmasked; clean-cut

Popular Expressions: A close shave; By a whisker; Razor sharp; Cut to the bone

Wouldn't you like to meet the genius who invented shaving! Why can't we just walk around hairy and still be considered cute?

Is the shaving a chore or a pleasure in your dream? This may indicate the value you place on outward appearance. The shaving in your dream may also signify that you've managed to scrape through a very challenging or embarrassing situation in your life—that is, it was a close shave.

Sheep

Quick Interpretation: Conformity; simplicity; warmth

Popular Expressions: Black sheep of the family; Being sheepish; A wolf in sheep's clothing; In like a lion, out like a lamb; Lamb to the slaughter; Pull the wool over someone's eyes

The most obvious symbol meaning for sheep is group consciousness. Sheep aren't renowned for their individuality. Do you feel that you're being led by the group, or are you lost in it? Perhaps you're involved in a project that's mindless.

Also consider whether someone has made you feel ill at ease about the way you look, or if you judged someone by his or her appearance. For example, you may wish to stay young at heart, so you dress to keep up the latest fashion. If someone thoughtless says that you look like mutton dressed as lamb, you may experience a feeling of inadequacy, and a symbol of a sheep/lamb may appear in a dream.

A sheep can also signify hidden danger, because sometimes a wolf wears sheep's clothing. Is someone pretending to be harmless and friendly, but underneath you know they're predators who could put you at risk?

If you feel as though you're in a dangerous financial situation, you may dream of shorn or clipped sheep—as if someone has taken the shirt from your back. A feeling of vulnerability may be associated with seeing a lamb in your dream, because lambs are defenseless. Do you feel like a lamb to the slaughter?

If you dream that you're a shepherd who herds a flock of sheep, perhaps you wish to look after a flock, be it family, co-workers, or friends.

A flock of sheep could also have religious significance—the flock is often a symbol of the congregation. Perhaps you're alone or see a lone sheep. Does it symbolize a "soul" who needs to be brought back to the flock? Do you feel like a lost soul, or is someone you know a lost soul?

Sheep can also signify blind faith because they run around in a flock believing that all will be okay. Are you questioning your faith, or blindly accepting it?

The sheep in your dream may symbolize receiving or giving warmth—after all, the wool from a sheep's back can warm us to the tips of our toes.

Shell

Quick Interpretation: Protection; being bombarded (to be shelled); simple pastimes

Popular Expressions: Come out of your shell; Crawl back into your shell; Clam up

No matter which way you look at it, a shell has a very tough exterior that usually protects a very soft interior. Is the shell in your dream a means of protection, or does it signify a desire to hide? It may indicate that you wish to change your character and become more extroverted and well known—in other words, come out of your shell.

Ship (See *Boat; Sailing; Yacht.*)

Shoe

Quick Interpretation: Travel; movement; protection

Popular Expressions: Waiting for the other shoe to drop; If the shoe fits; Put one foot in front of the other; Toe the line

Do the shoes we wear reflect our moods, who we are and what we're doing? What kind of shoes are in your dream? Who's wearing them and for what purpose? Is someone expecting something, waiting for the other shoe to drop? Perhaps the shoe indicates a change in fortune—meaning that the shoe is on the other foot?

Shoulder (Also see *Body Parts.*)

Quick Interpretation: Support; connections; sympathy

Popular Expressions: Shoulder to shoulder; Get/give the cold shoulder; A shoulder to lean on; Shoulder responsibility; The whole world on your shoulders

Shovel

Quick Interpretation: Delve; reveal; be practical (down to earth)

Popular Expressions: Dig up dirt; Dig deep; Dig your heels in

One thing's for sure: When you see a shovel in a dream, there's exploration or excavation taking place. Is someone digging up the dirt on you, or do you want to uncover something?

Shower

Quick Interpretation: Hygiene; rejuvenation; success

Popular Expressions: Shower praise upon; Right as rain

To wash things away quickly, all you have to do is hop under a shower. Therefore, dreaming of a shower indicates that if you address challenges early enough, they can simply be washed down the drain.

Are you taking a shower in your dream or is someone else? Does it symbolize hygiene? Do you feel dirty? Or do you feel that the person who's taking the shower is dirty? Why?

A shower can also symbolize rejuvenation, indicating that it's time to slow down, take time out, and relax. You can't? Well, at least your dream is giving you a little respite.

Also, consider that the shower may represent success. Do you feel particularly successful in your life at the moment? Is everyone showering praise upon you?

Silk

Quick Interpretation: Precious; sensual; soft

Popular Expressions: As smooth as silk; A silk purse out of a sow's ear

Dreaming of silk indicates that something can be made out of nothing. It can also signify that someone is so set in their ways that trying to change their mind is like trying to make a silk purse out of a sow's ear.

Silver

Quick Interpretation: Quick fix (silver bullet); valuable; standing the test of time

Popular Expressions: Born with a silver spoon in your mouth; Every dark cloud has a silver lining

Silver is a symbol of quality without pretension. Does someone in your dream like the finer things in life without needing to show off? Also consider that dreaming of silver may indicate that you desire a long-lasting relationship and the opportunity to celebrate a silver wedding anniversary.

Sin

Quick Interpretation: Bad behavior; transgressions

Popular Expressions: The original sin; Snake in the grass; Forbidden fruit

If you've partaken in reprehensible behavior or have transgressed, you may dream that you've sinned. What has happened that morally offended you? Is the transgression out of character?

Sink

Quick Interpretation: Being fooled; feeling weighed down; clean-up

Popular Expressions: Sink into something; Everything but the kitchen sink; Sink or swim; Hook, line, and sinker; Go down the drain

There was a time when the family would bond around the kitchen sink. But with dishwashers, that family pastime of washing and wiping the dishes has dried up! Does the sink in your dream indicate a desire for a family get-together?

The kitchen sink is one of the items that is usually left behind when people move on. Does the sink in your dream signify that you want to move on in your life?

The sink may also be a symbol of looming danger. Are things around you sinking, or is something that you've been trying to keep afloat slowly going under? Do you feel that you're all washed up, or that someone else is?

Maybe you've just experienced a situation where someone has fooled or misled you and you feel that you've been taken in—hook, line, and sinker.

If you're at a crossroads in your life and have to make a difficult decision, you may see a sink full of water. It's time to decide whether you're going to sink or swim.

Siren (Also see *Ambulance*.)

Quick Interpretation: Warnings; temptation (a siren); right of way

Popular Expressions: Blow your own horn; On the alert; Sound the alarm

Whenever you hear a siren, it means that someone is trying to get somewhere fast—and has good reason to do so! Who or what needs your urgent attention?

A siren can also symbolize temptation that could lead to a very precarious situation. The sirens sang to the sailors, resulting in their eventual demise.

Sister (See *Family*.)

Skeleton (Also see *Body Parts*.)

Quick Interpretation: Support; foundation; secrets

Popular Expressions: Skeletons in the closet; Bag of bones; See right through you

Skipping

Quick Interpretation: Playfulness; disregard; exertion

Popular Expression: A hop, skip, and a jump

Whenever we feel the need to take shortcuts or get things done quickly, we start to skip. The question is, is it a good idea to do this or not?

Skipping can also symbolize a desire to loosen up. Perhaps it's time to take yourself less seriously, and go back to the days when you skipped through life.

Sky

Quick Interpretation: Limitless; peace (heaven); an expression of mood

Popular Expressions: Up in the air; Pie in the sky; Not a cloud in the sky; The sky's the limit; Head in the clouds

Inspiration often hits out of the blue; therefore, if you see a blue sky in your dream, you may be looking for illumination. Dreaming of a sky can also indicate limitlessness. Is this how you feel about your life at the moment? Do you see it stretched out in front of you without any bounds? Is this an exciting or daunting prospect?

What color is the sky in your dream, indicating an expression of mood? For example, gray skies suggest a melancholy mood, while blue skies indicate a joyful, light mood.

The sky is a symbol of peace, as many associate it with God's resort. Do you associate the sky in your dream with heaven? What is your impression of heaven?

Are you feeling particularly positive in your life at the moment—as if the sky's the limit? Or perhaps you're feeling ungrounded and uncertain, as everything is up in the air.

Could it be that you have a dark secret, a skeleton in the closet, and are concerned that things may be blown sky high?

Skydiving (See *Parachute.*)

Slaughterhouse

Quick Interpretation: Completion; mortality; calculated massacre

Popular Expressions: A fate worse than death; A matter of life and death; Easy meat; The lamb to the slaughter

A slaughterhouse is a place where the victims have no chance of escape. The question is, are you the lamb being led to the slaughter, or are you the slaughterer?

Chief executives often dream of slaughterhouses when they have to prune their workforce. Like a slaughterer who's paid to do a job quick and simply, the chief executive must do the same, remaining detached from the outcome. It's a means to an end, a way of ensuring that a company stays afloat and profitable.

To dream of a slaughterhouse may signify fear. Perhaps you believe that you're going to be massacred in a shady deal. Or maybe you're frustrated with a deal that's going down in your life at the moment, and the slaughterhouse suggests that although you're being threatened with death, it's a bluff.

How do you feel about the slaughterhouse in your dream: Did it ignite fear or frustration, or a desire to escape?

If you dream that you escape from a slaughterhouse—or that someone else does—it may be confirmation that you'll survive against all odds.

Slip

Quick Interpretation: Protection; sensuality; disguise

Popular Expressions: Give someone the slip; A cover-up; Slip-up; Slip of the tongue

P utting fashion trends aside, a slip is a symbol of modesty. Who or what do you feel needs to be more virtuous? What needs to be covered up?

Slum (Also see *Poverty.*)

Quick Interpretation: Poverty; overpopulation; under achievement

Popular Expressions: To slum it; On the wrong side of the tracks

S ome of the most incredible individuals on the planet grew up in slums. They had the determination to succeed no matter what the odds. Is your dream telling you that it's possible to succeed regardless of your apparent limitations?

What are you doing in the slum in your dream? If you're living in it, does it symbolize underachievement? Do you feel that you're there because of circumstance or fate? Or are you passing through the slum? How do you feel about it? This may indicate how you feel about poverty.

A slum is also associated with overpopulation. Perhaps the slum in your dream indicates that you feel cramped and crushed by other people in your life. If you are in the slum with people you know, take careful note of how they make you feel in your waking life. Are they stifling you?

Whenever we feel as though we're moving in circles that don't enhance who we really are, then we may feel as though we're slumming it. Perhaps it's time to do something about your social situation before it affects your self-esteem.

Smog (See *Fog; Pollution.*)

Smoke (Also see *Fire.*)

Quick Interpretation: Signal; spirituality (holy smoke); camouflage (smoke screen)

Popular Expressions: Go up in smoke; Where there's smoke, there's fire

Smorgasbord (See *Buffet.*)

Snail

Quick Interpretation: Slow moving; self-contained; visible movement (snail trail)

Popular Expressions: At a snail's pace; Come out of your shell; Go back into your shell; Slow as molasses

Dreaming of a snail can signify that the worst is over and smooth sailing is ahead, as the snail slides with ease over most surfaces. It can also indicate that one should slow down and do things at a snail's pace.

Snake (Also see *Anaconda.*)

Quick Interpretation: Transformation; fertility; rebirth

Popular Expressions: Lower than a snake's belly; Snake in the grass; Original sin

A snake dream suggests transformation. We all know that it was a snake's handiwork that transformed Adam and Eve from naive and blissful residents of the garden to a busy young couple with a family to feed and a world to populate.

Snakes are also cold-blooded. Is someone giving you the cold shoulder, or are you freezing someone out of your life?

Because the snake crawls along the ground, it suggests a feeling a being grounded. It also signifies paradox—it's deadly but revered.

The snake sheds its skin, which is a symbol of transformation—dumping the old and adopting the new. Where is the snake in your dream, and what is it doing? Is something about to be transformed or reinvented in your life? Or would you like to be transformed or remade?

Snakes rely on the sun for energy. This may suggest you're letting outside forces run your life. For example, do you wait until someone compliments you to feel good about yourself? Who else appears in your dream? What is your relationship to them?

As a final consideration, the snake is also fork tongued. Are you or is someone else being two-faced about something?

Snow (Also see *Ice.*)

Quick Interpretation: A cooling down; individuality; feeling overwhelmed

Popular Expressions: Left out in the cold; As pure as the driven snow; Snowed under

Too much of a good thing can be dangerous. As beautiful and invigorating as snow can be, if you get too much of it, it will stop you in your tracks. Snow also symbolizes individuality, as no two snowflakes are alike. Dreaming of snow is a great reminder of how special you really are.

Soap (Also see *Cleaning; Washing.*)

Quick Interpretation: Cleansing; agitation (lathered up); desire to be heard

Popular Expressions: Good clean fun; Squeaky clean; Cleanliness is next to godliness; On your soapbox; Wash your mouth out with soap; In a lather

Whenever you dream of soap, something is getting cleaned up. Who is the person getting rid of the dirt? Who wants to clean up their image? Is someone in your dream unnecessarily getting worked up about trivial matters, and they're all in a lather?

If someone has something to say and they want to announce it publicly, the first thing they look for is a soapbox. Are you listening to the opinions of others, or are you sharing your opinions with people? How do you feel about it?

Sofa (See *Couch.*)

Soldier (Also see *Military; War.*)

Quick Interpretation: Following orders; discipline; risk

Popular Expressions: Soldier on; At your command; Get your marching orders

The chain of command is the backbone of an efficient and well-functioning army. Do you want to be part of a chain that's bound by honor and tradition, or do you want to break loose?

What is the soldier doing in your dream? Protecting or attacking you? If you accept that the soldier symbolizes following orders, do you feel that this is a form of protection or an attack?

The soldier also symbolizes discipline. If you're the soldier in your dream, do you want to be more disciplined in your life? If someone else is the soldier, do you admire and respect their level of discipline?

Also think of the soldier as a symbol of risk. Soldiers risk their lives to save other people. Do you feel that you're taking risks for others?

At times in our lives, we feel like giving up or putting a project aside for a while. Is your dream telling you to discipline yourself and soldier on?

Son (See *Family.*)

Soup

Quick Interpretation: Nutrients; warmth; predicament

Popular Expressions: Too many cooks spoil the broth; In hot water; Whet someone's appetite

Many things tempt us in this world; many things whet our appetites. As an entrée, soup performs this function, and in a dream it indicates that something in your life is just beginning—your appetite has been stimulated and there's more to come.

To dream you're sipping soup indicates nourishment. Is it time to slow down and take care of yourself? If you're feeding soup to someone else, do you hope to nourish them? Or if someone is feeding soup to you, are they trying to nourish you?

Soup is also associated with warmth. Are you trying to warm yourself or someone else up? Why?

You may also dream of soup if you're in a particularly vulnerable situation—that is, you're in the soup, up to your neck in hot water.

Spider (Also see *Cobweb.*)

Quick Interpretation: Misunderstanding; predator; creativity

Popular Expressions: Web of intrigue; Oh what a tangled web . . .; Spin a web; A sticky situation

The spider is one of the most creative insects on the planet. It can build a web that's not only an engineering masterpiece, but a work of art. The spider has an enormous amount of patience, diligently building its web and waiting for its food to show up. Do you need to be patient, or do you wish to be more creative?

Spiders are often misunderstood and feared, but did you know that according to the statisticians, there's as much chance of getting hit in the head by a popping champagne cork as there is being bit by a poisonous spider? Do you feel misunderstood, or is there a misunderstanding in your life that's creating fear? Maybe you're afraid of something.

It's important to consider the location of the dream. Where is the spider—in your bedroom, your workplace, or in nature? Also consider how you feel. If you're afraid, ask yourself if the fear is unrealistic or if there really is something to be afraid of. What web are you being drawn into? Are you getting yourself into a sticky situation that's making you feel uncomfortable, or are you setting a trap for someone else? Perhaps someone or something seems scary in your life but is quite harmless on closer inspection.

Splinter

Quick Interpretation: Breaking away; small aggravations; parting company

Popular Expressions: Splinter group; Get under your skin

Splinters are very annoying. In a dream they represent letting little things get under your skin. Is the splinter on the surface of the skin or a lot deeper? The deeper the splinter, the more emotional you may feel about the circumstances in your dream.

How do you get the splinter—through carelessness, or is it accidental? This may indicate that you should either take more responsibility for what happens in your life, or simply accept that accidents do happen.

Do you try to remove the splinter in your dream, or do you endure the pain? A splinter, if left untreated, can fester and cause the loss of a whole limb. Is your dream reminding you that you need to face things as they arise and not let them build up until they become gangrenous?

The splinter may also represent a splinter group—one that chooses to break away from a larger group to assert its independence. Is the splinter in your finger pointing to this? Do you wish to assert your independence and individuality?

Sport(s)

Quick Interpretation: Recreation; exertion; competition

Popular Expressions: Be a good sport; It's just a game; Lift your game; Run for your life

We've all felt unfairly treated at some time in our lives. We've either been judged or people have second-guessed our emotions. Does the symbol of sport indicate that you'd like to be given a sporting chance to clear away any misconceptions?

Sport also symbolizes recreation. What sport are you playing? If you don't play this sport in your waking life, is it time to?

If you're watching someone else play a sport, how do you feel about it? Are you letting them do all the work while you sit back and watch? Are you taking pleasure from their exertion and effort? Perhaps it's time to get up and do something yourself.

Sport is also associated with being a team player. How do you feel about being a team player in your life? Do you like being part of a team, or do you want to stand out from the crowd and be counted?

Also consider that sport indicates competition. Are you being particularly competitive in your life at the moment, or is someone else? How do you handle the competition?

Perhaps your subconscious is telling you to chill out and not take things so seriously, to be a good sport and stop keeping score.

Spy

Quick Interpretation: Mind games; hidden agenda; untrustworthiness

Popular Expressions: Wolf in sheep's clothing; Behind closed doors; Hide in plain sight; Go undercover

You've just woken from an exciting dream that involved a car chase and shady dealings à la James Bond; except the spy in your dream was in more trouble than Bond ever imagined—and is without the nifty gadgets to help him out.

What does it mean to dream of a spy or secret agent? First, consider whether the person who's the secret agent in your dream is trustworthy. People who aren't as they seem can leave you on edge, making you wonder what their ulterior motive is. Does their loyalty depend on the highest bid? If you're the spy in your dream, does this relate to you? Why can't you show people your true colors? Do you feel that you must keep your feelings buried, as exposure may be life threatening?

What kind of spy are you? Are you a sneaky rat who creeps through the streets eavesdropping? Or are you suave and sophisticated like Agent 007? If you're the latter, you may be searching for some spine-tingling adventures in your life. Or perhaps you feel that you've been called on to help someone in great need and you're ready for the challenge.

If you're not the spy, then who is? Is it someone you know? Do you feel that they're spying on you, watching you like a hawk because they don't trust you? Perhaps you feel betrayed. Or do you feel guilty about something you don't want the secret agent to find discover?

Do you admire the spy in your dream? If so, perhaps you'd like him or her to confide in you and trust you enough to share secrets.

A STREAM OF DREAMS

Finally, the symbol of a spy may be wish fulfillment. You may want to be seduced by a mysterious and suave stranger who will show you a good time—no strings attached.

Stabbing (Also see *Knife.*)

Quick Interpretation: Betrayal; pain; guesswork

Popular Expressions: A stab in the dark; A stab in the back; Like a knife to the heart; Cuts to the bone

Stadium (Also see *Sports.*)

Quick Interpretation: Recreation; competition; observation

Popular Expressions: One of the crowd; Birds of a feather flock together; Mob mentality; A ringside seat

If you'd like to associate with people who have the same purpose, a stadium is the best place to find them, as it's where the multitudes gather to see the same event. What group do you want to join or be a part of? Does the stadium symbolize a desire to surround yourself with like-minded people?

Stadiums are modern-day coliseums. Do you want to go to a place where winning is everything?

Stage

Quick Interpretation: Period of time; exposure; performance

Popular Expressions: Set the stage; A stage in someone's life; All the world's a stage . . .

We all play on different stages. What do you see on the stage in your dream? A comedy, a mystery, or a tragedy? This is a perfect symbol of all things coming to pass, since what takes place on a stage is short-lived.

Stairs

Quick Interpretation: Ascent/descent; graduation; effort

Popular Expressions: On the up-and-up; Put your best foot forward; One step at a time; Step lightly; Watch your step; Move up (or down) in the world

To see stairs in a dream indicates that you're making connections between one level and another. Are you going up or down the stairs? If you're going up, it may signify ascendancy, growth, and expansion. If you're going down, it may be a symbol of moving backwards or probing deeper.

Moving up the stairs may also indicate a desire to deepen awareness, develop your intuition, or pursue higher spiritual ideals.

Is the climb arduous and difficult, or is it effortless? The amount of exertion required to move up or down the stairs may indicate the extent to which you're resisting change. If the stairs are difficult to climb, it may mean that your journey is tiresome.

If you're at school and find study tough going and concentration difficult, you may experience a difficult climb. But if you see yourself ascending three or four steps at a time, you may feel that you've mastered your work.

Are the stairs solid and strong, or are they in disrepair, rickety, and shaky? This may indicate how you feel about your life right now and the direction it's moving in.

How inviting are the stairs? Are they open and wide, or narrow and spiraling? This may also indicate how your life is unfolding.

Stairs are also a reminder to proceed with caution—that is, to take one step at a time.

If there's someone or something on the stairs with you, it may indicate whether the dream is based on relationships, work, or travel. For example, if you see a co-worker on the stairs, the dream is obviously work related.

In business you can end up with a new title instead of a pay raise—all that happens is you get kicked upstairs. Maybe it's time to descend the stairs to see what's really happening.

Stamp (See *Envelope; Letter; Post Office.*)

Star (Also see *Celebrity; Galaxy.*)

Quick Interpretation: Celebrity; ambition; destiny

Popular Expressions: Reach for the stars; Stars in your eyes; A rising star; Star-crossed lovers; It's in the stars

When we see a bright star in the sky, it's often the case that it actually died millions of years ago. Bright stars remind us that even though our loved ones may have departed, they can still shine brightly in our eyes.

A star can also symbolize ambition. Where do you see the star or stars in your dream? What is your response to it (or them)? How you feel about the star or stars in your dream may indicate how you feel about ambition in your life; or if the star belongs to someone else in your dream, how you feel about other people's ambitions.

Stars also indicate destiny. Do the stars in your dream represent your evolving future? What do you feel is about to come in to your life?

Also consider if it's time for you to step out of your day-to-day life and reach for the stars, or if you have stars in your eyes.

Today, it's easy to get star status. With home videos and reality TV, getting our 15 minutes of fame has never been easier. Are you getting ready for stardom?

Steel

Quick Interpretation: Resolve (nerves of steel); confrontation; strength

Popular Expressions: Nerves of steel; Steely determination; Steel yourself to something

Where would we be without steel? Its strength is the reason why it's so important to us. Does the steel in your dream indicate that it's time for you or someone else to have nerves like steel?

The great thing about steel is, the more you hit it, heat it up, and cool it down, the stronger it gets. It's a great reminder that no matter how many times you get knocked, you can always get up again, stronger and sharper than ever.

Stereo (See *CD Player.*)

Steps (See *Stairs.*)

Stinginess

Quick Interpretation: Meanness; stringency

Popular Expressions: Tight with money; Tightwad

If you or someone else is acting stingy in your dream, it indicates that you or they are stringent with money and/or possessions. What don't you want to share in your dream? Who's being greedy or tight in your life?

Storm

Quick Interpretation: Disturbance; commotion; outburst

Popular Expressions: Tempest in a teapot; Steal someone's thunder; The calm before the storm; Take by storm

It's common for people to dream of storms when what they really want is the calm that follows.

Dreaming of a storm suggests a disturbance. How you feel about the storm may indicate how you're responding to or dealing with a disturbance in your waking life. Do you feel that you're in the midst of the storm, confused and disoriented, or are you watching the storm from a safe distance?

A storm is also a symbol of commotion. Do you feel that you're caught up in the chaos of life at the moment? What's happening around you that you feel is out of your control?

Also consider the storm as an outburst. Does it represent an emotional flare-up in your life that's quick to pass, just like a tempest in a teapot?

Stranger

Quick Interpretation: New faces; the unknown; being out of place

Popular Expressions: Truth is stranger than fiction; A stranger in a strange land; A stranger in the mirror

Every one of us has dreamed of a stranger at one time or another—unless of course you're someone who knows everyone!

Look at any emotions or feelings that come up when you dream of a stranger. Does this individual frighten and threaten you, or excite and please you? Where are you? Your emotions and the setting of the dream will give you insight into your relationship with the stranger. Are you reluctant and fearful of strange ideas, people, or places, or do these types of things exhilarate and motivate you? Consider the context of the dream to determine the area of your life that's being influenced.

Are you being chased by a stranger in your dream, or are you chasing someone? What are you running away from, or what you are trying to catch?

How often have you looked in the mirror and seen a stranger staring back at you? Perhaps the stranger in your dream is an aspect of you. If so, what aspect of yourself are you being confronted with? How do you deal with it in the dream?

Again, ask yourself what you're feeling. Does the experience leave a bad taste in your mouth?

If you have fun with the stranger in your dream, ask yourself if you have a desire to kick off your shoes with new friends, new lovers, and new experiences.

Finally, I like Carl Jung's view of strangers in dreams. He suggested that we dream of our animus (for a woman, her male counterpart represented as a male stranger) or anima (for a man, his female counterpart represented as a female stranger) to express aspects of ourselves that we feel are inappropriate to express in everyday life. For example, a man may dream of a female stranger sobbing as a way to release pent-up emotions he feels are otherwise inappropriate to express.

Strawberry (Also see *Fruit.*)

Quick Interpretation: Being grounded; romance; easy pickings

Strength

Quick Interpretation: Determination; power

Popular Expressions: As strong as an ox; The strength of one's convictions

When you feel strong, it indicates that you're not easily swayed from opinion or action. What is the focus of your determination?

Stubbornness

Quick Interpretation: Intractability; inflexibility

Popular Expressions: Stubborn as a mule; Bullheaded; Won't budge; My way or the highway

When you're stubborn, you obstinately adhere to an opinion regardless of reason. In your dream, what idea or action are you attached to despite arguments to the contrary? Why can't you be flexible?

Study (Also see *School.*)

Quick Interpretation: Focus; deliberation; expansion

Popular Expressions: Hit the books; It's never too late to learn; A quick study

This symbol is about the acquisition of knowledge. What do you want to absorb for future use? Is the study tedious and forced upon you, or are you engrossed in what you're learning? What are you studying, and more important, for what purpose are you studying?

Submarine

Quick Interpretation: Delving deeper; disguise; claustrophobia

Popular Expressions: Beneath the surface; Going deep into something; Under the radar; That's over my head; Keep your head above water; A real dive

Dreaming of a submarine often indicates that someone is sneaking around, or you want to be sneaky. Most people accept that water is a symbol of emotion, so perhaps the submarine in your dream indicates diving deeply into someone's emotional state? If the submarine is on the surface, has everything been dealt with and brought to the surface, or is the submarine about to dive down?

A submarine could also symbolize a desire to put a stop to a situation or a relationship—meaning that you want to torpedo it.

Success

Quick Interpretation: Happiness; overcoming obstacles

Popular Expressions: The sweet smell of success; Everybody loves a winner

When you experience success, you know you've attained a favorable outcome to a situation, project, or event. What perceived failure have you overcome?

Sugar

Quick Interpretation: Sweetness; decay; love (romantic)

Popular Expressions: Sweetness and light; Sugar wouldn't melt in his mouth; Sugar daddy; Taking your lumps

When situations or individuals need sweetening, you can expect to see sugar in a dream. What is leaving a sour taste in your mouth that needs to be sweetened? Does someone in your dream wish to be looked after—that is, they desire a sugar daddy?

It could be that a very painful task is at hand and needs to be addressed. Just remember that a spoonful of sugar will help the medicine go down.

Suitcase (See *Luggage.*)

Sun

Quick Interpretation: Illumination; masculinity; light

Popular Expressions: Everything under the sun; A ray of sunshine; Sunny-side up; A place in the sun; Rise and shine; Getting burned by someone

Each and every living organism on this planet is looking for their place in the sun. Does the sun in your dream signify that you've found yours?

The sun is also a symbol of illumination. What do you want to illuminate in your life? Take note of where the sun is and how you respond to it to determine what it is. It may be a career prospect or a relationship.

If you're going through a particularly challenging time in your life right now, you may dream of the sun, indicating strength, determination, and reliability. We can count on the sun to rise and set every day.

Also consider whether the sun is rising or setting in your dream. If it's rising, it may indicate that certain situations or concerns are coming to the forefront (or emerging) in your life. And if it's setting, think about it in relation to going deep within and perhaps taking time out to explore your subconscious.

The sun is also a symbol of masculinity, of taking care of everyday concerns and getting ahead in the world. Is this what it represents in your dream? Or is the sun simply a symbol of lightness in your life?

The sun may also be a reminder not to wish too hard for what you want . . . as you might get it—too much sun causes everything from droughts to sunburn.

Of course, I prefer to think of the sun as a symbol of the end of a long period of darkness. That finally, in the immortal words of George Harrison: "Here comes the sun."

Sunglasses (Also see *Glasses*.)

Quick Interpretation: Mystery; protection; shadiness

Popular Expressions: On the nose; Blinded by the light; Look at life through rose-colored glasses

Sunglasses were designed to stop us from squinting, and now they're the ultimate fashion accessory. We choose our sunglasses as carefully as our hairstyles.

If you dream of sunglasses, it may indicate that you're not seeing something clearly. Do you choose to look at life through rose-colored glasses? Perhaps you don't want people to know what you're looking at or where your focus is. Are the sunglasses a mask, hiding your true intentions?

If you're wearing reflective sunglasses, who in the dream needs to know what you think of them? Do you need to tell this person something in your waking life?

Are you wearing sunglasses in a dark room? Where are you? This may help you to determine what you feel you must hide from. Do you feel uncomfortable, or cool and trendy, suggesting that you like to do little things to lift your self-esteem?

Essentially, sunglasses protect us from being blinded by the light. Is there something in your life so bright and illuminating that you can't look at it with the naked eye?

Sunrise (Also see *Sun; Sunset.*)

Quick Interpretation: New beginnings; inspiration; elevation of spirits

Popular Expressions: The early bird catches the worm; On the up-and-up; Rise and shine

Sunset (Also see *Sun; Sunrise.*)

Quick Interpretation: Release; farewells; closure

Popular Expressions: Set the scene; Down to earth; Down-and-out

Supermarket

Quick Interpretation: A multitude of choices; lining up; checking out

Popular Expressions: Variety is the spice of life; Check someone out; Cart someone off; Cart something away

The supermarket is the place to go when you want to stock up on food and creature comforts.

In the past, you had to go to a butcher, grocer, and baker to get what you needed, but not anymore. The supermarket is a symbol of being able to get everything you want under one roof. How do you feel about this? Are you excited by the selection you have before you, or are you annoyed, wishing you were back in the good old country store?

What are you doing in the supermarket? Do you feel overwhelmed, finding it difficult to make up your mind about what to buy and which aisle to go down? (This may suggest that you're at a crossroads in your life.) Or are you a bargain hunter with a good eye for value and quality—that is, you know what you want in life?

Do you have a shopping list with you and know what you're looking for? This may indicate that you know your future plans/goals and what you want to achieve.

After bars, nightclubs, bookstores, and Laundromats, the supermarket is one of the best pick-up joints there is. A subtle bump into a person's cart or a casual comment in the checkout line are perfect icebreakers. Is your dream telling you to get to the supermarket to meet that perfect partner?

Suspicion

Quick Interpretation: Distrust; lack of faith

When you feel suspicious, you doubt or distrust people's words and actions. What has instigated your distrust? Are your suspicions well founded?

Swan (Also see *Animal.*)

Quick Interpretation: Transformation; beauty; serenity

Popular Expressions: Whiter than white; Swan song; From an ugly duckling into a swan

Swimming (Also see *Swimming Pool.*)

Quick Interpretation: Exercise; competition; survival

Popular Expressions: Staying afloat; Keep your head above water; Sink or swim; Take a dive

The thing about swimming is, you've got to get everything right—the breathing, the coordination, and the buoyancy. Dreaming of swimming indicates that you're in charge of your life and dealing with your emotions well. It also signifies that it's time to get cracking and stop talking about what you should be doing. The choice is to either sink or swim.

Swimming Pool (Also see *Swimming*.)

Quick Interpretation: Fun; competition; risk

Popular Expressions: Staying afloat; Take a dive; Tread water; Keep your head above water; Get in over your head; In the deep end; Sink or swim; Pooling your efforts

The swimming pool is a place of pleasure or pain. An athlete would view the pool as a place of determination, achievement, competition, or perhaps injury. If you're a parent, you may view the pool as a place where you're constantly looking over your shoulder. You associate it with responsibility and diligence. If you're a reasonable swimmer, the pool may symbolize relaxation and exercise.

For non-swimmers, the swimming pool is a place of possible danger. It's associated with the fear of getting in over your head. However, the fear may be in your mind, because you do have the resources to float. The swimming pool is also a place of social activity, whether you're having a barbecue around the pool or a pool party.

For people who own outdoor swimming pools, the symbol in a dream may signify chores, because they relate it to pool maintenance—dropping chemicals in and dragging leaves out.

The swimming pool may also symbolize courage. How many of us have jumped in the deep end when taking a chance in life? It may also indicate emotional control—that is, the water represents emotion; and the pool, contained emotion.

Do you see someone else around the pool? If you see your accountant, your partner, or someone who works for you skimming leaves from the top of the water, consider whether they're siphoning things from you either physically (money) or emotionally.

If you see someone diving in at the wrong end of the pool, are you worried about them, or do you think that they have no depth?

The pool is also a symbol of bringing people together—"pooling" resources or combining ideas. Are you involved in a project that involves working with a group?

Sword

Quick Interpretation: Power; protection; honor

Popular Expressions: A double-edged sword; Live by the sword, die by the sword

Hasn't each of us secretly wanted to be the person to remove the sword from the stone to gain mystical powers? Does the sword in your dream indicate that you want to overcome challenges with magic and mysticism?

The sword is a symbol of power. Who's holding the sword in your dream? If it's you, how do you feel about holding it? Think of it in relation to being able to hold your own power.

If someone else is holding the sword in your dream, how do you feel about it? Do you feel they're abusing their power, or are they claiming it? Are you under their power?

The sword is also a symbol of protection. Do you feel you need the sword to protect you? From what? Or is the sword a symbol of honor? Who's being knighted?

We all make sacrifices in our lives, either for others or to achieve a desired result. Is it time to take stock of a situation and make the ultimate sacrifice by falling on your sword?

Syringe (Also see *Needle.*)

Quick Interpretation: Addiction; something that's life giving; injection

Popular Expressions: Hit a nerve; Injecting new blood; A shot in the arm; Needling someone

If something needs to move beyond its present predicament, then you may dream of a syringe, as it indicates that a new injection of something is required or called for.

Table (Also see *Desk*.)

Quick Interpretation: Conference/mediation; deception; exposure

Popular Expressions: Lay your cards on the table; Drink someone under the table; Turn the tables on someone; Table your thoughts

Whenever you want to get things off your chest and present your point of view, you table your thoughts. What is it that you want to display or exhibit? Perhaps someone wants to get their way at all costs and they're dealing under the table.

There are right and wrong ways of doing things, especially if you have a desire to become more sophisticated in the world. Someone's manners around the table in your dream may indicate their degree of sophistication.

Tablet (See *Pill*.)

Tap

Quick Interpretation: Quick pace; discovery; attention

Popular Expressions: Down the drain; Tap in to; Tapped out; On tap

If we're off the mark or doing something wrong, sometimes all we need is a tap on the shoulder to put things right.

Nothing controls water better than a tap. In your dream, does the tap symbolize a desire to regulate your emotions?

Whenever we want something to be available, fresh, and in abundant quantities, we want it to be on tap. Do you wish something in your life was more free flowing?

Tape (Also see *CD Player.*)

Quick Interpretation: Indisputable record; to stick together; bureaucratic dealings

Popular Expressions: Red tape; Off (or on) the record

I don't think there's anybody on this planet who likes red tape . . . oops, I forgot about the bureaucrats. Is someone or something tied down with ridiculous questions and unnecessary obstacles? Is the tape strong and holding things together in your dream? Or is it old and tattered, indicating that things are precarious and about to fall apart? Does the tape signify a desire to record something to ensure that it's on the record?

Target

Quick Interpretation: Accuracy; victim; achievement of goals

Popular Expressions: Drive your point home; Shoot for the same target; Right on target; Target practice; Aim and fire; Find your mark

We've all felt, at some time in our lives, that we've been the target of someone else's thoughts. Do you think the bull's-eye on your back makes you a victim or an object of desire? Is the target a symbol of achieving your goals? Do you feel that you're right on target, or are your goals still out there and the target merely gives you something to aim at?

Tattoo

Quick Interpretation: Statement; permanence; identification

Popular Expressions: Bleed red ink; Get under someone's skin; Skin deep

If you want to make a statement about whom you love or what you think, there's no better way to do it than with a tattoo. What is it that you want to expose for all the world to see?

Who has the tattoo in your dream? How do you feel about it? If it's your tattoo, do you want to let the world know that you're in love, or is it a symbol of your pain? If you have a tattoo, think of the dream in relation to how you feel about it. Have you outgrown it?

Tattoos are the perfect identification marks. Is the tattoo in your dream a symbol of wanting to be identified, or of wanting to identify someone else?

Today, tattoos are fashion statements, and because they're permanent, dreaming of a tattoo indicates that you feel that your choices will always be in fashion.

Taxi (See *Cab.*)

Tea

Quick Interpretation: Refreshment; time-out; change

Popular Expressions: Not your cup of tea; Not for all the tea in China; It's not in the tea leaves; A new leaf

Tea bags have simplified the whole tea-drinking process. What do you do on a regular basis that can be simplified and made more convenient?

Are you drinking tea in your dream, indicating refreshment and time out. What do you feel you need time out from? What type of tea is it? If it's herbal tea, perhaps your subconscious is urging you to drink it in your waking life.

Are you drinking the tea with a friend, indicating togetherness and sharing? How do you feel about it? If you're drinking tea with a friend you're fighting with, perhaps it's time to make amends.

The tea may also be a symbol for something that isn't to your liking ("not your cup of tea").

Teaching (Also see *Lecture.*)

Quick Interpretation: Shared knowledge; support; punishment

Popular Expressions: Those who can't, teach; Teach someone a lesson

Tears

Quick Interpretation: Flow of emotion; open expression

Popular Expressions: Crocodile tears; Tear up; Cry me a river; Sob story

Feeling teary indicates an uncontrollable flow of emotion, regardless of whether you're expressing joy, pain, or anger. Are they happy tears, or are you sad? Are you happy to display your emotion, or do you wish you'd held back? Tears in a dream indicate how much of yourself you're willing to expose to the world.

Teeth (See *Tooth.*)

Telephone (Also see *Cell Phone; Telephone Book.*)

Quick Interpretation: Communication; bridging distance; intrusion

Popular Expressions: A close call; Get through to someone; Ring true; Answer to someone

Nothing eliminates distance like a telephone. You can communicate even though you're miles apart. Dreaming of a telephone may indicate a desire to be brought closer to someone.

What are you doing with the telephone in your dream? Are you trying to call someone? Many people dream that they're trying to do so but are unable to dial the numbers, or they dial them incorrectly. If you have such a dream, ask yourself what you'd like to communicate. Whom do you want to get through to?

If a telephone is ringing in your dream, do you answer it? If you don't, perhaps it indicates that you don't want to communicate with people right now. Talking on the telephone indicates that you wish to communicate with someone else or an aspect of yourself.

At times there isn't anything more intrusive than a telephone call, especially if you're in the middle of a conversation or in the shower when the phone rings. Dreaming of a telephone may be a reminder that you have a choice. You don't have to pick it up. You can continue to do what you're doing.

Telephone Book

Quick Interpretation: Accessibility; listings; choices

Popular Expressions: At your fingertips; Let your fingers do the walking . . .

The phone book is so handy. Anything you want is available in alphabetical order.

Dreaming of the phone book may indicate that you can instantly manifest what you want and that you have an abundant number of choices. What are you looking for within these pages?

Television

Quick Interpretation: Information; entertainment; distraction

Popular Expressions: Change your tune; Tune in (or out); Picture perfect; Down the tubes; The picture of health;

Sight unseen; Change the channel; Turn someone on; On the same frequency

The symbol of a television is, in itself, not as significant as what you're watching. Is it a soap opera, or are you being alerted to an important piece of news?

What does the television in your dream symbolize? Is it a symbol of mind control (it dictates your life) or choice (you can always change the channel).

How do you feel about watching TV? Is it your only source of entertainment, or does it sabotage your social life in some way? Do you *choose* to watch it, or do you feel that it's your only option? Is the picture in black and white or in color, indicating that outside stimuli are dull and mundane or vibrant and full of life?

Also consider what you're inviting into your world that you wish to keep at a safe distance. If you're watching someone familiar on the screen, what fascinates you about them? Or what is it about their performance that's teaching you something?

If you're on television, does it indicate that you desire fame and fortune, or do you wish to spread the word—your word? There's no better way to get people's attention than to appear on TV.

If you happen to be watching a television commercial, it may indicate that something in your life has lost its flavor or has become over-commercialized.

Tension

Quick Interpretation: Feeling unnerved; pressure

Popular Expressions: A tension headache; Uptight

When you feel tense, it indicates that you're unable to express your feelings appropriately. What is unnerving you in your dream? Why is it so hard to articulate your feelings?

Tent

Quick Interpretation: Camping out; being a nomad; simplicity

Popular Expressions: Pitch a tent; A foot in each camp; Under cover of night

We've all been indecisive at times, or unsure whom to give our allegiance to. The tent in your dream may indicate that you want to keep a foot in each camp to ensure that you're on the winning side.

The tent is also a symbol of the great outdoors. Does the tent in your dream symbolize a desire to get back to nature and away from your everyday life? How do you feel about camping out? This may indicate how you feel about your own nature.

A tent can also suggest a desire to be nomadic. Do you feel a need to uproot and go traveling? Or do you wish to return to a simple life, where you're free to move with your possessions on your back and the world at your feet?

Test (Also see *Examination.*)

Quick Interpretation: Validation; understanding; trial

Popular Expressions: Stand the test of time; Test one's mettle; A test of wills

Thief (See *Burglar.*)

Throat (Also see *Body Parts.*)

Quick Interpretation: Speech; swallowing; passage

Popular Expressions: Bring a lump to your throat; Jump down someone's throat; Take someone by the throat; A frog in your throat; Swallow your words; Swallow your pride

Thunder (Also see *Storm.*)

Quick Interpretation: Emotional outburst; threat; warning

Popular Expressions: Steal someone's thunder; A clap of thunder; Thunderous applause

Dreaming of thunder may indicate the release of emotional tension. Have things been particularly intense in your life at this time? Also consider that the thunder may be a warning. Is it time to slow down before things erupt?

The thunder in your dream may signify a threat. Who's in the dream with you? Do you see them as a potential threat? Or are you a potential threat to them?

Perhaps the thunder indicates standing in another person's limelight. Have you stolen someone else's thunder, or has someone stolen yours?

Ticket

Quick Interpretation: Admission; vanity; inclusion

Popular Expressions: Just the ticket; That's the ticket

It's not the ticket itself but its purpose that's significant in a dream. What kind of event or situation have you gained access to? Is the ticket a gift, or did you have to pay for it? Do you feel special and singled out, or at one with the mob? Perhaps the ticket is a symbol of punishment, like a parking or speeding ticket. Or is it a return ticket, indicating that it's time to come back, since you've been away long enough?

Tidal Wave (Also see *Disaster, natural.*)

Quick Interpretation: Feeling overwhelmed; extreme force; intuition

Popular Expressions: On the crest of a wave; Riding a wave; A wave of emotion; Over one's head; In troubled waters; All washed up; Swept away

Tiger (Also see *Animal; Cat.*)

Quick Interpretation: Solitude; fierceness; confronting challenges

Popular Expressions: Have a tiger by the tail; A paper tiger

Time (Also see *Alarm Clock; Watch.*)

Quick Interpretation: Change; movement; infinity

Popular Expressions: Right on time; On borrowed time; The test of time; Crunch time; Time is slipping away; No time like the present; Running like clockwork

One of the things that most of us experience is that there's so much to do and so little time to do it. Is your dream an indication that you feel you're always running out of time? There's only one solution: Move your clock five minutes forward, and forget that you did it.

If you're fortunate enough to dream that you have all the time in the world and that time is actually on your side, then it's either wish fulfillment or you've finally managed to get organized.

It's often said that time is money. Is your dream about time really about money? Do you have plenty of money and plenty of time, or are you running out of them both? If you see yourself saving time in your dream, is it an indication that you want to start saving money?

To dream of time may also indicate that you need to take a break—to smell the roses.

Toilet

Quick Interpretation: Privacy; flushing away the unwanted; relieving yourself

Popular Expressions: Flush your troubles away; Flush with anticipation; Going down the toilet

When you think about it, you're not really what you eat, you're what you don't eliminate. A toilet is a positive dream symbol, as it shows you're getting rid of unwanted feelings, emotions, or thoughts.

If in your dream people are watching you sit on the toilet, and you just can't go, consider that you feel limited in your ability to truly express yourself. There's a desire to let everything out, but you're not going to do it publicly.

Tongue (Also see *Body Parts.*)

Quick Interpretation: Language; taste; sensuality

Popular Expressions: Bite your tongue; Hold your tongue; Cat got your tongue

Tooth (Also see *Dentist.*)

Quick Interpretation: Youth; power; strength

Popular Expressions: Get your teeth into something; Show your teeth; Bare your fangs; Give your eyetooth for something; Losing face

It's extremely common to dream of teeth falling out. Whenever I mention such a dream to my mother, she runs for cover. She thinks catastrophe, but my instant reaction is to advise the dreamer to make a dental appointment. If your dentist gives the all-clear, then it's time to explore other possible dream meanings.

The first question is: Do I feel like I'm *losing* face? In many cultures, this indicates embarrassment, being put in a position that lowers your feeling of self-worth. This can include feeling isolated from others. Think about where you are when your teeth fall out. Is it a family situation, or are you at work? What embarrassed you? I've found that the more high profile an individual is, the more often these dreams occur.

Another popular dream theme is rotting or weak teeth. This may indicate that you feel as though your youth is slipping away. It could be a vanity issue—appearance counts for a lot in this world, and anything that detracts from our appearance can be upsetting. If you feel overweight or ugly during the day, then you may have a rotting-teeth dream.

If you're involved in a major project, or trying to start a new relationship, you may dream that your teeth are loose. It suggests that you're not able to "get your teeth" into the situation.

Perhaps you dream that someone else's teeth fall out (your dog, the lady next door, or a family member). If so, you may have concerns about their health or general state of well-being. If it's a dog, you may be concerned about the health of a very good friend.

If another person's teeth fall out in a dream, it may relate to an aspect of yourself. For example, if you dream that, say, Arnold Schwarzenegger's teeth fall out, you may feel that the strong and muscular part of yourself is in decay.

If it's a relationship dream—for example, your partner's teeth fall out and he or she is in good health (with no teeth problems)—it may signify that there are communication problems within the relationship.

Teeth falling out in a dream has a number of possible meanings. To this day I try and convince my mother that she doesn't have to hide out in the nuclear bunker under her house every time she hears someone dreamed that a molar dropped from their mouth.

Torch

Quick Interpretation: Illumination; focus; shining light

Popular Expressions: Carry a torch for someone; Carry the torch; Torch song; Pass the torch; Shine light on a situation

The torch, unfortunately, can indicate that you or someone else has a broken heart and that they're still carrying a torch. Is it time to shine the light on a new path?

Often, when someone flashes a torch, it ends up in your eyes. Does this symbolize that someone doesn't want you to see the whole picture? Also consider that it could be time for someone to retire or move aside, as the torch must be passed on.

Torture (Also see *Interrogation.*)

Quick Interpretation: Withholding of secrets; brutality; torment

Popular Expressions: For the hell of it; Give someone hell; Tighten the screws on someone

Even though torture can be quite horrific in a dream, try to look at it as a symbol of determination and willpower. Is someone willing to go through a lot of pain because of what they believe or who they are?

Who's being tortured in your dream? If it's you, why are you being tortured? Is someone trying to extract information from you? Can you withstand the torture, or does it symbolize that someone in your waking life is giving you hell? Who is it, and how are they torturing you?

Are you torturing someone else in your dream? If so, perhaps you want to uncover withheld secrets. Do you feel that torture is the only way to extract the information?

Torture is also a symbol of brutality and torment. Who's behaving brutally toward you? Do you feel that your life is torturous right now?

Often we'd love to let people know how we really feel about them and not refrain from showing our disapproval. Perhaps you want to give someone in your life a tongue lashing.

Tower

Quick Interpretation: Strength; danger; imprisonment

Popular Expressions: An ivory tower; A tower of strength; Tower over someone

I f it's time to be a bit more courageous and make difficult decisions, you may see a tower of strength in a dream. Who's
depending on you, or who are you depending on? A tower can also
symbolize completion.

In the old days in Great Britain, if the king or queen got tired
of what you were saying, they would send you to the Tower of
London. If someone has a desire to stand head and shoulders
above the crowd, then you may see them towering over everyone
in your dream.

Toy (Also see *Play.*)

Quick Interpretation: Plaything; to not take seriously;
manipulation

Popular Expressions: To toy around with; Child's play

T oday, everything is like rocket science, and you need a degree
to program your VCR. The toys in your dream may represent
a desire to return to the days when everything was child's play.

Dreaming of toys indicates playing around. Is this what you're
doing with your life right now? Is it time to lighten up a little and
not take life so seriously? Perhaps you're watching someone else
play with toys in your dream. Does it mean that you don't take
this person seriously?

The toys may also indicate that someone is manipulating you
right now ("toying with you"). Or are you toying with someone
else? Are you playing with fire, perhaps?

Traffic (Also see *Traffic Lights.*)

Quick Interpretation: Congestion; feeling stuck; illicit trade

Popular Expressions: Bumper-to-bumper; Traffic jam; to traffic
drugs

H ow did you end up in a traffic jam? There isn't anything
pleasant about being caught behind someone else's bumper.

If you're stuck in traffic in your dream, does it indicate that you feel stuck in your waking life? Perhaps you feel as though you know where you want to go and how to get there, but other people are slowing you down with their own agendas and destinations.

Traffic also signifies congestion. Do you feel that you're taking too much in at the moment and don't have enough time to digest it all?

Today, if you're a trafficker, it doesn't mean you have a habit of getting caught in busy streets, it means you move illicit drugs. Does the traffic in your dream symbolize that you or someone else may be involved in something illegal?

Traffic Lights (Also see *Traffic.*)

Quick Interpretation: Intersection; stopping/going; permission

Popular Expressions: Get the green light on something; See the light; See red; Run a red light

Red often symbolizes passion and lust, but in relation to traffic, it means stop! What color are the traffic lights in your dream, and what are you being directed to do? Do you have to stop and wait, or prepare to stop, or can you just go ahead? How do you feel? Are you annoyed because you have to stop at a red light? This may indicate that a project or relationship is at a standstill. If you feel okay about waiting at the lights, it may indicate that you feel it's time to pull back and stop and think things through before you go any farther.

If the lights are yellow, do you feel that you have to slow down when you really want to speed up? Or do you see it as a warning to proceed carefully? If the light is green, do you feel that it's safe to proceed, and you can move with invigorated passion? Or do you feel apprehensive and unsure about moving forward?

Traffic lights also signify control, and are synonymous with hidden cameras. Do the traffic lights in your dream indicate that you're careful not to do the wrong thing because you might get caught?

Trailer

Quick Interpretation: Freedom; mobility; lack of foundation

Popular Expressions: Driving your point home; A foot in each camp

Aren't turtles fortunate—they never have to tow a trailer, as they already have them conveniently placed on their backs! How do you feel about the trailer in your dream? Is it a symbol of pleasure, because you can handle the load with ease, or do you feel that it's a burden? Is it difficult to maneuver through life because of the weight you're towing? Does this indicate that it's time to get rid of some of your possessions in order to lighten your load?

What is the trailer like? Is it old and run-down, sitting in the middle of an empty lot, uninhabitable? Or is it modern, new, and well equipped for a long journey? Your answer will help you determine what you're towing (or perhaps no longer towing) around with you.

Determining whether the trailer is moving or stationary may help you identify whether you feel you're going somewhere or you've gone as far as you can go.

If you've got a point to make and you feel it's important that people understand something about you or your intentions, the trailer may symbolize wanting to drive your point home!

Train

Quick Interpretation: Movement; being on track; straight-forwardness

Popular Expressions: Train of thought; Getting off track; One-track mind; Ride the rails; Rail against something

Trains symbolize fast movement, and achieving a goal quickly with direct action. A train can also signify a one-track mind, and a lack of flexibility when it comes to changing direction.

If you're the train in your dream, are you on track with your goals and aspirations, or are you too rigid and set in your ways? If you're traveling by car, bike, or scooter, you can change direction in seconds, but it's not possible when you're traveling by train—it doesn't allow you to make spontaneous changes.

What kind of train is it—a stream engine, a locomotive, or an electric train? If it's a steam train, are you under stress or pressure, ready to explode? Or do you feel old, antiquated, and superseded?

Perhaps you're an overburdened diesel train with too many carriages to pull. Does this reflect your waking life? Do you feel as though you have a ridiculous number of hangers-on in tow who expect you to do all the work while they enjoy the ride? Or do you feel powerful enough to handle any challenge or burden that comes your way?

Are you about to catch a train? Where are you going? Whom are you traveling with? Is this person a help or a hindrance?

If you just missed a train, what's stopping you from being/getting on track? Where do you want to go?

Trampoline

Quick Interpretation: Spring into action; anger (jumping up and down); exercise

Popular Expressions: Bounce back; On the up-and-up; Experiencing highs and lows

A trampoline symbolizes the ups and downs in life. Because of the world we live in, everything that goes up must come down. The important thing is to keep on bouncing. Why are you on a trampoline? Is it for exercise or fun? Do you feel insecure or in control?

Transportation (See *Airplane; Bus; Car; Driving; Train.*)

Trap (Also see *Cage.*)

Quick Interpretation: Confinement; ambush; control

Popular Expressions: Fall into a trap; Caught with your pants down

Wouldn't it be wonderful if all traps in life were like the one's in James Bond movies? They all had an escape hatch!

What are you trying to trap in your dream? Or is someone trying to trap you? Think of the thing or person you want to trap in relation to what you want to control in your life. Or are you tieing to ambush someone?

A trap also suggests confinement. Do you feel confined in your dream, or are you trying to confine someone else? Most of the traps we see are in our imagination. Is your dream reminding you not to be scared of your shadow?

Trash (See *Garbage*.)

Treasure

Quick Interpretation: A search; something in reserve; in hiding

Popular Expressions: Good as gold; Strike it rich; One man's trash is another man's treasure

Films with treasure maps in them are so wonderful. The X always marks the spot, and once you see the spot, you wonder why it wasn't found without the map. What hidden treasures are there for the pickings? What valuable thing is hidden away waiting for you to discover it? Do you feel that you're being led on a wild-goose chase, or are you on a real treasure hunt?

Tree (Also see *Forest; Jungle*.)

Quick Interpretation: Nature; sustenance; hidden resources

Popular Expressions: Down to earth; Put down roots; Out of your tree; Bark up the wrong tree; Out on a limb; Don't have a limb to stand on; Branch out

Trees are only as good as their roots. It doesn't matter what the tree looks like above the ground, if it hasn't got a strong root system, it's not going to survive.

The tree is a symbol of getting deep into a matter: into the soul, into the psyche, into the earth. Look at the tree in your dream and its foundations. Is it wobbly, can it be blown over, or is there enough support?

What kind of tree is it? Is it one that experiences the seasons: blossoms in spring, looks alive and abundant in summer, is like a burning bush in autumn, and a dead twig in winter? If so, it may indicate that you want people to see what's going on in your life.

If it's an evergreen, then maybe you prefer to keep things personal and make changes in your life quietly. Is the tree ornamental, such as a Christmas tree, or is its purpose to bear fruit and nourish people? Has the tree got lots of branches, indicating a desire to expand in some way—perhaps your career or family? Is the tree inflexible in the presence of powerful winds? Does it run the risk of being snapped in half? Does this represent your own inflexibility?

Are you climbing up the tree or falling out of it? Is the tree a place of nurturing and new life, full of nests, ants, and insects, or is the tree dead?

Perhaps you're barking up the wrong tree. This may indicate that a current endeavor needs to be reconsidered because you're on the wrong track or someone has outfoxed you.

The tree may also represent the tree of life, and be a reminder of your connection to the universe and all living things.

Trial (Also see *Interrogation; Judge; Lawyer.*)

Quick Interpretation: Being examined; defense/attack; on probation

Popular Expressions: Get off my case; Put words in someone else's month; A trial balloon; Trial and error

If there was ever a room full of judgments, it would certainly be a courtroom. Does the trial in your dream signify that you're making too many assumptions and judging others too harshly?

Who is on trial, and what are they on trial for? If *you're* on trial, do you feel as though someone or something in your life is putting you under the microscope? Do you feel unfairly examined, or is someone trying to put words in your mouth?

Trip (See *Excursion; Vacation.*)

Trophy (Also see *Winning.*)

Quick Interpretation: Award; acknowledgment; validation

Popular Expressions: Trophy wife; Everybody loves a winner

Dreaming of a trophy is a wonderful reminder that someone has achieved or excelled in their endeavors. Whose name is on the trophy, and what did they do to get it? Do you feel that you need proof to support your claims of success? Do you feel that you're the trophy and someone is showing you off?

Truck

Quick Interpretation: Heavy loads; transporting goods; barter

Popular Expressions: In for the long haul; A load on your mind; Carrying a heavy load

If you've got a heavy load to carry, then a truck will do the job. Do you need help with the heavy burdens that are weighing you down? Is it time to pull up at a truck stop, refresh, and revitalize yourself? The truck in your dream may also symbolize that you should pull up stakes and go trucking across the highways of adventure.

Trust

Quick Interpretation: Honesty; confidence

When you trust, you have faith and confidence in yourself and your relationships. Who or what do you have supreme confidence in?

Tunnel

Quick Interpretation: Escape; breakthrough; shortcut

Popular Expressions: Light at the end of the tunnel; Tunnel vision

If you want to get from point A to point B quickly and without interruption, then a tunnel is often the answer. What do you want to overcome by digging deeper into an issue or situation? Why can't you go around the obstacle instead of through it? It's wonderful to see a tunnel in a dream, as there's always a light at the end of it.

Turkey (Also see *Animal; Bird.*)

Quick Interpretation: Fool; feast; gratitude

Popular Expressions: Talk turkey; A turkey shoot; Like turkeys voting for Christmas; Gobbledygook

Turtle (Also see *Animal; Shell.*)

Quick Interpretation: Longevity; thick skin; patience

Popular Expressions: Home free; Slow and steady wins the race; Go into your shell; Shell-shocked

Umbrella

Quick Interpretation: Protection; union; contingency plans

Popular Expressions: Save for a rainy day; Right as rain; Take a rain check; Take cover; Under one umbrella

Why is it that you've always got an umbrella when it's sunny, but can never find one when it starts to rain? What is showering down on you that you need protection from? Do you feel that your protection may be blown away, or do you have a good grip on things?

Perhaps you wish to be part of a bigger organization or group of people so that you can place yourself safely under one umbrella?

Uncle (See *Family.*)

Unicorn

Quick Interpretation: Magic; fantasy; unattainability

Popular Expressions: The best of both worlds; The horns of a dilemma; Living in a fantasy world

The unicorn is a symbol that transcends geography and culture. No matter who or where you are, it reflects majesty and beauty. Does the unicorn in your dream indicate that you want to see beauty in all things?

Where does the unicorn appear in your dream? If it's a place you recognize, is this a magical place for you? Perhaps your dream is telling you to let up, let loose, and let magic happen.

The unicorn also represents fantasy. Are you living your life in a fantasy world at the moment? How do you feel about it? Is it escapism? Of course, your dream world may be influenced by a book you're reading or a film you saw recently. Why has the book or film influenced you so strongly?

The unicorn may signify unattainability. If you can't get near the unicorn in your dream, what do you feel you can't attain in your life?

No one has actually seen a unicorn, yet many of us believe in the possibility of its existence. Can it be a symbol of accepting things with blind faith?

Vacation (Also see *Excursion.*)

Quick Interpretation: Time-out; reward; release

Popular Expressions: Give me a break; Rest on your laurels; Trip the light fantastic; No rest for the weary

The best thing about dreaming of a vacation is that when you wake up you actually feel like you've been away. It's just a pity that you can't collect frequent-flyer points! The first question to ask yourself is whether it's time to take a vacation. This is probably the case if you dreamed of your favorite vacation destination.

Also, think of the vacation as a reward. Perhaps it's time you recognized that you've worked hard and deserve a break. Or maybe your dream vacation is enough, as it's giving you the release you need to get back into your work life.

If someone else is taking the vacation in your dream, how do you feel about it? Does it mean that you need a break from this person?

Vacuum Cleaner

Quick Interpretation: Extraction; deception; capture

Popular Expressions: Getting sucked in; It's in the bag; Suck it up

Today, if you get fooled or tricked in some way, it's said that you got "sucked right in." Does the vacuum cleaner in your dream symbolize that someone is trying to con you, or are you trying to take advantage of someone else? It can also signify that someone is trying to suffocate you and wants you to exist in a vacuum.

Vagina (Also see *Body Parts; Genitals; Penis; Sex.*)

Quick Interpretation: Birth; pleasure; monthly cycle

Popular Expressions: Don't put all your eggs in one basket; Down the hatch

Vampire

Quick Interpretation: Darkness; immortality; myth

Popular Expressions: Go for the jugular; Bleed someone dry; Out for someone's blood; Baring one's fangs; Give my eyetooth for that; Sink your teeth into something

It's interesting that a mythical creature can seem so real. Has anyone ever seen a vampire? Even vampire bats aren't as scary as legend would have you believe. The first question to ask is: Who is trying to suck the life force out of you or a situation? Is someone trying to exploit you, or do you feel someone else is being exploited?

Do you feel that you're more powerful at night than you are during the day? Whom would you really love to sink your teeth into? Do you have a wish to stay in the shadows?

Perhaps you believe you're someone's mentor. You see yourself as a vampire and the other person as your prey—maybe you'd like them to be more like you. You don't kill them but instead initiate them as a vampire.

Is the vampire in your dream a celebrity? Do you wish to emulate him? Perhaps the celebrity vampire is biting you in your dream, indicating that you want them to be more like you?

Vampires also signify being protected by simple means. Garlic wards off vampires. Could it be that a simple, natural approach to a dangerous situation will be more successful than a high-tech one?

Who is in the dream with you? Do they drain you of life? Do you feel they're leeching you? Perhaps it's a guest who has lingered too long, or you have to work with incompetent people?

If the vampire, or the person being bitten by the vampire, is a family member, it may mean that you want to establish a stronger bloodline or connection with them.

Vampires are closely related to bats, which have an acute sense of hearing. Could it be that you should be quiet and listen more?

Vanity

Quick Interpretation: Focus on outward appearances; self-absorption

Popular Expressions: Doing something in vain; A vain attempt

The experience of vanity indicates an excessive focus on outward appearance—physical and/or social. Is someone in your dream excessively preoccupied with themselves? How do you feel about it?

Vehicle (See *Car; Trailer; Truck.*)

Veil

Quick Interpretation: Mystery; commitment; anonymity

Popular Expressions: Draw a veil over something; A veil of secrecy; Behind the veil; Keep someone in the dark

The thinner the veil, the more sensuous it is. Does the veil in your dream symbolize seduction or control? Who's wearing the veil in your dream, and what are they trying to cover up? If you are wearing the veil, what don't you want other people to see? Are you keeping your emotions veiled?

The veil also symbolizes mystery. Do you want to keep a sense of mystery about you? Or if someone else is wearing the veil in your dream, do you feel that they want to keep you in the dark about something?

Also consider the veil as a symbol of commitment, worn when a bride gets married. Do you wish to commit to a new relationship or work opportunity?

The veil may also signify anonymity. Do you wish to be anonymous in certain situations? Or, if you're lifting the veil in your dream, does it symbolize a desire to reveal something you've been keeping to yourself?

Veterinarian

Quick Interpretation: Caution (to vet); compassion; creature comforts

Popular Expressions: In the doghouse; Animal magnetism

Why does it cost more to see a vet than it does to see a brain surgeon? Is there something wrong with your pets, or is someone treating you like an animal? It could be that someone is scrutinizing you, checking out your character or reputation, and you feel like you're being vetted.

Victimization

Quick Interpretation: Oppression; self-pity

Popular Expression: A victim of circumstance

When you feel victimized, you feel injured, destroyed, or sacrificed. Who's inflicting the pain? Why do you feel oppressed?

Vulnerability

Quick Interpretation: Emotional or physical wounds; sensitivity

Feeling vulnerable indicates that you believe that you're open to physical or emotional wounding. Who has physically or emotionally wounded you? Why do you feel at risk?

Vulture (Also see *Animal; Bird.*)

Quick Interpretation: Scavenger; being picked on; untrustworthiness

Popular Expressions: Circle in; Have a bone to pick with someone; Soothe the savage beast

Wall

Quick Interpretation: Confinement; being cornered; barriers

Popular Expressions: Climb the walls; Back to the wall

Where does the wall appear in your dream? This will help you to determine the area of your life in which you feel confined or cornered. It's important to consider whether you climbed or went through the wall in your dream. How you interacted with the wall will give you insight into how you approach or deal with challenges in your life.

The wall or walls in your dream may also symbolize putting up barriers. Do you need to create a boundary or two in relation to the people around you? Or do you need to pull a couple down?

If you're climbing the walls in your dream, it may indicate that you're experiencing a frustrating time in your life. If you've had your back to the wall, perhaps you feel that there's nowhere to turn in your life at the moment.

Wallet

Quick Interpretation: Identification; possessions; finances

Popular Expressions: Cash in hand; In the money; Holding the purse strings

Times are a-changin'. We used to carry paper in our wallets; now we carry plastic. Do you feel that the wallet in your dream is safe, or can it be easily removed? Does the wallet contain everything that represents who you are: your driver's licence, your medical card, your credit cards? Are you taking good care of your wallet, or are you treating it flippantly, indicating that you're not taking care of yourself?

Perhaps you're looking for a wallet in your dream, indicating a search for your possessions. Or do you find a wallet? If so, and the wallet isn't yours, what do you do with it? Do you hand it in or keep it?

War (Also see *Military; Soldier.*)

Quick Interpretation: Conflict; loss of communication; uncompromising

Popular Expressions: Fighting mad; On the warpath; Fight to the finish

Dreaming of war indicates that diplomacy has been exhausted, and the only way to resolve differences is on the battlefield. Where is the war being fought in your dream, and who's involved? If you live in a country that's at war, is your dream helping you make sense of what's happening?

Perhaps your dream indicates that a battle is going on in your personal life. Who is in the dream with you? Are you in conflict with this person/people in your waking life? The battle may also be with yourself. Are you of two minds about something?

War suggests loss of communication, and the breakdown of diplomatic relations. What do you feel you can't talk through? What must be dealt with by force?

War can also symbolize an uncompromising situation. Do you feel that you're in this type of situation in your waking life? Who's expecting you to compromise? Or has something in your life made you mad with rage? What is it you're fighting mad about?

Dreaming of war can also signify that it's time to really think about the consequences of your actions, as some battles simply result in a Pyrrhic victory, and the cost is simply too great.

Washing (Also see *Cleaning; Soap.*)

Quick Interpretation: Purification; completion; renewal

Popular Expressions: Wash your dirty linen in public; It will all come out in the wash; Wash your hands of the matter

This dream symbol may indicate that the truth is about to be revealed, as something underhanded has come out in the wash. To wash in a dream may also suggest purification. What are you washing? If you're washing yourself, are you trying to wash yourself clean of something? What has made you feel dirty and soiled?

If you're washing something else, why are you washing it? Does it represent something you want to wash your hands of?

If you're feeling particularly jaded and flat at the moment, you may dream of washing to suggest feeling washed out. But remember, once you've been hung out to dry, you'll be as clean as a whistle.

Watch (Also see *Alarm Clock; Time*)

Quick Interpretation: Timeliness; being scrutinized/scrutinizing; keeping vigil

Popular Expressions: Look before you leap; On someone else's watch; Watch out for something/someone

When it's time to pay attention and stay focused, you keep watch. Do you want someone to watch over you, or do you want to watch over someone else? Most of us like to be noticed and desired. Does your dream indicate that you want to be watched?

Water (Also see *Beach; Ocean; Waterfall.*)

Quick Interpretation: Hydration; emotion; life

Popular Expressions: Blow something out of the water; Can't keep your head above water; Stay afloat; The tide will turn; In too deep; Drowning in my sorrows

I don't think I've met anyone who hasn't had a water dream, experienced as either a vapor (mist), solid (ice), or in liquid form.

The first thing to consider is that you may be dreaming of water because you're dehydrated physically or spiritually. Drinking more water will help quench a physical thirst, but quenching a spiritual thirst isn't as easy. Are you feeling dissatisfied with your life?

Water is aligned with emotion, the ebb and flow of life, influenced by the waxing and waning moon. (The moon influences the "tides" of the human body just as it does the ocean tides.) During times of emotional turmoil, it's common to see tidal waves and/or rough seas in a dream. If life is smooth sailing, you're likely to see still waters.

If we replace the word *water* with the word *emotion,* it speaks volumes. For example, if you dream of stormy waters, ask yourself if you're experiencing tempestuous emotions.

When water appears as a mist, it may indicate that you're not seeing things clearly. Is something or someone clouding your vision? What emotional experience is blinding you to reality? Mist is dissolved by sunlight and warmth. If you're feeling melancholy, what can you do to dissolve the mood and cheer yourself up?

If you dream of ice, think about it in relation to frozen feelings. What will help you defrost these emotions?

Over the years I've noticed an increase in the number of people who have water-sport dreams. These dreams speak of competition and a desire to feel and conquer emotions.

Diving dreams suggest a willingness to sink to the depths of despair to reach the bottom of a painful or fearful emotional experience. The upside is exhilaration upon reemergence.

Water is a universal symbol, as rich in meaning as the Christian cross or the Star of David, yet simple, too—after all, it's the most satisfying thirst quencher.

Waterfall (Also see *Water.*)

Quick Interpretation: Descent; being cleansed; mystery

Popular Expressions: Over the top; Drop off the face of the earth

It's incredible to think that we can stare at water dropping from a great height for a long time and feel exhilarated by it. Does the waterfall in your dream signify that you're beautiful even though you're falling on your face?

Waterfalls can also symbolize hidden beauty and mystery, because what lies behind the waterfall is often a secret. There aren't many waterfalls in a big city; they're out in nature. Does the waterfall in your dream indicate that you wish to get away from it all?

Weakness

Quick Interpretation: Easily persuaded; lack of power

Popular Expressions: Weak in the knees; Give in to temptation

When you feel weak, it indicates that you're unable to withstand temptation and are easily persuaded. Who's stopping you from exerting your will in your dream? What can't you endure any longer?

Wealth (See *Abundance; Money.*)

Weapon (See *Gun; Rifle.*)

Wedding (Also see *Bride/Bridegroom; Marriage; Ring.*)

Quick Interpretation: Communion; public announcements; celebration

Popular Expressions: Stand on ceremony; To have and to hold; Till death do us part; A meeting of the minds; A shotgun wedding

Weeds (See *Garden.*)

Well

Quick Interpretation: Deep inspiration; wishful thinking; good health

Popular Expressions: All's well that ends well; Get into deep water; Go to the well and drink; Welling up with tears

How do you feel about seeing a well in your dream? No doubt your answer will depend on where you're standing in relation to the well. For example, if you're standing at the top of the well looking down, you may feel safe. Whereas if you're lying at the bottom of the well looking up, you may feel afraid and uncertain. Same well, different views and feelings.

The well may also symbolize creativity, nourishment, and abundance. Is it a wishing well, and with the toss of a small coin your heart's desire will be granted? Are you thirsty, and the well offers refreshment?

If you're at the bottom of the well looking up, do you feel confined, helpless, and trapped? How did you get there? Was it by your own doing, or is someone else responsible for placing you in this predicament? Are you being reminded that the only way out of a predicament you're facing in your waking life is to look up? That to get ahead you need to claw your way to the top, step-by-step, inch-by-inch? Perhaps it's time for you to call out for help.

Is the well full of water? What is the water like? Is it clean and refreshing, or green and stagnant? Your answer will reflect the present state of your emotions.

Also, consider whether the symbol of the well is a pun for feeling well. Are you concerned about someone else's well-being or your own? How is your health?

Whale (Also see *Animal.*)

Quick Interpretation: Power; migration; being endangered

Popular Expressions: Have a whale of a time; Have bigger fish to fry

Wife (See *Family.*)

Wig

Quick Interpretation: Camouflage; protection; enhancement

Popular Expressions: Something on your mind; Flip your lid; Wig out; A head for something; A good head on your shoulders; Off the top of my head

Can you believe that for centuries people thought that putting (dyed) white horsehair on their heads was a good look? Most of these individuals had perfectly good heads of hair themselves, so why didn't they just dye that?

Is the wig in your dream a symbol of vanity gone berserk? If you wear a wig or are contemplating wearing one, how will it affect your image or self-esteem? Is the wig a disguise that allows you to act differently from how you normally would? A wig may also signify that you feel you're being judged, or judgment is going to be passed down upon you, because in many courts throughout the world, judges still sport a lovely head of white horsehair.

Wind

Quick Interpretation: Being blown over; talking too much (long-winded); turbulence

Popular Expressions: Get wind of; A second wind; Throw caution to the wind; Blowing in the wind; Pass wind; Blow it out your ear; A blow to the system; Old windbag

The difference between a breath of fresh air and a tornado is the velocity of the wind. Does the wind in your dream signify that someone needs to slow down?

Sometimes, if we swallow things too quickly, or devour something that should be savored, the consequence is bad wind. Are there circumstances around you that you can't digest?

Wind can also indicate that it's time to count your blessings and trust, because it's an ill wind that doesn't blow somebody some good.

Window

Quick Interpretation: Breakthrough; clarity; opportunity

Popular Expressions: Window of opportunity; Missed the window; Window-shopping; Window dressing; Window seat; See through something (or someone)

From time to time, we're given an opportunity to succeed in a certain situation. But we have to be quick and catch the window of opportunity.

Is someone trying to impress you without putting in any real effort—that is, are they window dressing? Perhaps someone is indecisive and leading you on because they're merely window shopping. To see things from a different perspective and get a full view of what's going on, it's best to get a window seat.

Wine (Also see *Alcohol.*)

Quick Interpretation: Intoxication; communion; complaints (whining)

Popular Expressions: Sour grapes; Pop your cork; Wine, women, and song

Wing (Also see *Bird.*)

Quick Interpretation: Liberation; flight; movement

Popular Expressions: On a wing and a prayer; Take someone under your wing; Just wing it; Spread your wings; Rise above it all

If you suddenly sprout wings, it indicates that you want to get above something. What do you want to rise above? Perhaps it's time to leave your comfort zone and truly spread your wings. Can wings symbolize a sense of achievement, because you feel as though you've earned your wings?

Winning (Also see *Success; Trophy.*)

Quick Interpretation: Good fortune; desired outcomes

Popular Expressions: Come out on top; Get the better of something; Win hands-down

From the moment humans started to keep score, there have been winners. Dreaming that you win indicates good fortune. Is your life particularly fortuitous at the moment? What is happening to make it so?

Winning is also associated with success. Do you feel particularly successful in your life at the moment? Or if someone else is the winner in your dream, does it represent a recent success in their life? How you feel about it will indicate how you accept other people's achievements.

Does the win signify how you'd like to see things turn out in your life? Take careful note of the circumstances of the dream to find out what you feel will result in good fortune.

If you feel particularly positive in your life at the moment, you may dream of a win to suggest coming out on top. Do you share this good fortune with the people around you?

Wolf (Also see *Animal.*)

Quick Interpretation: Wildness; pack mentality; loner

Popular Expressions: A wolf in sheep's clothing; To throw to the wolves; Wolf something down

Wool (Also see *Sheep.*)

Quick Interpretation: Warmth; deception; financial loss

Popular Expressions: Pull the wool over one's eyes; Being fleeced; A wolf in sheep's clothing

Do you have a feeling that someone is trying to trick you or that they're trying to pull the wool over your eyes?

Work (Also see *Office.*)

Quick Interpretation: Commitment; expression; livelihood

Popular Expressions: Have your work cut out for you; All in a day's work; Work your fingers to the bone; All work and no play . . . ; Workhorse; Working man (or woman)

Who invented work? We try so hard to enjoy our lives, but somebody is always sending a bill that has to be paid! What type of work are you doing in your dream? Is it a new line of work, perhaps indicating a desire to change jobs or professions?

Work is associated with commitment, so think of it in relation to what you feel committed to in your life. Also consider work as a symbol of expression—a way to make your mark in the world. If this is what it indicates in your dream, take careful note of how you feel. This will help you to determine whether you're in the right or wrong line of work.

Livelihood is also associated with work. Is your work simply a means to get by in life?

Today, when you ask for "the works," it usually means you want every single topping on a pizza or a hamburger. Perhaps work in your dream signifies that you don't want to miss out on anything.

Workplace (See *Office.*)

World Wide Web (See *Internet.*)

Worm

Quick Interpretation: Recycling; distrust; scholar

Popular Expressions: To open a can of worms; Worm your way out of something; Bookworm; The early bird gets the worm

What an unsavory creature the worm seems to be! They do so much good, yet they have negative associations. Does the worm in your dream signify that you're not seeing the value and importance of someone? Or is the worm a reminder to be on your toes and prepare to act because the early bird gets the worm?

Is someone trying to worm their way out of a relationship or arrangement with you?

Also consider that the worm could symbolize a situation that's infecting you and preventing you from working to your fullest capacity.

A worm is a computer program that's designed to damage your system by duplicating itself. At some point in our lives, we've all taken a deep breath and stood up for ourselves or some injustice; finally, the worm turns, and we stop accepting the negative situation.

Worry

Quick Interpretation: Concern; agitation

Popular Expression: Worrywart

Feeling worried indicates that you're overly concerned about someone or something; you're fretting. Who or what agitated you to the point of distraction in your dream? What's nagging at you?

Worship (places of)

Quick Interpretation: Confession; salvation; answered prayers

Popular Expressions: Practice what you preach; On a wing and a prayer

Visiting a place of worship in a dream doesn't necessarily mean that you're religious, although these dreams are common among pious folk.

How do you feel about the place of worship in your dream? Is it a sanctuary, a place of love and care? Are you there to confess, to get something off your mind? Do you need to forgive someone or get over something in your life?

Where is the place of worship? Is it in the middle of nowhere, or in the middle of the city? Are you alone, or are other people around? Is the dream experience exhilarating and purifying, or does it feel like a chore? Are you afraid?

Is there a particular faith associated with the place of worship? Are you of this faith? Consider its significance—perhaps you're feeling disillusioned, or maybe you're dealing with an issue right now that involves this place of worship.

If you find yourself in a place of worship that's not your own, perhaps it's time to explore other belief systems or schools of thought. If you visit the Vatican in a dream, think about power and authority in your life. Do you feel powerful, or does someone have power over you?

Dreaming of the Taj Mahal may suggest completion, yet dreaming about a Japanese temple may suggest a time of peace and quiet. Find out what the place of worship in your dream means to you to uncover its unique symbolic meaning.

Worthlessness

Quick Interpretation: Lack of self-esteem

Feeling worthless indicates that you believe you lack value. You feel unimportant. Who cannot see your true worth? What incident is affecting your self-esteem?

X-Rated (Also see *Pornography*.)

Quick Interpretation: Voyeurism; forbidden pleasures; adult entertainment

Popular Expressions: X marks the spot; X something out

When you see the X on a film, you know you're going to see lots of scenes that some people believe are unsuitable for your eyes. Does the X-rated symbol indicate that you should decide what is suitable or unsuitable for you, or does it mean that you should take other people's word because they have the authority to judge?

Perhaps you feel that someone is being exploited, or forced to do something unnatural for money. Also consider that something marked X-rated in your dream could mean that you're stimulated by watching other people do things you wouldn't necessarily do.

X-ray

Quick Interpretation: Transparency; exposure; examination

Popular Expressions: To see through something; The bare bones

If you really want to see through things and not be influenced by what's on the outside, an x-ray will do the job. What do you see on the x-ray? Is it a part of the body that you should be paying attention to? Perhaps you may even need to consult a health professional.

The x-ray in your dream may indicate a desire for extra security and peace of mind, as nothing gets through customs today without being x-rayed.

Yacht (Also see *Boat; Sailing.*)

Quick Interpretation: Being on course; escape; easygoing mentality

Popular Expressions: Smooth sailing; Above board

A yacht is one of the ultimate status symbols. It has luxury written all over it. Does the yacht in your dream symbolize that you're moving up in the world? What is happening on the yacht? Are you in a race for a prize, or are you relaxing and enjoying the fruits of your labor?

Yellow Pages   (See *Telephone Book.*)

Yogurt

Quick Interpretation: Sour taste; culture; good health

Popular Expression: To sour on something

It's incredible to think that yogurt can be so nutritious and taste good, too. Dreaming of yogurt may indicate that even though you think things have gone awry, it's not too late to salvage the situation and create a successful outcome.

Perhaps you want to be considered more cultured. Remember, all you need is time to mature.

Youth

Quick Interpretation: Freshness; vitality

Popular Expression: Youth is wasted on the young

When you feel young, you're vital and full of life. Just because you live for a long time doesn't mean you're old. What has made you recognize this fact of life?

Yo-Yo

Quick Interpretation: Indecision; fool

Popular Expressions: String someone along; Leave dangling; Someone who's a real yo-yo

The yo-yo is the ultimate symbol of indecision. What has an upside and a downside, preventing you from making a decision? Does the yo-yo symbolize that you're trying to lose weight but no longer want to be on a yo-yo diet?

Perhaps you feel that someone has complete control over you and has put you on a string—meaning that he or she is playing with your emotions. Also consider that the yo-yo may signify a desire to be less serious and more childlike, since children are greatly amused by the simple yo-yo.

Zebra

Quick Interpretation: Wildness; safety (zebra crossings)

Popular Expression: A horse of a different color; See things in black and white

Forget about the chicken and the egg; the real teaser is whether the zebra is a black horse with white stripes, or a white horse with black stripes!

To see a zebra in a dream may indicate that the last thing you want to do is camouflage your feelings or intentions. Nothing stands out as vividly on the Serengeti as those black-and-white stripes.

The zebra may also symbolize that wild, untamable spirit within us all. As much as we'd like to have a pet zebra to ride, no one has managed to break one in.

Also consider that the zebra in your dream could be a symbol of authority, like in the military, where you can tell someone's rank by the stripes.

The zebra may also indicate that you want to get from one point to another safely (the zebra crossing), whether it be in a relationship, your career, or with your finances.

The zebra is also a great symbol signifying that you've come to terms with all aspects of yourself, your light side and shadow side. You've integrated them perfectly, and you're quite happy to openly display the light and dark side of yourself without fearing judgment.

Zipper

Quick Interpretation: Fastener; practicality; enclosure

Popular Expressions: Zip your lip; Zip code

The zipper can be a symbol of modesty. Sometimes it allows for quick concealment of something that's very private. It can also indicate that someone should keep their mouth shut and think before they speak—that is, zip up. Or perhaps the zipper in the dream signifies that you want to deliver a message and what you need is a zip code.

Zoo (Also see *Animal.*)

Quick Interpretation: Protection; display; confinement

Popular Expressions: Behind bars; Animal house; It's a zoo out there

Why is it when things go haywire, we call it a zoo, when zoos are well organized and run according to a tight schedule? It must be the noise. What appears to be well organized in your life, yet is making a real racket and requires constant attention?

Do you feel that the zoo in your dream is protecting endangered species, or do you see it as a prison for human gratification? Do you need protection, or do you feel that you're the object of someone's amusement?

Do you try and escape from the zoo in your dream, or do you assist the animals in escaping, indicating that your desire for free expression far outweighs your need for security and creature comforts?

The zoo may also represent relationships you've formed in your life. At times we're forced to live with individuals with whom we're incompatible, but we choose to stay and endure the situation because it's a lot safer than going out in the jungle.

ZZZ

What better way to end a dream book than with a good night's sleep!

EMOTIONS AT A GLANCE

It's often difficult to find the time to truly sit with and appreciate our emotions in the rush of everyday life. Yet at night, we get the opportunity to slow down, sleep, and dream. And it's in our dreams—and the change in rhythm of our minds—that we often tap in to emotions that may have been trying to get our attention during the day.

To identify the emotions that pop up in our dreams provides a wonderful opportunity to connect with how we feel, and to better understand what's happening in our lives. Our dreams may reflect difficult times, but they can equally reflect joyous ones, and every experience in between.

But what is an emotion? Most of us have an intuitive sense of what an emotion is, and we're quick to define people as "emotional." It seems to describe a person's state when they're caught up in an emotion—whether it be fear, pain, anger, joy, or sadness. Indeed, *The Macquarie Concise Dictionary* defines emotion as "an affective state of consciousness in which joy, sorrow, fear, hate, or the like is experienced." Feelings, on the other hand—although the words can be interchangeable—most commonly describe the sensate experience of the emotion. "I feel sad, angry, joyful, fearful," and so on. So, an emotion is a state of feeling, and a feeling is the sensate experience of the emotion. Phew!

Although very simplistic, I was fascinated with theorist Robert

Plutchik's (1980) approach to the classification of emotions. He suggested that there are eight primary emotions—joy, acceptance, surprise, fear, sorrow, disgust, expectancy, and anger—and that other emotions are a mixture of these. So, for example, pride = anger + joy; love = joy + acceptance; hate = anger + surprise; guilt = joy + fear; shame = fear + disgust; and so on. It's not surprising, then, that we often feel confused when we're emotional, which is why it's often important to ask, "What exactly am I feeling?"

When an emotion is identified, we become aware of what it is that brings us joy, peace, wonder, and so on in our lives, and if we identify a particularly difficult emotion, it can help us find out what needs to be done (if anything) to work through it.

Like a magnet with a positive and negative end, we're a mix of "positive" and "negative" emotions. We don't judge each end of the magnet as good or bad; similarly, it's counterproductive to judge an emotion as good or bad. And if you put a magnet under the most powerful microscope, you wouldn't find a bunch of negative atoms and a bunch of positive atoms . . . they're simply atoms.

Defining emotions as either "positive" and "negative" is misleading. It's more appropriate to define them as either a time of expansion (the so-called positive emotions) or a time of contraction (the so-called negative ones). We each know that when we feel sad, confused, lonely, and so on, it's extremely difficult to reach out to other people. It's a time of contraction; whether we feel closed down and reflective, or maligned and aggressive, we often feel cut off from other people, and protective or defensive. When it's a time of expansion, on the other hand, we often feel generous and loving, confident and complimentary.

To help you better work with your emotions, most particularly the emotions that accompany your dreams, I encourage you to spend a few minutes each morning to sit with them before you get up. The idea is to help you clarify your dream and get in touch with your emotions so that you can center your thoughts and begin your day with insights that bring about self-empowerment. Following is an alphabetical list of commonly experienced emotions to assist you in identifying the ones you feel in your dreams.

List of Emotions

Acceptance
Agitation
Alertness
Altruism
Ambition
Anger
Anxiety
Apathy
Arousal
Attachment
Blessings
Bliss
Boredom
Calmness
Charity
Cheerfulness
Clarity
Compassion
Composure
Confidence
Confusion
Contentment
Cursed (feeling)
Depression
Detachment
Disappointment
Dissatisfaction
Empowerment
Failure
Faithfulness
Fear
Flexibility
Forgiveness
Frigidity
Fulfillment

Genuineness
Gloominess
Gluttony
Gratitude
Grief
Guilt
Ignorance
Ill treated (feeling)
Impatience
Innocence
Insensitivity
Inspiration
Intuition
Invincibility
Irrationality
Irritation
Jealousy
Joy
Judgment
Lack
Laziness
Lethargy
Liberation
Loneliness
Luck
Lust
Miserliness
Moderation
Modesty
Negativity
Negligence
Obsession
Obstinacy
Optimism
Pain

Paranoia
Passion
Patience
Pessimism
Pity
Pleasure
Positive feelings
Praise
Protection
Rationality
Reassurance
Relaxation
Resentment
Respect
Sadness
Secretiveness
Selfishness
Self-pity
Serenity
Sin
Strength
Success
Suspicion
Teariness
Tension
Thoughtfulness
Trust
Vagueness
Vanity
Victimization
Vulnerability
Weakness
Worry
Worthlessness

My intention when writing this book was to make you, the reader, a dream interpreter. Like any good coach, my role is to help you develop your skills so that you can excel to whatever level you choose. A good music coach shows you where the notes and chords are, and it's up to you to go ahead and create your own symphony. I've given you a variety of dream-coaching tools so you can construct your own interpretations. I truly believe that it's very rare that a student does not exceed the master. With that in mind, I welcome you as a colleague and a dreamer.

ABOUT THE AUTHOR

Leon Nacson is one of the pioneers of the self-help movement in Australia. He's the publisher of *The Planet* newspaper and the author of nine books. Leon specializes in dream coaching and regularly contributes to national newspapers, magazines, and radio programs. His popular Website: **www.dreamcoach.com.au** enjoys millions of visits each year.

NOTES

NOTES

Sign up via the Hay House USA Website to receive the Hay House online newsletter and stay informed about what's going on with your favorite authors. You'll receive bimonthly announcements about: Discounts and Offers, Special Events, Product Highlights, Free Excerpts, Giveaways, and more!
www.hayhouse.com

We hope you enjoyed this Hay House book.
If you would like to receive a free catalog featuring
additional Hay House books and products, or if you
would like information about the Hay Foundation,
please contact:

Hay House, Inc.
P.O. Box 5100
Carlsbad, CA 92018-5100

(760) 431-7695 or (800) 654-5126
(760) 431-6948 (fax) or (800) 650-5115 (fax)
www.hayhouse.com

Published and distributed in Australia by:
Hay House Australia, Ltd. • 18/36 Ralph St. • Alexandria NSW 2015
Phone: 612-9669-4299 • *Fax:* 612-9669-4144
www.hayhouse.com.au

Published and distributed in the United Kingdom by:
Hay House UK, Ltd. • Unit 62, Canalot Studios • 222 Kensal Rd.,
London W10 5BN • *Phone:* 44-20-8962-1230 • *Fax:* 44-20-8962-1239
www.hayhouse.co.uk

Published and distributed in the Republic of South Africa by:
Hay House SA (Pty), Ltd., P.O. Box 990, Witkoppen 2068
Phone/Fax: 2711-7012233 • orders@psdprom.co.za

Distributed in Canada by:
Raincoast • 9050 Shaughnessy St., Vancouver, B.C. V6P 6E5
Phone: (604) 323-7100 • *Fax:* (604) 323-2600